SAYING GOODBYE

A Guide to Coping with a Loved One's Terminal Illness

BARBARA OKUN, PH.D., AND
JOSEPH NOWINSKI, PH.D.

BERKLEY BOOKS, NEW YORK

THE BERKLEY PUBLISHING GROUP
Published by the Penguin Group
Penguin Group (USA) Inc.
375 Hudson Street, New York, New York 10014, USA
Penguin Group (Canada), 90 Eglinton Avenue East, Suite 700, Toronto, Ontario M4P 2Y3, Canada
(a division of Pearson Penguin Canada Inc.)
Penguin Books Ltd., 80 Strand, London WC2R 0RL, England
Penguin Group Ireland, 25 St. Stephen's Green, Dublin 2, Ireland (a division of Penguin Books Ltd.)
Penguin Group (Australia), 250 Camberwell Road, Camberwell, Victoria 3124, Australia
(a division of Pearson Australia Group Pty. Ltd.)
Penguin Books India Pvt. Ltd., 11 Community Centre, Panchsheel Park, New Delhi—110 017, India
Penguin Group (NZ), 67 Apollo Drive, Rosedale, Auckland 0632, New Zealand
(a division of Pearson New Zealand Ltd.)
Penguin Books (South Africa) (Pty.) Ltd., 24 Sturdee Avenue, Rosebank, Johannesburg 2196,
South Africa

Penguin Books Ltd., Registered Offices: 80 Strand, London WC2R 0RL, England

PUBLISHING HISTORY
Berkley hardcover edition / January 2011
Berkley trade paperback edition / January 2012

Berkley trade paperback ISBN: 978-0-425-24518-7

The Library of Congress has cataloged the Berkley hardcover edition as follows:

Okun, Barbara F.
    Saying goodbye : a guide to coping with a loved one's terminal illness / Barbara Okun and Joseph
Nowinski. — 1st ed.
        p. cm.
    Includes bibliographical references.
    ISBN 978-0-425-23322-1
    1. Bereavement—Psychological aspects.   2. Families—Psychological aspects.
3. Death—Psychological aspects.   I. Nowinski, Joseph.   II. Title.
    BF575.G7O34 2011
    155.9'37—dc22

                                                                                2010037151

PRINTED IN THE UNITED STATES OF AMERICA

10 9 8 7 6 5 4 3 2 1

PUBLISHER'S NOTE: Neither the publisher nor the authors are engaged in rendering professional
advice or services to the individual reader. The ideas, procedures, and suggestions contained in this
book are not intended as a substitute for consulting with your physician. All matters regarding your
health require medical supervision. Neither the authors nor the publisher shall be liable or responsible
for any loss or damage allegedly arising from any information or suggestion in this book.

All names and identifying characteristics have been changed to protect the privacy of the individuals
involved.

"[An] emotional road map to steer families through their early reactions, the medical and social and financial issues, the ways caregiving reawakens old family dynamics, the need for communication. They point out the broad array of reactions, including anxiety, ambivalence, and resentment, that qualify as normal. They suggest exercises and strategies. . . . *Saying Goodbye* [is] very useful."
—*The New York Times*

"A new paradigm on dealing with death and dying . . . *Saying Goodbye* helps guide individuals and families on next steps and processes when confronted with a potentially fatal but chronic disease."
—David S. Rosenthal, M.D., medical director, Harvard University
and past president of the American Cancer Society

"This exceptional book for families and healthcare professionals is a valuable contribution to the field of survivorship. As patients share their unique stories, the authors offer a plethora of suggestions for managing grief and loss so individuals and families become empowered as they navigate their way through a most challenging period in their lives. An excellent reference and recommended reading list is also included."
—Kenneth D. Miller, M.D., director of cancer survivorship,
Dana-Farber Cancer Institute, and Joan E. Heller Miller, Ed.M.,
author of *Healing Grief: A Story of Survivorship*

"This important book calls attention to the changing face of grief. Now that modern medicine prolongs survival time from many illnesses, we must cope with impending loss in new ways. Okun and Nowinski offer excellent suggestions to individuals and families passing through that process."
—Irvin D. Yalom, M.D., author of *Staring at the Sun:
Overcoming the Terror of Death*

"For more than thirty years, I have worked daily with cancer patients and their families. At least once, in every single one of those days, I have wished that a book like *Saying Goodbye* were available. This long-needed book will give frightened and grieving patients and their families a road map and a guide to the best possible management of the many challenges awaiting them. The authors never turn from the truth and painful realities, but offer wise and practical strategies and support that surely will help their readers to live through and beyond loss."
—Hester Hill Schnipper, author of *After Breast Cancer:
A Common-Sense Guide to Life After Treatment*

In loving memory of Sherman
from B.O.

and

In grateful memory of all those whose lives touched
mine before saying goodbye
from J.N.

SAYING GOODBYE

Bereavement is a universal and integral part of our experience of love. It follows marriage as normally as marriage follows courtship or as autumn follows summer. It is not a truncation of the process but one of its phases; not the interruption of the dance, but the next figure.

—C. S. LEWIS

CONTENTS

STAGE 3 UPHEAVAL

STAGE 4 RESOLUTION

STAGE 5 RENEWAL

THE NEW GRIEF

If you are reading this book, it is probably because someone in your family—or someone you love—has been diagnosed with an illness that is terminal or life threatening. Although you've learned this alarming news, you really don't quite know what it means. Is death imminent? Is the condition treatable, and if so, what are the options and what is the prognosis? What does the ill family member need to do now? What do you need to do?

If the above describes you, rest assured you are not alone. Thanks to ongoing advances in medical diagnosis and treatment, life expectancy in countries like ours continues to grow. These advances have resulted in a sea change in the nature of death, which has evolved into a process rather than a more or less sudden event. Consequently, dying has created changes in the way we grieve. Those changes are the subject of this book.

In her groundbreaking book, *On Death and Dying,* first published in 1970, Elisabeth Kübler-Ross identified a process that she believed individuals pass through when they are confronted with death. This process begins with *denial* of the loss and ends in its *acceptance.* At the time her book appeared, sudden and unexpected death was much more common than it is today. The grief associated with that kind of loss is captured powerfully in Joan Didion's memoir *The Year of Magical Thinking,* which recounts her reactions to her husband's sudden death and which is dominated by a persistent element of disbelief. Didion's husband, the writer John Gregory Dunne, collapsed and died of a heart attack in the midst of eating dinner. Although he had a heart condition—indeed, he had a pacemaker—John apparently was experiencing no symptoms up to the moment of his collapse.

Didion's initial response to her husband's death typifies what Kübler-Ross called *denial.* She refused, for example, to read his obituaries. She refused to throw away his clothes. And she avoided going places that would remind her of him.

As useful as the Kübler-Ross model may have been in its time, the realities of death and dying have changed dramatically in the intervening forty years. If the kind of grief that Kübler-Ross wrote about—and Joan Didion experienced—represents what we could call *traditional* grief, then it stands in contrast to what could be called *contemporary* grief, which is defined by a very different set of circumstances. You could also call this *the new grief.* This new grief exists today as a direct result of the increasing ability of modern medicine to stave off death.

Today, having a loved one live with a terminal diagnosis for an extended period of time is fast replacing sudden and unexpected death as the norm. Consider, for example, the fact that two thirds of those who are diagnosed with cancer currently have a five-year survival rate. Thanks to an ever-growing body of medical advances, doctors are able to successfully cure—or arrest—a number of illnesses that once were likely to lead to sudden or quick death. The good news is that a diagnosis of cancer (or coronary artery disease) no longer means that death is imminent. In fact, today over 1.4 million cancer survivors are more than twenty years past their initial treatment episode. The same is true for heart disease: The number of deaths immediately following a heart attack has decreased dramatically and continues to do so.

The result of all of this is that death has become less and less a sudden and unexpected *event*. In its place has come a *process* that begins with a life-threatening diagnosis, proceeds through a period of treatment (or treatments), and ends eventually in death. This process means that both the terminally ill individual and the family are increasingly confronted with the need to "live with death" for a prolonged period of time.

For an example of contemporary grief, consider the experience reported by Eleanor Clift in her memoir *Two Weeks of Life: A Memoir of Love, Death, and Politics*. Clift's husband, Tom, was diagnosed with kidney cancer fully five years before he died. Tom spent the last ten weeks of his life at home, in a bed that hospice services had set up for him.

Eleanor's situation describes what more and more people are experiencing. Unlike Didion, Clift had a good idea at least four months in advance that her husband was approaching death. She knew this when her husband's oncologist advised them to discontinue chemotherapy.

———————

Regardless of whether it comes suddenly and unexpectedly or slowly with much advanced notice, the death of a loved one leaves us with a feeling of loss. That is unavoidable, given our human capacity to form attachments. In a sense, our attachments define us. They help us know our place in the world. When we lose an attachment, the connection to that part of our identity is broken. In a word, we lose a part of ourselves. And we grieve that loss. That said, there is also a case to be made that contemporary grief differs in significant ways from traditional grief.

The New Grief

So the reality is that sudden death has been replaced by a process that begins with a terminal diagnosis. But what exactly does that word—*terminal*—mean? Typically, it refers to a process that can last anywhere from months to years. The process of dying may be interrupted—once, twice, or many times—by periods of remission. It may be extended by increasingly sophisticated pharmacological, medical, and surgical technologies.

Because the nature of death and dying has changed so dramatically, the way we grieve has also changed. The new grief differs from traditional grief in significant ways, not the least of which is that it includes the terminally ill person. In addition, what has increasingly become a protracted process as opposed to an event not only leaves individuals to mourn but typically draws in the entire family of the dying person for months or even for years. This process has the potential to alter lifestyles and force families to confront issues that once were dealt with only after the death of the loved one. It can easily evoke issues from the past that were never fully addressed or resolved.

The fact is that grief today is a *family* matter as much as it is an individual one. What is needed is a new template—one that is relevant to families and their experience. That is what we present here. This model is intended to be a road map that you and your family can turn to as you navigate your way through the current realities of death and dying. And by the way, when we use the word *family*, we include not only blood relations but all those who have a significant connection to the person who carries the diagnosis.

The challenges that families must face when confronted with a terminal diagnosis of a loved one are complex. They include evolving new structures and dynamics as the person they love slowly slips away. It means learning how to cope with setbacks and deterioration as well as periods of seeming remission. It means dealing with the complexities of extended grief, which can wear individuals down and lead at times to ambivalence or the unpleasant feeling we get when we find ourselves wishing that the process would end. It means talking with a dying loved one about mortality and other issues that do not arise when death strikes suddenly and unexpectedly. It means learning to make space for extended grief in lifestyles that are typically busier than those of earlier generations.

Perhaps most important, the new grief involves confronting family issues that may have been dormant but unresolved for many years. These issues typically reemerge as families move past their initial reactions to a terminal diagnosis and are forced to interact and work together through a process of extended grief.

Finally, it means moving forward together as a stronger family after a loved one passes.

Most if not all of this probably describes your own situation today.

Without understanding, and without guidance in each of these areas, family members who are forced by circumstances to cope with prolonged grief are vulnerable to serious psychological consequences, including depression, guilt, and debilitating anxiety. These circumstances can even lead to physical illness. Whole families are vulnerable to rupture as a result of a resurgence of unresolved issues that are unearthed as a result of a prolonged terminal illness in a loved one. Even loving couples may find their relationships in jeopardy as a consequence of unwanted lifestyle changes. What families need now—and will need in the future—is guidance for how to anticipate and deal with such issues. This book provides you and your loved ones with that guidance.

A NOTE ON REMEMBRANCES

The authors are indebted to a number of men and women who were kind enough to share their personal stories of loss for this book. The reader will find these stories interspersed throughout the book. These individuals not only share their experience of loss (with permission) but also offer their thoughts as to what they wished they had known at the time they were going through it. These stories serve to illustrate the phenomenon of family grief. Beyond that, it is our hope that readers may identify (in part or substantially) with some of these stories and thereby find them helpful as they work their way through their own journey of grief.

Chapter One

GRIEF AS A FAMILY MATTER

Although both authors of this book are experienced therapists who have counseled many individuals and families facing death, there is perhaps no substitute for personal experience when it comes to focusing one's attention and providing the motivation to write a book on the topic of death and grief. Like most everyone else, both authors have had such experiences.

⚡ *Joe's Story*

I was a freshman in high school. I, of course, knew about death, but it had never yet touched me personally. Until that call came one day at 4 A.M. It was Christmas Eve.

The ringing woke the entire family. It was as if we all instinctively knew that no one calls with good news at that hour, for the tension in the air was palpable. My father answered the phone. It was my uncle, Bruno, calling from Brooklyn, New York. By chance Bruno had spent the night at my grandparents' apartment—the result of a heavy December snowstorm that had made commuting back to Long Island all but impossible. The sun had not yet risen on that Christmas Eve day when I learned that my grandfather had passed away in his sleep.

Faced with such sudden and unexpected losses, many people respond initially with what has been called denial. Simply put, denial refers to the difficulty we have accepting reality: that a person we love has just died, that we have just lost an attachment that is part of ourselves. That was pretty much the way I initially reacted to the news of my grandfather's death. It seemed unreal, as though I were only dreaming it. I insisted on accompanying my father to Brooklyn, to see my grandfather for myself, and it was not until I did so that the loss began to become a reality for me. Even then it was difficult for me to get my arms around this loss, and my recollection of the next several days—spent attending the wake and funeral— retain that dreamlike quality to this day.

Although sudden and unexpected death certainly still happens, as in Joe's story, living with death is increasingly becoming the norm. The nature of death has changed, and therefore, the way we grieve must also change. And although each of us must grieve the loss of a loved one in our own personal way, the fact is that because it can be so prolonged, grief is more and more an issue that affects both the one with the illness and the entire family for an extended period of time.

Here is another, rather different story:

✿ Barbara's Story

When my husband first felt a lump in his groin, I thought immediately of lymphoma. I have worked with so many families coping with illness that I think I was waiting for it to hit my own family. It was several weeks before Sherman had a biopsy. He and his buddy then went off on a long-anticipated fishing trip to a remote part of Mexico, leaving me to wait for the test results. I received them a few days later, and by the time Sherman returned from Mexico, our grown children and close friends (many of whom are physicians who provided invaluable loving support and help) had already been apprised of the situation.

When I picked the men up at the airport, they were so excited about their successful adventure that it reminded me of greeting the kids when they returned home from summer camp. We were almost home before I finally asked Sherman if he wanted to know the results of his biopsy. And that was the start of a two-year journey navigating through uncertainty, amazing love, and friendship, wonderful and disappointing medical care, and most important, the strength of family connections. We were determined to live as fully as possible. We took a trip to Bhutan and India, as previously planned, after the first course of chemotherapy; visited our sons and grandchildren in their new home in San Francisco; and generally enjoyed an active social life and our usual activities up until the last few months. I continued my busy professional life, and Sherman continued teaching and studying at the Brandeis and Boston College lifelong learning institutes.

During what we thought was a remission shortly after year one, we planned a Mediterranean cruise, recognizing that this would most likely be our last trip together. Three days before we were to leave, we were informed by hospice that my mother only had a few days left to live. My mother lived in New Orleans and had spent three months in Boston during Hurricane Katrina. She had been ill for several years and had had several close calls, but she insisted on returning to New Orleans when her residence there was restored. As with others in her generation who had satisfying lives in New Orleans, the devastating changes in New Orleans life resulted in a decline in mental and physical health. My sons and I went immediately to New Orleans to find her in agony. It was a weekend, and hospice could not send anyone to help because of post-Katrina staffing shortages. With the aid of a dear physician friend, I was able to lessen her suffering, and her last few hours of sleep were peaceful. Since none of us lived in New Orleans and since there were no available services, emptying her apartment and settling her affairs were difficult. However, we prevailed, and I returned to Boston to find a very sick husband. It was a lucky thing that we had not gone on our cruise because Sherman now had a different kind of lymphoma, which took weeks to be diagnosed and treated.

At the beginning of his illness, I asked Sherman to prepare a manual for me, explaining that there would be so much I would need to know and before he felt the effects of treatment he could perhaps think about some of the pragmatics of our life. Since his retirement ten years earlier, he had taken over all of the financial and household management responsibilities. He kept putting the project off, and I let it go even though it was on my mind to lessen tensions.

Six months before the end, Sherman suffered a stroke, and my children and I realized that bills had not been paid and that records were disorganized. My sons organized the papers and set me up with online banking, and I did the best I could to maintain the household while Sherman valiantly fought to regain his language capacities. We met with our attorney, and I consulted with our accountant

regarding income tax matters. Unfortunately, these attempts to pre-
pare were unsuccessful, and I later had to start from scratch with
different professionals.

Sherman died a peaceful death—it wasn't from cancer, but from
heart failure most likely attributed to his cancer treatments. Just ten
days before, we had arrived at our home on Martha's Vineyard (his
favorite place in the world) for the summer, when he suddenly
seemed pale and fatigued. I phoned a physician friend who lived
nearby, and she called an ambulance. He was flown by air ambu-
lance to a Boston medical center and spent a week in the cardiac
ICU. It became clear that we were coming close to the end, and
friends came to say goodbye. Meanwhile, the medical team went to
great lengths to see that he returned to the Vineyard to die in his own
bed, hearing the ocean and surrounded by children, his brother, and
his grandchildren. I was accompanied back to the Vineyard by
friends, one of whom is a physician. Both Sherman and I felt well
protected and cared for throughout. Because another close physi-
cian friend involved in his care told us there were just a couple of
days left, my son was able to get our daughter home from Europe
and our other son and his family in from San Francisco thirty-six
hours before the end. His Vineyard friends also had the opportunity
to say goodbye those last two days. Sherman's only regret was that
he couldn't go on his next fishing trip.

In hindsight, yes, I wish we had talked more about some details
related to burial, but we had selected a graveyard and talked to
those who would officiate at the services. I'm glad we cried and
laughed together and that we talked about our grandchildren and
what life would be like for me. We had years earlier decided to
move to a lifelong community (which had independent, assisted,

and skilled nursing living on the same campus), and three months before he died, he picked out the unit that I now live in, knowing that he would not be going with me.

We miss Sherman terribly, but my children (including their spouses), grandchildren, and I feel his presence and believe that we are richer for having been together openly sharing those last two years. We talk about Sherman a lot, sharing memories, photos, and wonderful stories. One of those things we've talked about a lot is the fact that Sherman lost a twin brother to a staph infection when he was nine. He never spoke about his own loss until our children accidentally discovered some photos under their grandmother's bed. That discovery opened the door to the sort of healing communication that we advocate in this book.

After Sherman's passing, our youngest grandchildren—twin girls who were then age three and a half—would draw pictures of Grandpa and talk about hugging and kissing him before they went to bed, knowing that "Grandpa is going to live with the dinosaurs."

With Sherman gone, I found myself overwhelmed with all of the estate, house management, and other responsibilities and tasks that awaited me. I had heard stories from my patients, but had not fully appreciated all that was involved in the process of grieving and reorienting one's identity and life until I experienced it myself. Just about everyone with whom I have shared my experiences has urged me to write a book, the kind of book I wish I'd had from the beginning. For example, I would have liked to have had Sherman's military discharge papers on hand, to have known his computer passwords so I could cancel accounts and transfer airline miles, to have had knowledge of the types of insurance policies he had along with the names and numbers of the agents, to have been prepared for the paperwork and immediate decisions that needed to be made.

Barbara's story illustrates how death has changed, largely as a consequence of advances in medicine. Death now refers to *process* more than it refers to an *event*. Moreover, Barbara's story shows us how grief has become a *family* matter as much as it is an individual one.

Her story also captures the essence of why we have written this book. What we are proposing here are *five stages* that all families, including yours, will likely go through as they find themselves caught up in the process of having a loved one die, not suddenly and unexpectedly, but slowly as the result of a terminal condition. It is intended to serve as a guide or handbook for your family to turn to as a resource as you head down this road. We do not claim that every family or family member will experience these stages in lock-step fashion. Also, the stages we define are not separated by bright lines; rather, they tend to blend into one another. That said, we sincerely hope that this book will be for you the one that Barbara wished she'd had.

Before we move on, here's one more example that shows some of the issues associated with contemporary grief:

🌿 *Hank and Betsy's Story*

Betsy and her husband, Hank, were members of an increasingly rare breed: They owned and operated a working farm. It was a fruit and berry farm. Each year they raised and harvested crops that included apples, peaches, and pears as well as strawberries, raspberries, and blueberries. They employed a staff of thirty, some of whom worked in a kitchen preparing jams, pies, and muffins and others who worked the fields. In the fall they made cider. All of these goods were sold wholesale to a variety of stores as well as retail to people who cared to stop by a small roadside store they operated.

Hank, an only child, had inherited the farm from his parents. Never particularly good in school (or much interested in it), he didn't finish high school, but he had worked full-time on the farm since he was fourteen and loved it.

Hank and Betsy had been childhood sweethearts. They married at age eighteen and had one child, a son, Mark. Whereas Hank had always been nothing but a straight arrow and a man who kept his nose to the grindstone, from childhood Mark had a history of being something of a cut-up. As a result, parents and son had long endured a contentious relationship.

Mark worked on the farm, but his work ethic could be described as on-again, off-again. When he was there, he did a good job. The trouble was he was not consistent. Literally days could pass without Mark showing up. That meant, of course, that work that needed to be done had to be put on hold. Betsy and Hank were of the opinion that Mark really didn't earn the salary they paid him and that, if he were not their son, he would have been fired many times. However, being their only child (and the potential heir to the farm), they had always hesitated to take that step.

Betsy, like Hank, was committed to the farm, and between the two of them they had, over thirty-five years, converted what had once been a farm on the verge of bankruptcy into a thriving business. Betsy concentrated on the business side of the operation, while Hank did what he'd always done best, which was to grow and harvest crops.

Then Hank's troubles began. First, at age sixty-five, he was diag- nosed with cancer in one kidney. The kidney was removed, and the cancer appeared to have been contained. That notwithstanding, Hank was nevertheless aware that his prognosis for remaining cancer free forever was not 100 percent.

A little after a year following his surgery, Hank's other kidney began to fail, and within nine months he was told that he would have to go on dialysis. Hank found the dialysis to be somewhat draining, not to mention causing a major disruption in his and Betsy's lifestyle. But they were comforted by the knowledge that, without dialysis, Hank could not have survived long with only one kidney functioning at 5 percent of normal.

Things went along fairly smoothly for the next six months, and then Hank began experiencing chest pain and shortness of breath. The pain started off as a minor annoyance, but it grew worse remarkably fast. A CT scan confirmed the worst: Hank's cancer had returned, this time in his lungs. Hank found himself now confronted by two realities. First, he could no longer actively work on the farm. Second, he had no way of knowing if he might live for another year or another decade.

Hank began a course of chemotherapy and radiation therapy, but midway through he suffered a blood clot that lodged in his lungs and that necessitated his being hospitalized and placed on a respirator. He lasted another month. Betsy was grateful, however, that Hank at least spent his last few days at home, and that he died in his sleep. When she awoke at dawn, as farmers usually do, she was at least relieved to see that there were no signs of distress on her husband's face.

The time that elapsed from Hank's initial cancer diagnosis to his death was a little shy of three years. His and Betsy's situation epitomizes many of the issues that we address in this book, and you may find yourself relating to some of them. What is most instructive in Hank and Betsy's story, though, is not only how they handled the long and arduous process of his decline and eventual death but how they approached it as a family.

Betsy and Hank were very attached to their two grandchildren. Unfortunately, Mark was divorced from their mother, which meant they had to depend on him for any contact they had with the kids. They were also keenly aware of the fact that whenever they tried to confront Mark on his unreliability, he'd blow up and stalk off. Then they would find themselves not seeing their grandchildren again for anywhere from a week to a month.

Rather than allow this frustrating situation to continue, after he underwent his kidney surgery, Hank summoned Mark, and the family had a long talk, right there, bedside at the hospital. Despite the fact that Hank had never sought counseling for anything in his life, it was he who suggested during that meeting that they seek a family therapist to help them. The facts were, he said, that he was not going to be around forever. He did not want his current relationship with Mark to be the way it was when he died. Moreover, he and Betsy wanted to have a relationship not only with Mark but with their grandchildren. Finally, they needed to decide collectively what would happen to the farm after Hank died. If Mark was ambivalent about farming, as Hank suspected he was, then it was better to be honest about it so that Betsy could make plans to hire professional help.

We want to point out several key things about Hank's situation and how he and the family handled it:

- Although it was true that Hank was in fact dying, it was not a sudden event. His dying was more typical of what people experience now, which is a *process* rather than an *event*.

- Hank decided to approach the issue of his own mortality and decline as a *family* issue, rather than allowing each person to deal with it separately.

- Hank included *himself* in the process.

- Hank and Betsy's goal was for the *family* as a whole to emerge from Hank's eventual death better off than it had been before.

- The focus was on the *future*, including what would happen to the family after Hank was gone. One of the things Hank did, for example, was to devote a couple of hours every day to writing a long journal about the farm. In it he detailed not only everything that needed to be done, and when, but he included anecdotes about how he had confronted crises over the years, ranging from floods to droughts and hailstorms and from frosts to pestilence. Eventually Hank's journal became a hefty handbook about farming for those who might follow him.

We want to help you approach the issues of dying and grief as a family, and with the same goals that motivated Hank and Betsy. You can think of this book as a kind of handbook or road map for anticipating and dealing with what may lie ahead, much like Hank's journal evolved into a handbook for running the farm and dealing with whatever crises might arise.

To finish their story, Hank, Betsy, and Mark learned through counseling that one reason for Mark's unreliability was his secret belief that he could never do as well as his father had. Even though he was bright and talented—especially mechanically—he had never openly expressed his insecurity and lack of confidence. Instead, he expressed it indirectly, through his inconsistent work ethic.

As it turned out, Hank's handbook for farming proved to be a blessing to Mark, who came to make a true commitment to taking on the responsibilities of the farm before Hank passed on. Betsy took this as a blessing as well. She had been fearful that as much as she knew about the business aspect of the farm, the idea of trying to keep it going by herself after Hank was gone seemed utterly overwhelming. What she and Hank had always hoped was that Mark and his own family would inherit the farm and that it would provide the family with financial security for generations. However, as Hank became more and more incapacitated, Betsy had begun to think that she might have to end up selling it. The sad fact was that it wasn't easy to find someone willing to take on the responsibilities that a farm demanded, and it would not fetch nearly as much money as would selling the land.

Mark remarried two years after Hank's death. His second wife was a woman very much like Betsy, who was more than happy to be mentored by her mother-in-law in the ways of running the farm. It was beginning to look like Hank and Betsy's dream might be fulfilled after all.

Death and dying are sad events to be sure. Yet the story of Betsy and Hank and, we hope, your story as well show us that the process of dying need not be limited to sadness. This idea is captured in the following quotation:

> *I saw Grief drinking a cup of sorrow and called out, "It tastes sweet, does it not?"*
>
> *"You've caught me," Grief answered, "and you've ruined my business. How can I sell sorrow, when you know it's a blessing?"*
>
> —RUMI

Chapter Two

THE FIVE STAGES OF FAMILY GRIEF

We are proposing here a five-stage model for family grief. However, as said earlier, we want to caution readers not to expect that there will be hard-and-fast boundaries separating these stages. While virtually every family will experience each stage, you should not expect one stage to simply end and another to begin. On the contrary, anticipate finding yourself dealing with issues associated with more than one stage at any given time. In addition, the stages vary in length and intensity, depending, for example, on the length of the terminal illness and whether there are any significant periods of remission.

We want to give you an overview of the five stages of family grief before we go into each one in greater detail.

Stage 1: Crisis

The process of family grief begins when the family learns that a loved one has a terminal diagnosis. When we talk about family members, we are including the person with the diagnosis (the *patient*) as well as loved ones who are not blood relatives. Family members' experiences and reactions are significantly shaped by the patient's reactions and responses to the diagnosis. The diagnosis itself may have been somewhat expected—for example, if it was preceded by a long period of testing—or it may come as a total surprise, which can happen when a person goes to the doctor for treatment for a minor ailment only to discover a short time later that he or she has cancer.

In either of these scenarios, the diagnosis of a terminal illness (say, a stage 4 cancer) or a potentially terminal illness (a stage 1 cancer) creates a *crisis* for the family. It disrupts the family's equilibrium, just as a rock thrown into the middle of a still pond disrupts its equilibrium. Factors that affect how you may react at this stage include

- The history of as well as the current status of your relationship with the ill family member.

- Whether the loved one is a spouse, a parent, or a child.

- What your and the patient's past (and current) roles in the family are.

As an example, consider those people who are commonly referred to as "parental children." These are individuals who, often since childhood, have taken on responsibilities for managing family conflicts, caring for siblings, cooking and cleaning, and so on. Parental children will react differently to the news that one of their parents is terminally ill from children who have been estranged or less involved in family matters and activities. Similarly, if the loved one is a child, or a young parent, reactions of family members can be expected to be different from what they would be if the loved one who is now facing death has had what one could call a full life.

Anxiety is the most common initial reaction to the news that a family member is terminally ill. However, if your relationship with the terminal family member has been strained or alienated, you may also find yourself feeling guilty, resentful, or angry. If the terminally ill person is a child or young adult, anger at the seeming injustice of early death may be the dominant emotion shared by family members at this initial stage.

Very often, memories of past interactions with the dying loved one will be evoked in this first stage. These memories have particular significance because they typically reflect the various family members' image of where they believe they stand in relation to one another and to the terminally ill person. Often, both happy and unhappy memories will come to mind. One woman, for example, on learning her mother had lung cancer, found herself flooded with memories of taking horseback riding lessons with her mother when she was a child. At the same time she recalled how angry and scared she was when her mother divorced her father and left her and her brother in his care while she pursued a new life and a new career elsewhere.

At this first stage of the new grief, all adult family members benefit from guidance in issues such as what to expect in terms of their own emotional reactions, whom to seek support from, whom to share memories and emotions with, and what to expect when they meet with the dying loved one and other family members.

Stage 2: Unity

The reality of impending death has the effect of pressing family members to put even longstanding complaints or grudges on hold as they pull together to move into this second stage of grieving. Any unpleasant emotions that may have been evoked in the crisis stage are typically suppressed as the family gets down to the business of doing what is necessary to care for the dying loved one. Any resentments, sibling rivalries and jealousies, and wounded egos are usually forced (temporarily) into the background.

Because today's families may be scattered over the world, physical distances can complicate the achievement of unity. This can complicate the grief process for a couple of reasons, First, on a practical level, distance can make it difficult for some family members to pitch in and help. Second, distance may limit the kind of contact you have with a terminally ill loved one. While phone calls and e-mails can provide support, the family members living closest to the ill member will have more demands, both practical and emotional. Family members who live away are not always able to come for every scary episode or procedure, and this can stress everyone. How do you know when to come? For how long? How do you know whether it is okay to go on vacation or to leave the country on business and/or pleasure? Travel insurance may well become more of a necessity than an option at this point.

In Stage 2, the needs of the dying become paramount. This may be no problem for family members who have no conflicted feelings or unresolved issues of their own with the loved one, such as favored children. On the other hand, if you feel that you were always a less favored child (or the family scapegoat), you should not be surprised if you experience a complex combination of emotions even as you strive to be a good team member.

A major issue for all family members in Stage 2 is how they will define their roles with respect to one another and the terminally ill member. If they do not give some thought to this—a situation that is quite common—they may quickly find themselves having regressed into roles they played years earlier, as children and adolescents, but that they would not consciously choose now.

In this second stage of the grief process the family has much work to do, including

- Choosing and working with a medical team.

- Navigating the social services maze.

- Pursuing and qualifying for entitlements.

- Ensuring that critical legal work (wills, living wills, and so on) is completed.

How the family organizes itself so as to complete these tasks can have powerful psychological and emotional effects on each member, depending on how comfortable each feels with the role he or she is playing. Two issues that will be addressed in depth in the part of this book that explores this stage of family grief are

- Defining your new family role.

- Defining your role with respect to the terminally ill family member.

Stage 3: Upheaval

The family will eventually enter this third stage of grieving if the process of dying goes on for some time, which it typically does today. At this point, the unity that characterizes Stage 2 begins to wear thin as the lifestyles of all involved, whether they recognize it or not, gradually undergo some significant changes. Whereas thoughts and feelings about these changes may have heretofore been put on the back burner, they can no longer be suppressed and begin to leak out. One such feeling is *ambivalence*, meaning the mixed feelings that many people experience when the process of dying evolves into a protracted one in which the loved one's overall quality of life slowly deteriorates. At the same time they become increasingly aware of the ways in which this process has put an added burden on them, and possibly their own families. If they then find themselves wondering if it wouldn't be better for all concerned if the process came to an end, they may feel guilty.

Emotions such as guilt, anger, and resentment are likely to emerge in Stage 3. For example, spouses who heretofore have been supportive of one another may begin to resent the ways in which a terminal illness is affecting their marriage, their family life, or both. By the same token, some family members may feel that they have carried too much of the burden as compared to others.

Meanwhile, as all of these issues begin to rear their heads, the

work of caring for the needs of all involved, including the terminally ill loved one, continues. The terminally ill individual needs
to be treated with dignity and not left out of important discussions. For their part, family members need to turn some of their
attention to learning to balance caretaking with self-care, their
own marriages, and their family life.

At this stage the most important issue becomes being able to
communicate honestly with other family members and with trusted
loved ones. Immediate family of the terminally ill loved one as well
as their spouses (and children if they have any) need to be given
a voice without fear of recrimination. Issues that need to see the
light of day include not only how each immediate family member's lifestyle may have been affected by the prolonged grief process but also how their marriages and families may have been
affected. Suppressing thoughts and feelings about such upheavals
can lead to strained relationships and eventually can cause the
entire family to fall apart.

Successfully negotiating the upheaval stage is easier when
families have relevant guidelines and prescriptive advice. We provide these in the chapters that cover this stage in depth.

Stage 4: Resolution

As a family moves into the fourth stage of grief, the terminally ill
loved one's health is typically marked by gradual deterioration,
punctuated perhaps by periods of stabilization or temporary
improvement, and the effects of the prolonged grief process can
and should no longer be ignored. If some family members' lifestyles have been significantly changed for the worse as a result of

a protracted terminal illness, for example, then that must be acknowledged; otherwise it will fester and create resentments. Stage 4 represents the point at which issues such as this are either successfully addressed or else left to slowly undermine the bonds that keep the family together.

As they enter Stage 4, family members often find themselves having more memories—both good and bad—of past experiences and events. Unlike the memories most often evoked in Stage 1, which usually reflect relationships with the patient, these important memories are different, typically telling the story of how family members have viewed their place and role in the family. Often they point to unresolved issues. Some of these memories may evoke feelings of joy or nostalgia; others, however, may evoke anger, jealousy, or envy. Others still may cause feelings of pride or, alternatively, of shame or embarrassment.

Stage 4 sometimes finds family members questioning themselves as to whether they have been a good enough spouse, parent, friend, or child. This process of introspection can be harmful—for example, if it leads to needless guilt, resentment, or second-guessing. Alternatively, it can set the stage for personal renewal if it opens the door to change and/or reconciliation.

Stage 4 represents an unprecedented opportunity, if families only choose to seize it. It is an opportunity to resolve longstanding issues, heal wounds, and redefine one's role in the family—indeed, to alter a family member's very identity. Every family, as they say, has its share of skeletons in the closet. It is in this fourth stage of the grief process that the skeletons can be brought out of the closet, exposed to the light of day, and cast forever into oblivion.

Regardless of whether the terminal family member is a sibling, a parent, or a child, chances are that there are some loose ends that have never been properly tied up. As children grow and move into adulthood, sibling-sibling and parent-child issues often are left behind, swept under the rug as it were. There they remain, potentially hidden but ever present, forever, unless some opportunity occurs for resolution. Contemporary grief, because of its protracted nature, presents families with just such an opportunity.

In particular, Stage 4 is a time when the following can be addressed and resolved:

- Old rivalries and jealousies.

- Long-held resentments.

These two issues stand in the way of families being able to bond together as strongly as they could and love one another unconditionally. Some family members, however, may react to this opportunity with anxiety instead of with enthusiasm. Rather than seizing the opportunity, they may try to avoid facing these issues. However, facing up to them offers the best opportunity for the family as a whole to move on together to a happier future. In this way the process of family grief can set the stage for growth and renewal for all involved.

In the chapters that cover Stage 4 we provide guidelines for bringing these issues into the open, where they can be resolved, and suggest ways of talking about them so as not to elicit unnecessary defensiveness. This process includes unresolved issues that family members may have, not only with one another but also with the loved one who is terminally ill. We emphasize the power of honesty and the ability to admit to personal flaws as well as recognize personal strengths.

Stage 5: Renewal

The final stage of grief actually begins with the funeral and the celebration of the life of the now-lost family member. This is a time of mixed emotions, to be sure, including both sadness and relief. If the family has successfully negotiated the previous four stages, however, this final stage also opens yet another door: to collective as well as personal renewal. It can be a celebration of life as much as it is a marking of a loss. It can be a time of creativity and planning, as the family decides, for example, how it will commemorate anniversaries and birthdays.

As much as Stage 5 is a time for remembrances, it is also a time for looking forward, to revitalized relationships and to new family traditions. We encourage just such activity, and we provide examples of families who, in the long run, emerged more vibrant and resilient despite the pain of their loss.

✍ *Lauren's Story*

Lauren's father passed away from acute myelogenous leukemia (AML) one year after the diagnosis. He was sixty-two years old and had been diagnosed several years earlier with testicular cancer. He underwent treatment at that time and had no relapse that Lauren was aware of.

Lauren's parents divorced shortly after her father recovered from the testicular cancer. The divorce was very difficult for Lauren and her younger sister, as they had been under the impression that their parents were very happy together. To Lauren's surprise, the divorce appeared to have been her father's idea. He met another woman shortly after the divorce was finalized, and Lauren and her sister were not able to develop any kind of relationship with the woman. "We felt like she was taking my mom's place," Lauren explained, "and so soon after he was sick. It didn't feel right to either of us."

Lauren's father, Paul, was diagnosed with AML in 2004, soon after he had moved in with his new girlfriend. At the same time, Lauren and her husband were trying to conceive their first child but were having a difficult time.

Lauren lives in New Hampshire; her father lived in Rochester, New York, closer to her sister. Because of the distance, much of the caretaking responsibilities for their father during his final year fell on Lauren's younger sister and her father's girlfriend. Lauren's mother was not allowed to see her ex-husband, reportedly a demand of the new girlfriend. This hurt Lauren deeply. "My mom and dad were married for thirty years," she explained. "He was dying, and she wasn't allowed to see him. I hated that. I wish someone could have helped me to deal with that at the time."

Lauren and her sister had to ultimately make the decision to take their father off of life support, as they were his blood relations and their mother was out of the picture. After his death, his girlfriend demanded that Lauren's father, Paul, not be buried in the plot he had originally chosen and paid for, explaining that she wanted to be buried next to him, in a different cemetery, when she died. Lauren's uncle, who was the executor of Paul's will, complied with the girlfriend's wishes despite the daughters' protests. This was extremely painful for Lauren. To make matters worse, her father had been in the process of selling his house. After his death, the girlfriend refused to move out for nearly a year, and when she finally did, it was clear that she took with her many items that had

*belonged to Lauren's father. Some of these items were of no conse-
quence, but others would have had great meaning to Lauren had she
been able to keep them.*

*Her father's death felt to Lauren "like my world had fallen apart.
My dad had always been my rock, and then he was gone. Nothing
was the same again." She felt it was all the sadder due to the fact
that she was trying to have a baby and that her child would never
know his grandfather. Lauren did get pregnant six months after her
father passed away. Her son's middle name is Paul, to honor his late
grandfather.*

*"I am so sad that Parker will never get to know his grandfather,"
Lauren said. "He looks so much like my dad, and part of me feels like
he is going to grow up feeling a void because my grandparents meant
so much to me."*

Looking back, Lauren wished she had known the following at
the time of her father's terminal illness:

- Who the executor of her father's will was (she learned this
  only after his death) and what rights his children might
  have regarding the process of divesting of her father's properties and belongings and selling his practice (he had been
  a dentist).

- How to help her mother cope with her loss after the divorce
  and then losing her ex-husband after so many years of
  marriage.

- How to communicate better with her younger sister and
  support her despite the geographic distance.

- How to manage the relationship with her father's girlfriend, who was not legally entitled to assets but who fought the family to receive money.

- How to manage her own marriage during this tremendous time of loss as well as during a time when she was trying to have a child.

- How to interact with medical staff, especially around the process of ending her father's life per his request but dealing with the associated grief.

Lauren stated that she has always had a difficult time asking for help because she is a very private person. She spoke about her closest friends and sister letting it be known that they were available to her, but because she did not like to depend on anyone outside of her husband, she made little use of them. This was a decision she regretted because talking with friends (or her sister) might have pointed her in the direction for dealing with the issues cited.

Nearly another year passed before Lauren learned that her sister was harboring some resentment, for two reasons: because Lauren had been relatively unavailable to help out and because Lauren and she had communicated very little during that last year of their father's life. In other words, their father's death and the way the family had handled it had left an emotional residue. Fortunately for Lauren, she loved her sister and sensed that some distance had come between them. She suggested seeing a family therapist together and offered to pay for it. She volunteered to drive from New Hampshire to Rochester—weekly, if necessary—to meet with the therapist.

Lauren's sister was touched by this offer and agreed to it. It took only a few trips (and therapy sessions) for the sisters to vent the complexity of feelings that they had experienced during their father's terminal illness. Lauren was able to acknowledge the work that had fallen on her sister's shoulders, as well as how it had been all the more difficult because of the animosity both women felt toward their father's girlfriend. Last, but not least, Lauren was able to take responsibility for her difficulty in reaching out to others, and vowed to make inroads in that area, at least in her relationship with her sister.

⛥ STAGE 1 ⛥

CRISIS

When I go down to the grave, I can say like many others, "I have finished my day's work," but I cannot say, "I have finished my life's work"; my day's work will begin the next morning. The tomb is not a blind alley. It is an open thoroughfare. It closes in the twilight to open in the dawn.

—VICTOR HUGO

Chapter Three

GETTING THE NEWS/ SHARING THE NEWS

THE NEW GRIEF BEGINS

The process of family grief begins when we get the news that a family member is either terminally ill or has an illness that is clearly life threatening. Regardless of whether we've already considered this possibility, as Barbara did (see the Introduction), hearing this kind of news never fails to shock us on some level. Perhaps we are shocked because hearing such words—*terminal, life-threatening*—forces us to confront mortality head-on, to stare death in the face, as it were. Perhaps it is natural for us to live in denial of our own mortality (and perhaps that of our loved ones as well), so that we resist facing it until we can no longer do so.

In any case, the bottom line is, getting the news that a family member is facing death tends to galvanize our attention. It throws the family—no matter how large or small—into a state of *crisis*. For some, it will mean that their worst fears have been confirmed.

For others, the first reaction may be a flood of fears. They may feel suddenly vulnerable and helpless. Still others may think, "This is a mistake. This can't be happening, not to *me*, not to *my* loved one, not to *our* family."

Many people report that their first awareness that a loved one is dying was accompanied by a sense of dreamy unreality. Some, in contrast, experience an immediate and intense feeling of panic or dread. It may take a while for this to pass, but eventually their minds and emotions settle down and reality sinks in. They realize that this is no mistake. Then they think: "What do we do now?"

Exactly what you (and each family member) will experience— how you will feel, what you will think—and how you will respond to the crisis depend to a large extent on the nature of your relationship with the terminally ill person, that person's reactions to his or her own diagnosis, and the roles that you and the patient have each played in the family in the past.

Often, the person who is ill is accompanied by a family member when going to the doctor's office, and this family member is therefore the first to experience the shock and pain on hearing the diagnosis. This person is also typically the one who shares the bad news with the rest of the family. But what if the one with the terminal diagnosis does not want to share his symptoms—or diagnosis—with loved ones, not wanting to worry them? Then what? Do the patient and the family member simply put aside a terminal diagnosis and pretend that nothing has happened? What would it be like, in that scenario, to be in either of their shoes?

Our advice to family members who find themselves being made aware of a terminal diagnosis but being asked to keep it secret is to take some time to see if you can live with this without feeling unduly burdened and distressed. If you can, then you might do so, unless and until you no longer feel comfortable. On the other hand, if keeping such a secret would cause you significant distress, the best course of action is to share your feelings with your ill loved one and frankly state that you can't keep quiet. It might be possible for you to reach a compromise regarding whom you feel obligated to share the news with. Or you might feel okay keeping the diagnosis secret for a limited period of time. If no such compromises are feasible, then you must respect your own feelings and share the news, even over your loved one's objections.

✑ John's Story

John was someone who wanted to keep his diagnosis a secret. Interestingly enough, the one person he chose to call after leaving his doctor's office and learning he was terminal was his therapist. He had gone to the doctor's appointment alone. Immediately on leaving the office, he called and asked his therapist if he could stop by that day. His therapist recognized this immediately as a sign of some sort, for in the three years that she and John had worked together he had never once made such a request. She vaguely recalled John mentioning that he was scheduled for a chest X-ray—the result of a persistent, chronic cough. But John had said this was to check for pneumonia.

As soon as John entered her office, the therapist knew that there was bad news. She quickly learned that John had not only had an X-ray but that its results had led to an additional half day in the hospital and many more tests, all of which ended in a preliminary diagnosis of advanced lung cancer.

John had been seeing his therapist primarily for support while he went through a divorce from his wife, who had an alcohol addiction. After he had decided to leave his wife, a friendship he'd had with a colleague had blossomed into a loving relationship, and at the time of his diagnosis, he and she were talking about a permanent relationship. Now this!

John's immediate reaction was that he did not want Francine, his woman friend, to know. The therapist asked why. "I don't want anyone to have to take care of me," he explained. "The very thought of that makes me sick." So, John told his therapist, he thought it would be better to end the relationship now, without an explanation, before it went any further.

The therapist sat bolt upright in her chair. "Whoa!" she said. "Let's slow down a minute! Before you make that decision, let's consider all the available information and prioritize what you need to do. And let's keep your options open."

John's initial response to his diagnosis was based largely on panic and guilt. He had always been a caretaker, not someone who needed to be taken care of. Moreover, he hadn't even had time to absorb all of what the doctors had told him, and he was now considering desperate, impulsive action as a way of managing his overwhelming emotions.

First Steps

Imagine that John's story is yours. The very first part of your plan—whether it is obvious to you or not—is to decide *whom to tell* and *what to say*. This is true certainly for the one receiving the diagnosis, but it is also true, by extension, for those family members or significant others who are the first to get the news.

However, depending on your emotional state, you may or may not be in a good position to make these decisions immediately. That's why we offer the following advice.

Slow Down. The first step to take in a crisis is to *slow down*. Accept whatever emotions are washing over you. Allow your body and mind some time to recover from the initial shock. Try taking some slow, deep breaths. Don't try to resist your anxiety; rather, let it pass through you in waves that are separated by these deep breaths. Feel the air fill your lungs as you breathe in, and then feel it leave as you exhale. As you do this, let your muscles relax, at least for that moment.

If you continue to breathe evenly and deeply like this and let your muscles relax while you do, you will find that your anxiety gradually diminishes and your mind gradually clears. Until now, sheer unrelenting anxiety may have made clear thinking impossible or distorted your perspective, as John's thinking was distorted by his initial reaction to his diagnosis.

Next, try to imagine yourself someplace that is or has been special and relaxing for you: watching a sunset, sitting in front of a fire, or watching the waves crash on a beach. Imagine the sights, sounds, and smells. Every so often shift your attention back to your breathing. Take in and exhale deep breaths, at the same time relaxing your muscles.

This exercise is a good stress management tool that you should keep in your back pocket, ready to be taken out and used whenever you feel the panic returning. Its purpose is to allow yourself to experience your feelings in a calmer state. Your emotions are natural and necessary and a part of coming to terms with your very real impending losses. At the same time, this exercise can set the stage for clearer thinking and decision making. Last, it is something that can be used by everyone: the terminally ill family member, other family members, and significant others.

Break the Ice. The second step is to find at least one person you trust with whom to share the bad news. *Don't keep it secret.* Maybe this first person will be your spouse, an adult child, a sibling, a dear friend, or even a helping professional (the person John opened up to). Looking back on it, John realized he chose his therapist because he knew she would help him get grounded before he did anything else. Having expressed intense emotions to her as he went through his divorce, John believed that his therapist could also handle his initial feelings of terror, panic, and immense sadness. The first person you choose to share the news with ought to be someone you think can handle it.

Sharing and communicating feelings and thoughts increases the likelihood of navigating the uncertainties and disruptions of the days, weeks, months, or perhaps even years that lie ahead. The first person you turn to will be your icebreaker, making it easier to move on from there.

Decide What to Share. John got his diagnosis rather quickly, and indeed sometimes it happens that way. Sometimes, however, an individual is faced with deciding how much to share—about both the illness and the emotions he or she may be experiencing— while waiting for a definitive diagnosis. Similarly, loved ones must make this same decision regarding what to say to whom about a family member who *might* have a terminal illness.

Given the time it takes to work your way through our contemporary medical services system, it can take weeks to months from the first suspicion that something is wrong to a firm diagnosis, and those weeks involve scheduling appointments, undergoing procedures, and waiting for results and sometimes starting the cycle all over. During those weeks or months, everyone who knows about the possibility of a serious or terminal illness can be expected to be pre-occupied (at least some of the time and maybe a lot of the time), anxious, and frustrated. By the time you receive a diagnosis, it can actually be a relief to move from uncertainty to certainty.

If it appears that there may be a long wait-and-see period while tests are being conducted and a diagnosis is forming, it may be better to limit the circle of people who are aware of what is happening and to ask that they put a cap on the information they disclose to others. This decision is best made by the person whose illness is being assessed in concert with the first person or persons who learn the news. Going outside of the immediate family or closely trusted others may have negative consequences, as Martin's story shows.

✍ Martin's Story

Martin, a fifty-year-old successful independent management consultant, learned that he had stage 2 colorectal cancer. Since he was to undergo surgery and several months of intense chemotherapy, he canceled or postponed many meetings, declined to take on new clients, and was open with his existing clients about his illness. After his treatments were completed, he realized that most of his clients had established relationships with a different consultant, writing him off as gone. Two years later, after struggling to restart his business, Martin regrets having shared the news of his illness with his business clients.

At the opposite end of the spectrum, there can also be consequences for leaving close family members out of the loop. Here is an example.

✔ *Meg's Story*

Meg learned that she had lung cancer after literally months of diag-
nostic workups. A fifty-five-year-old divorcee who worked as a pub-
lic school teacher substitute, she decided not to share this news, or
her feelings, with her adult daughters. Given an economic downturn
in the state where she lived, she did not want to miss a day of sub-
bing; she was, therefore, resistant to any treatment that would
require her to stay home and miss more than one day of work. She
was terrified of her illness, of course, but also scared of the prospect
of having to rely on others, so scared in fact that her oncologist rec-
ommended she see a therapist.

Reluctantly, Meg accepted the recommendation, and it took sev-
eral months before she could bring herself to share the news of her
illness with her daughters (both of whom lived out of town with their
husbands and children). Meg had distrustful relationships through-
out her life and consequently had great difficulty accepting kindness
or help from anyone. Her daughters, even though they were aware of
their mother's emotional difficulties, were nevertheless angry at first
that their mother had not trusted them to keep her secret and had
chosen instead to not inform them of her testing or diagnosis.

What these two stories illustrate is that there is a delicate line
that sometimes must be walked when it comes to sharing a potentially terminal diagnosis. One needs to consider *who needs to*
know what. Obviously, close loved ones will want to know—and
probably should know—so they can be part of the ill person's support network. On the other hand, people who will not be part of
that network probably need to know only the basics, if that. For
example, neither Martin's clients nor the school system that Meg

worked for needed to know anything about their illnesses. Meg's daughters, though, did have a legitimate need to know.

Designate a Point Person. Physicians report that having at least one family member accompanying the patient to each office visit is helpful. This person should bring a pen and pad of paper to every appointment. Her role is to be a second pair of eyes and ears, to take notes, and to help the patient better grasp the nature of and likelihood of treatments and prognoses. This person can also help ensure that other family members are kept accurately informed.

Adult children are most often the ones to be called on to be the point person. One factor to consider, however, is the potential for sibling rivalry to erupt if there is more than one adult child. This can occur even in families where such rivalries have not been a problem for years. This issue will be discussed in detail when we address Stage 2. But it is something to be aware of from the outset.

Further Food for Thought

Psychological research has shown that people who have social and emotional support are typically better able to cope with crises. This includes family, but it also can include others who are in the same boat as the terminally ill person. It is an interesting phenomenon that once you become aware of a disease, you begin to hear multiple stories about others with a similar diagnosis. That is why disease-specific support groups have proven to be so successful, whether they are attended in person or via the Internet. These facts alone are good reasons for the terminally ill person to begin building a support network as soon as possible.

Research has also shown that there are personality differences that define *resilient* versus *fragile* people, with the former being better at coping with crises. We will address this more in chapter 5. For now it is enough for you to know that an individual's personality plays an important role in how they deal with a terminal illness and even their survivability.

🌿 Holly's Story

"My father-in-law was like the father I never had," Holly explained. "He was such a gentleman, and seeing him and my mother-in-law together made me see what a marriage could be like."

Holly's father-in-law, Matthew, was diagnosed with hepatitis C approximately two years before his death. She thought that he may have been an alcoholic, but his doctor said it was more likely that he was infected through a blood transfusion he received after surgery.

Matthew's diagnosis was made worse by the fact that he gave the disease to his wife. Hers was better managed, though, because she did not drink at all. "Matthew's attitude," said Holly, "was that he was going to die anyway, so he might as well enjoy himself. He ate whatever he wanted to eat, and he enjoyed his cocktails. He did stop smoking, though."

Matthew's death was a striking blow to the family, as he had always been the one to organize all of the family gatherings. He also had a way of keeping the peace between Holly's husband and his brother, who did not much like one another. All in all, Holly felt that after Matthew died the family "fell apart a little."

Matthew's death was made more painful for Holly, since her own father not only drank but was an abusive man, physically and verbally, toward her, her siblings, and their mother. Her father-in-law represented a better man and was a real source of love and strength

to her. Her husband also suffered greatly with the loss of his father,
which put a strain on the marriage.

Holly was fortunate to have had a great deal of support from her
friends, who also helped by watching her son, who was six at the
time Matthew was diagnosed. They also volunteered to help her
mother-in-law and even to take Matthew to doctors' appointments
when he was too weak to drive himself. Holly talked about her father-
in-law and his illness with people at work. She had worked there for
many years, and these people too felt like family to her.

Holly wished that she had known the following during the two
years her father-in-law was sick before he died. Some of Holly's
reflections, along with our suggestions, might be relevant and
helpful to you in your own situation.

- How to get therapy for herself and her husband. She
  felt that they each grieved alone and were not good at sharing their thoughts and feelings with one another. She believed that this had created a certain distance between
  them. A therapist, she believed, might have helped them
  come out of their shells, bridge the gap, and support one
  another better.

- What her in-laws' financial situation was. As it turned out,
  her mother-in-law became very ill soon after Matthew died,
  and Holly and her husband became her primary caretakers.
  It would have been very helpful, she said, to know how to
  qualify for entitlements such as home healthcare. They also
  ended up paying death taxes and getting caught up in a prolonged probate process before getting paid back.

• How to help her husband deal with his father's death and her son with the loss of his grandfather. Again, Holly wished she had sought some sort of counseling for dealing with these issues.

• Whether Matthew had a do not resuscitate (DNR) order and where it was. Such orders prevent medical staff from instituting extraordinary measures in the event a person dies. Holly knew that her father-in-law was not comfortable with having such methods used, but the hospital could not find such an order. It eventually showed up in a manila folder in Matthew's desk drawer.

• How to prepare for the loss of a central person in the family and particularly how to plan for major family events like holidays after losing the person who had always been in charge of these gatherings. Although there is no easy way to prepare for the loss of a family member who has played such a central role, adult children are wise to gradually begin to take on some of the financial, social, and emotional responsibilities. No one lives forever, and sooner or later these duties will need to be transferred to the younger generation. Families are like tribes, and tribes that survive find a way to pass down rituals, roles, and traditions from one generation to the next. We encourage families to welcome and facilitate this process, not resist it. Ideally, this process will have begun before a central family member gets a terminal diagnosis, but certainly it needs to begin once that happens. Rather than exclude the patient from this process, however, he or she should be included by being asked, for example, for advice or guidance about family traditions and how they are to be run.

Chapter Four

FIRST REACTIONS

In a story written for the *New York Times Magazine* (April 26, 2009), Christopher Buckley, son of the late William F. Buckley, Jr., described his experience of his mother's death. It was April 2007, and his mother, Pat, was in the hospital. She had fallen the previous November, breaking several bones. In addition she had been a lifelong smoker, and it had taken its toll. Once a high-profile socialite like her famous husband, Pat was now a frail shell of herself, hanging on to life by virtue of a respirator. She had fallen victim to a mortal infection that had set in after an unsuccessful operation to install a stent in an artery. Recovery, the doctors told Christopher, was impossible. The only issue was if and when to take Pat off the respirator.

In his article, Christopher described a contentious relationship with his mother (indeed, with both his parents). There were many periods of time, for example, when son and mother were not on speaking terms. He wrote: "Mum's serial misbehavior over the years had driven me, despairing, to write her scolding—occasionally scalding—letters." In his story he recounted some of these incidents, which paint a picture of a mother who was vain and given to making up stories—such as regular visits by the British royalty to her home—so as to make herself look as if she had a higher social status than she did.

He described Pat as someone who was "defiant—almost magnificently so—when her demons slipped their leash." An interesting woman, perhaps, but not necessarily an easy mother for a child to get along with.

As he sat at his mother's bedside, holding her hand after making the decision to withdraw the respirator—a decision Christopher and both his parents were in agreement on—he was flooded not with anger, but with tears, and the only words that formed in his mind and came out of his mouth were "I forgive you."

Expect the Unexpected

Christopher's reaction to his mother's death surprised him. Why? Probably because his relationship with Pat had been marked by so many incidents that had made him angry. He never expected to feel so forgiving toward the woman who he felt had tormented him so over the years.

In contrast to Christopher's reaction, we have heard stories where people surprised themselves by expressing unexpected anger when first learning of the death of a parent. That has led us to the conclusion that one should expect the unexpected when it comes to first reactions.

Of course, most people will experience a measure of anxiety mixed with sadness when they learn of a terminal diagnosis. However, depending on the nature of their relationship with the patient and other family members, they may also experience anger, guilt, resentment, or even panic. One man, for example, who had long harbored feelings of resentment toward his father—whom he saw as favoring an older brother while being harshly critical of him—expressed anger when he was told about his father's cancer, "Now he'll be someone I have to feel sorry for!" he exclaimed. He felt that his father's diagnosis meant that he would never be able to express his resentment over the past or seek some sort of resolution with his father.

Another man found himself burdened with unrelenting guilt when he learned that his mother was expected to live six months or less. Although he believed he'd been a reasonably good (attentive, thoughtful) son, he also believed he could have done a lot more to make his mother happy. "She loved to walk on the beach," he explained, "just like I do. But I only went out of my way once in the last three years to pick her up and take her to the beach."

Other examples of guilt as an initial reaction include the husband of a woman diagnosed with lung cancer who felt guilty that he had not been more forceful in trying to get his wife to stop smoking. The wife of a cancer patient, meanwhile, felt guilty because she felt the illness was God's punishment for an affair she had had during the marriage.

It seems that people believe it is appropriate to feel only

sadness as an initial response to a terminal diagnosis in a loved one, and therefore are caught off guard and feel bad if they also experience anger or guilt, as in these examples. However, if you think about it, it does not really make sense that we should feel only sadness. If your relationship with this family member has been especially good—close and mutually supportive—then anxiety and sadness would be expected. But what if you have been a son (or daughter) who felt you had always been a less favored child? Would it be so unreasonable for you to feel some anger or resentment mixed in with the sadness? What about the parent of a terminally ill child who has harbored doubts about how effective or nurturing or supportive he or she has been? And what about the adult child who has become dependent—emotionally, financially, or both—upon a parent who is suddenly diagnosed as terminally ill. Should this person not experience anxiety, even panic? Why, in other words, should we expect people to experience only sadness as a first reaction?

Expect Ripple Effects

Everyone in the family, in fact, will probably have a unique and somewhat different reaction to a terminal diagnosis. Moreover, each person's reaction will influence everyone else's. That's because a family is an interconnected, interdependent system. It is interdependent not only in terms of raising children, keeping a household, and so on but also emotionally. If one part of the family is crippled, for example by illness or a loss of income, the effects likely will ripple through the entire family. The same is true for emotions, including the reactions we are discussing here. If one family member is overcome with sadness, while others harbor feelings of resentment, guilt, or panic, these varied reactions will have ripple effects, causing family members to react to one another. The most common mistake families make at this first stage is to cast judgment on what emotions a person may initially experience when the news of a terminal illness throws the family into crisis. As a consequence, you may find yourself feeling guilty if you experience any emotion other than sadness. Yet this clearly is not necessarily the only emotion you will experience, and for good reason.

What we do know is that the emotions family members experience will very likely be intense, sometimes surprisingly so, and that there will a period of shock, unreality, and, in some family members, frenzied activity. The latter is more likely among so-called parental children who have long taken on major responsibilities within the family. Panic, in contrast, may well be the dominant emotion felt by dependent adult children.

Whether family members feel free to openly express their feelings will depend in large part on the *family culture*. If parents are models of stoicism, for example, the outright expression of intense emotion will be suppressed. On the other hand, more emotionally expressive parents open the door to freer expression of reactions. Families in which anger is an acceptable emotion open the door to that reaction. And so on. Generally speaking, a stoic family will minimize the immediate ripple effect, whereas an emotionally open family will promote it. Suppressing initial reactions, however, is no guarantee they will not emerge at a later time in even more virulent forms.

Expect Changes over Time

First reactions inevitably give way to many more as time goes by. Even reactions such as anger, resentment, guilt, and panic will change, becoming more nuanced with the passage of time. For that reason, many people have found it helpful to take a few minutes every few days to write down their thoughts.

STARTING A GRIEF JOURNAL

To avoid complications later on, it is best to admit—at least to yourself but preferably also to someone you trust—the full range of emotions you experience soon after learning that someone in your family is terminally ill. In addition, it can be very helpful in the long run to start a journal in which you periodically write down your thoughts and feelings.

The best journals are those that are by and large unedited testimonials about a person's thoughts and feelings. President Ronald Reagan kept such a journal throughout his eight years in the Oval Office. It is remarkable for its frankness. Clearly, writing in his journal was as useful for President Reagan as reading it is enlightening for those who care to get a glimpse of what goes on in the mind of a president—how one president reacted to events and to people.

A journal is, of course, private, and yours should be kept in a private place. All things considered, it is better not to advertise the fact that you are keeping a journal. At most, one or two of your trusted friends (or a spouse) should know about it. Use it as a place to freely express your thoughts and feelings. Try not to edit yourself too much; rather, assume your words will be read by only you. Write down your thoughts and feelings about the loved one who is terminally ill, about your interactions with this person as well as with other family members. Write down your thoughts about how you feel about yourself and your role in the family. And write down your thoughts about what, if anything, you would like to change about your role in the family, now and in the future.

Sometimes a parent who has received a terminal diagnosis and has young children will begin to write letters or start a journal—perhaps including photographs, video, and/or CD recordings—for their children to have when they reach an appropriate age. In *The Last Lecture*, Randy Pausch, the young father of small children, shared how he began to collect his thoughts and feelings for his children to read later in their lives.

Early Actions

🌿 Merry's Story

When Merry, age forty-four, was diagnosed with late-stage invasive breast cancer, her husband, John, immediately arranged to take a leave of absence from his sales manager job, which involved a great deal of traveling. Before Merry went to the hospital for surgery, she wrote out all of the caretaking and house management jobs she had handled, and even though John was capable of taking on many of these chores, together she and John decided to ask her recently widowed mother to come help, especially with their two youngest children, who still lived at home.

Jerry, their college freshman son who had always been a high-maintenance child, also wanted to come home, but John and Merry

decided that this would not be helpful, as they suspected he was moti-
vated less by a desire to help than by a desire to evade academic
difficulties at school. Meanwhile, Joey, their thirteen-year-old, volun-
teered to take over the pet management for the family's two dogs and
cat, while Suzie, their ten-year-old, asked to stay home with her
grandmother to help out, rather than going on a church trip to Wash-
ington, D.C., over spring vacation.

This family possessed two of the characteristics that we consider to be essential to a healthy, functioning family system: cohesion and adaptability. *Cohesion* refers to feelings of connection, of
being a family unit, and *adaptability* is the ability of individuals
within the system and of the system as a whole to be flexible in
terms of roles as circumstances warrant. In this case, Merry and
John were decisive and took immediate action to help the family
get itself in place to deal with the crisis at hand.

Other families do not take the kind of decisive action that
Merry and John did. These families are more likely to lack clear
leadership and so are left to flounder in the face of crisis. This
inevitably leads to an increase in the emotional reactions discussed earlier as well as in a significant increase in overall stress
levels in all family members.

How a family responds at this point is strongly influenced by
its history of dealing with crises. Thinking of your own family,
consider the following factors that play an important role in this
regard.

How Decisions Have Been Made in the Past. Historically, has
there been one primary decision maker in your family or have
important decisions been made in consultation with others? If
the terminally ill family member has also been the person who

has made all the important decisions, who else is ready and willing to step into this role, either independently or in coordination with others? The patient can still be part of this process, but the reality is that dealing with a terminal illness can easily become a full-time job, not to mention the fact that many treatments can sap a person's energy even as they aim to cure or arrest an illness. Obviously, the family would want those with the coolest heads to step up to the plate at this point. However, those family members who tend to be more emotional should not be delegated to the sidelines, for they too may be quite capable of containing their emotions in the interest of working together to get things done.

Dependent Family Members. Are there dependent family members—either adults or children—who can be expected to consume time and attention as opposed to being able to take on additional roles and responsibilities? Young children and teenage children of a terminally ill parent represent an additional responsibility the family must take on. Adult children who are dependent for one reason or another cannot be relied on too heavily during this crisis. At the same time, neither can they be allowed to drain too many of the family's resources.

The Flexibility of the Family's Roles and Rules. In highly patriarchal or matriarchal families, having a dominant parent hand over control to someone else, even if they are now terminally ill, may be very difficult for the entire family. In those instances, it is usually important to communicate respect for the ill person's status within the family while offering to be of assistance. You would be wise to consult with the historical head of the household even about relatively minor decisions, to minimize any chance that he or she will feel anxious about losing control. This in itself may be uncomfortable (and time consuming), but the alternative can cause a matriarch or patriarch who feels slighted to actually sabotage the family's efforts to cope with the crisis. And other members in the family may have feelings about who is chosen to take over control and how the decision was made.

The Family Routines and Rituals. Family rituals can be as significant as who plans and cooks the annual Thanksgiving dinner or as mundane as who walks the family dog and cleans up the poop in the backyard. These routines need to be maintained for two reasons: (1) to keep the family functioning on a day-to-day basis, and (2) because they promote family cohesiveness and strengthen family bonds. How many of these routines and rituals were handled by the ill family member? To whom can they be delegated during this time of crisis?

How Long the Family Has Been a Family. The meaning of illness, vulnerability, and mortality differs for a younger family than for a family in later stages of life. Parents who have raised children well into adulthood may have a family that extends to include in-laws and grandchildren, nieces and nephews. A terminal diagnosis in a parent over sixty carries somewhat different ramifications for the family than an identical diagnosis in a thirty- or forty-year-old parent. Generally speaking, there is a greater sense of urgency associated with the crisis when the ill individual is the parent of young children. In that case, other family members must seriously consider taking on surrogate parental responsibilities, beginning in Stage 1. A good starting point for this is a frank dialogue among family members as to who is willing and able to do what in terms of child care.

Religiosity. Some studies have shown that families who are actively involved in religions that promote family and community cohesiveness show less stress during a terminal illness and more acceptance afterward. That is not to say that a family should join a religion at this point in time; on the other hand, we have known families who discovered a renewed faith in response to the crisis posed by terminal illness.

Age of the Terminal Family Member. Few people would disagree with the contention that a terminally ill child is perhaps the greatest stress that parents and a family can bear. In a thinly fictionalized account of his daughter's terminal illness, titled *The Blood of the Lamb*, Peter De Vries captured the excruciating pain of such an experience. Parents and siblings confronted with this situation require as much support—from other family, from friends and clergy, from medical personnel and therapists—as they can get. Unfortunately (from our perspective at least), some parents elect to go through this kind of family crisis privately. We encourage them not to do so but to reach out instead to all of these sources of support as well as to support groups for parents who find themselves in a similar situation.

COLLECTING ACCURATE INFORMATION

One of the most important early actions that needs to be taken in Stage 1 is to collect as much accurate *information* as possible about the following:

* *Diagnosis:* Exactly what is the illness? How severe is it?

* *Treatment options:* In what ways is this illness treated? Are there alternatives? If so, what are the pros and cons of each alternative?

- *Prognosis:* What is the prognosis for this illness if it is not treated? What is the prognosis associated with each alternative treatment?

During this initial, crisis period, it is important that the family collectively learn as much as it can about the diagnosis and its possible ramifications. With respect to this, we recommend that at least one and preferably two family members other than the patient attend all medical appointments and *ask questions* and *take notes.*

Researching the diagnosis online can also be helpful if you focus on reputable sources. Gathering as much information as possible and organizing and sharing this information with family members can be invaluable. However, you need to be able to assess the quality of the information you find—particularly when you uncover conflicting information and hear different secondhand and thirdhand personal accounts from friends and acquaintances. Relying on national organizations such as the American Cancer Society and reputable medical centers can lessen misinformation, even though there may be disagreements about their recommendations. Each situation is different, and what works for one person may not for another. Your own family physician may also be able to recommend some websites. Finally, government-sponsored websites, such as the National Institutes of Health, can also be helpful resources.

Accurate information serves as a focus for the family during the crisis stage, while also providing something of a road map as to what to expect, generally speaking, in the weeks, months, or even years ahead.

Simultaneously, it is important to identify all potential *resources*. For example, CaringBridge (www.caringbridge.com) is an online site at which a family can register to provide updated information to the circle of people they wish to keep informed. This site (one of several such online sources) allows trusted friends to volunteer for such things as driving someone to medical appointments or treatments, bringing meals, and running errands. While many terminal patients are embarrassed and do not want a fuss made over them, they can get used to it if it is done in a respectful way. Furthermore, continuous support from family members, friends, and even colleagues has a salutary effect on the family's overall well-being.

TALKING TO CHILDREN

When to tell children that a beloved family member has been diagnosed with a terminal illness is one of the most difficult decisions facing the family in this crisis stage. Factors you should consider include the child's age, temperament, and developmental capacities. It is even more difficult if it is the child's parent who has been diagnosed. Not everyone in the family may feel up to this task. Indeed, some may feel that it is better not to tell children at all, at least at this point, in the hope that the illness may either remit or be arrested through treatment.

We have decided to include this topic here because we have come to believe that it is at this first stage that this dialogue should begin, even as we recognize that this is not the point at which many adults feel comfortable initiating such a dialogue.

It is important to appreciate that young children's understanding of illness in general, much less a terminal illness, is very different from that of an adolescent or an adult. The very concept of death is one that requires the ability to think in the abstract—something that emerges typically in late childhood (though there are exceptions). Accordingly, any dialogue with a child about a terminal diagnosis in a parent, sibling, or extended family member needs to take place in this developmental context.

Why Should They Have to Know?

Understandably, many parents' initial reaction to the idea of disclosing a terminal diagnosis is to reject the idea. One father of a twelve-year-old daughter and seven-year-old son responded exactly this way after learning that he had late-stage colon cancer.

✒ Ken's Story

Only forty-three years old, Ken had always been an active, vigorous, and athletic man. In twenty years, he could count on one hand the number of days he'd called out sick from his job as an engineer. He, his wife, Jean, and the children enjoyed snow skiing in the winter and water skiing in the summer.

Ken's symptoms were typical—weight loss and intense fatigue—but they came on suddenly. Diagnosing the cancer proved somewhat elusive as the malignancy had wrapped itself around Ken's colon. In any case, by the time it was diagnosed it was clear that he was terminal. Experimental treatments were available, but his oncologists were frank in sharing an extremely guarded prognosis.

As Jean recalled that meeting in which Ken's diagnosis was first confirmed, it seemed more like a bad dream than an actual meeting. "I heard Ken's doctor speaking to us. I could see the serious

*expression on his face. But I felt like I was floating instead of sitting
in that chair. Afterward Ken told me he felt the same way."*

*It wasn't until Ken and Jean had a second meeting with his doc-
tors, three days later, that reality began to sink in. Until then they
spoke very little about it. Jean cried, and Ken had comforted her, but
Ken had not cried or expressed much emotion at all. At that second
meeting, experimental treatment options and their side effects were
discussed, and despite the poor prognosis, Ken opted to travel to a
cancer center several hours away to pursue the treatment. Then Jean
asked him what he wanted to tell the children. Ken's curt reply: "I don't
think we have to tell them anything." Jean, surprised, responded by
explaining that Ken would expect to be drained after his treatments.
Besides, she argued, how would they explain his bimonthly trips?*

*Reluctantly, Ken agreed to tell the children that he had an illness
that required him to travel to another city twice a month for treatment. He was adamant, however, that they not use the word* cancer. *
Jean was skeptical that the children would quietly accept such
an explanation, but she acquiesced in the face of Ken's intense
resistance.*

Ken's initial response to the idea of telling the children about his
illness is not so unusual, especially when the terminally ill family
member has a history of relative good health and has taken on a
role as a leader in the family. This described Ken very well. He later
disclosed that he was motivated by a desire to protect his son and
daughter from the potential stress of learning that their father was
terminally ill. He wanted them to be able to go on with their lives
without the distraction of worrying about him. As noble as this
desire was, it was not really workable.

When Jean and Ken first sat the children down and told them that Dad had an illness that required him going for treatment every other week, his daughter's first response was "Do you have cancer?" Meanwhile, Ken's son, who had just turned eight, looked on, a blank expression on his face. As Jean recalled the moment, "It couldn't have been clearer just how different the children were at that moment, how far apart they were when it came to understanding what Ken's illness really meant."

Ken and Jean, struck dumb by their daughter's question, had looked at each other blankly. "I was caught completely off guard," Ken explained. "At first I didn't know what to say, then I just said yes. Then my daughter started crying, but I could tell that my son still had no real clue what was going on."

Guidelines for Talking with Children

Ken and Jean's experience illustrates why we advocate communicating early with children about a terminal diagnosis in a close family member, be that a sibling, a parent, or another member of the extended family. What follows are some suggested guidelines for doing this.

Obviously, if a terminal diagnosis is given to one parent of a young child or children, both parents need to decide when and what to tell the children. If the parent happens to be a single parent, that presents an even more delicate situation. As a rule, we have found that parents need to share very little with children under the age of six. They may acknowledge, for example, that Mom or Dad is ill or not feeling well, but that should suffice at least at this initial stage.

Older children and adolescents also need to have some basic information. However, parents may elect to protect these children from worry, at least until the final diagnosis and treatment options and implications are known.

As in Meg's story, given earlier, adult children should probably be given at least the essential facts as they become available. This approach communicates respect for them as adults. It also allows them to begin thinking about the future and to plan for how they may have to become involved as the terminal illness progresses.

As a rule, we recommend that children be told about a diagnosis if there is reason to believe that a parent's appearance will be affected by treatment or if the parent will soon not be able to function at the same level that they have been. The following are some things to consider talking to children about:

- *How the illness will affect the parent.* Will chemotherapy or radiation therapy cause fatigue? Will there be a loss of hair, and if so, how will the parent deal with that?

- *How the illness will affect the child's life.* Will parental roles change and in what ways? Will schedules or routines change? Will new caretakers be involved?

In addition to this basic information, children should be given as optimistic a prognosis as possible, at least at this first stage. It is not necessary to go into details, other than to explain that the family member (or parent) is ill, will be undergoing treatment, and how that treatment is likely to affect the parent and the child. It is also appropriate for parents to inform their children's teachers so that the teachers can be alert for any changes in behavior or performance and understand the likely cause for any such changes.

✒ *Brandon's Story*

Brandon and his wife, Jen, had been childhood sweethearts, and they had been married for forty years when she passed away. She was diagnosed with amyotrophic lateral sclerosis (ALS) only eleven months before her death, and she had declined rather quickly.

Jen and Brandon had two daughters, both in their late twenties, and both single. Brandon shared with us what a terrible loss Jen's death had been for all of them. Brandon said that there were days that he did not want to get out of bed in the morning, but that he was Jen's primary caretaker, so he always managed to roll over and get going. He felt that he had to be strong for Jen's sake, as it was so incredibly frustrating and humiliating for her as she began to lose function of her body.

"Jen was so active," Brandon explained. "She was always walking and hiking with the dogs. Everyone told me that I should continue to go on my walks while she was ill, but I couldn't bring myself to leave her side. At the time I was glad that I didn't leave her. I don't know how I will do those things now, without her."

Jen was Brandon's best friend, and he struggled mightily after her death. For a while he stayed with one of their daughters, who is a nurse. However, he spoke about how difficult it was to lean on his daughters or even talk to them about how he was feeling because he felt he should be strong for their benefit, as he had been for Jen. "I'm their dad," he said. "Fathers are supposed to be strong. I try, but I honestly don't know how successful I am. I'm afraid at times that they see through me—to how vulnerable and weak I really feel."

Brandon said that he and Jen had gone through the process of estate planning while she was still well and was relieved to have taken care of that so that he would not have to "waste time," as he put it, worrying about that while she was ill. He also said he was grateful that their daughters were at least adults and that he didn't know how people would get through what he'd been through if they had young children.

The religious community to which Brandon and Jen belonged is very close-knit and everyone knew about Jen's illness. "People were very kind. They would run errands for us, bring us meals, keep Jen company. One friend would come in and read to her for an hour or more three times a week." Brandon did not express any hesitation in asking for this help, but again he hesitated to call on his daughters. For some reason, he said, he felt that he and Jen were not a burden for their fellow parishioners but that they would be a burden to their daughters.

Brandon said that he thought it would be helpful for others in the same situation to know the following:

- Spend as much time with your family member as possible but take care of yourself as well. "You have to take care of yourself in order to take care of the other person. Looking back, I should have taken the dogs for a short walk at least once in a while. It would have done a lot of good for my mental health."

- Respect the dignity of your loved one, especially if and when the person loses bodily abilities and cannot care for him- or herself.

- Do not show your frustration; if you do, your loved one will feel guilty and so will you after your family member has passed away. The best way to avoid frustration is to just keep telling yourself, "It is what it is," meaning that you have to accept the situation for what it is, not wish that it were different, and not try to change it.

- Brandon wished that he had turned to his daughters more when he was suffering himself. He also wished that he and Jen had decided to rely on them more, as after Jen's death each daughter separately shared how she felt as if she were on the outside looking in a lot of the time. In retrospect, he thought that some personal or family counseling might have been helpful in breaking out of this pattern, which he attributed to some false sense of paternal protectiveness on his part. "Afterward I realized that I had sold them short. They're both really very strong individuals."

- Brandon also wished that he knew how to move on while still respecting Jen's memory. He said he feels stuck. He can't bring himself to get rid of her clothes, rearrange their bedroom, and so on. His daughters think it would be good for him to do both and have offered to help. He said that he was considering asking them to do it for him.

Chapter Five

THE RESILIENT FAMILY

PERSONALITY DIFFERENCES AND SURVIVABILITY

The subject of this chapter—what we call *family resilience*—begins to play a role right from the start of the crisis that a terminal diagnosis creates. It is essential, therefore, that you understand this important concept at the outset. Armed with that understanding, it is possible that not only you but your entire family can emerge from this crisis even stronger than you were before. It is even possible that the terminally ill family member can extend his or her life through an effort to become more resilient.

Family Resilience

Throughout the past twenty years, psychologists have learned a great deal about people who are able to weather life crises and emerge pretty much unscathed versus those who don't. They use the word *resilient* to describe the former group, in contrast to those whose personalities could be described as *fragile*. This work has its origins in the simple observation that not everyone is affected equally by trauma. Whereas some people come out of a crisis— death, divorce, loss of employment—with obvious and deep psychological wounds, others seem to be more capable of bending without breaking. Similarly, studies have found that some people who are exposed to chronic stress—for example, business executives—suffer from emotional and physical problems, while others do not, again depending in part on their personalities.

At the same time psychologists were studying the personality trait called resilience, physicians were becoming increasingly aware that a person's attitudes and outlook were significant factors in how they came through major surgery. Essentially, optimistic people who are determined to survive surgery do much better than those who enter surgery afraid, pessimistic, or both.

It makes sense that these concepts and observations are relevant to people who find themselves diagnosed with a terminal illness. Taking one more step, it is reasonable to assert that not only individuals but whole families can differ in terms of their outlook, and that some families are more resilient than others. In other words, some families deal with crisis more effectively and emerge from crises less damaged than others.

THE RESILIENT PERSONALITY

There are some fairly specific and identifiable differences between resilient and fragile men and women. Those who react to stress and crisis poorly—who report much higher levels of anxiety or depression and who have more problems with their physical health—are individuals whom we could call psychologically *fragile*. They stand in sharp contrast to people whose lives may be just as stressful, but who by and large do not suffer these problems.

As a group, more-resilient people have personalities that are characterized by the following beliefs.

Life Has Meaning. To some people, saying that life has meaning is a statement of spirituality. Perhaps they are correct, in the sense that those people we most often associate with being spiritual typically do believe that life has meaning. In fact, resilient people tend to believe that they are here for some purpose and that there is something to be learned from whatever life throws their way. That's not to say that spirituality is exclusive to any particular religion. On the contrary, virtually all religions endorse this idea of life having meaning.

When asked if they believed that their life had meaning or purpose, some responses we have gotten from terminally ill men and women include

"Yes, I have always believed that I was destined to have children and raise them to be healthy, happy adults. I can take some comfort now in knowing I have done that."

"I do believe that God meant me to put whatever talents He blessed me with to good use. I try to do that."

"I suppose if my life had a purpose it would be to leave the world a little better off after I'm gone than it was when I got here. I'm not sure I'm the best judge of whether I succeeded."

"I had very little growing up. That may be why it has been my goal for a long time to make sure that my children and grandchildren will have a financial safety net under them. I'm happy that I've accomplished that."

As it pertains to life crises, including a crisis such as terminal illness, truly resilient people will be inclined to believe that not only their life in general but the present crisis itself has meaning for them, if they are only open to finding it.

In contrast, psychologically fragile persons are inclined to seek no meaning in crisis and may struggle with the question of whether their life has meaning. They are much more likely to view themselves as victims: of bad luck, of bad genes, or possibly even of others' intentional efforts to make them ill.

Crises Are Normal. Have you ever met someone who acted as if they believed it were possible for life to be one long, smooth road? Do you believe that yourself? If so, you are destined to be disappointed.

As unrealistic as it may seem, there are people whose beliefs lean much more toward these expectations for life than toward the idea that life is a road that holds as many bumps and holes as it does smooth patches. It is not surprising that resilient people look at life in the latter way. Because they expect there to be rough spots in the road, they are not overly put off when they hit one, even a major one like a terminal diagnosis. They more or less keep their hands on the steering wheel. In contrast, psychologically fragile people are apt to react to a bump in the road—in other words, a life crisis—as if it were more than it is. They see doom and gloom in every frustration or roadblock that life throws their way. When faced with a true crisis, they are apt to throw up their hands and lose control of events.

Resilient people are able to maintain a sense of humor even in the midst of a crisis. Fragile people lack this ability. Ronald Reagan, for example, was reported to have joked with his wife about the bullet missing his heart as he lay in a hospital bed after an assassination attempt. This is a clear sign of his psychological resilience.

Crises Create Opportunities. The belief that crises present opportunities is also critical to being able to weather bad times to emerge stronger than you were before. When they encounter a crisis, psychologically fragile people immediately think, "Oh my God! This is terrible! My life is ruined!" In contrast, resilient people think, "This is bad. What can I do about it?"

Resilient people are not averse to taking risks, not necessarily any and all risks but calculated risks. They can do so because of their fundamental self-confidence. In contrast, psychologically fragile people avoid risk as much as possible.

As it pertains to the changing nature of death and dying, the resilient person who is faced with a terminal diagnosis will ask himself or herself questions such as:

- Are there any new or experimental treatments that are available to me?

- Are there any ways in which I and my family can possibly benefit from this ordeal?

The resilient person faced with a terminal diagnosis will of course recognize the downside of this event but will also look for the proverbial silver lining.

One man who was close to retiring had planned to receive his maximum monthly benefits. These benefits, however, would have ended with his death. After learning that he had stage 2 lung cancer, he immediately changed his option so that he received less in monthly payments but allowed the payments to go to his wife for her lifetime after his death. Between that, her Social Security benefits, and some mutual funds they held, she would not only be able to maintain the house they'd lived in for over forty years but have a financial safety net that would allow her to help out their three grown children if they needed it now and then. This is a good example of seeing an opportunity in the midst of a crisis.

We Can Survive. Resilient men and women never really doubt their ability to get through a crisis. Applied to the crisis that terminal illness presents us with, the resilient person will be strong in his or her conviction that there are things that can be done to extend life, even if death appears inevitable. They approach their illness with a fighting attitude, determined to fend it off as long as possible.

Death Has Meaning. When death is inevitable, resilient people seek meaning in the process of dying. Religion, spirituality, family traditions, and exposure to other families who have experienced terminal illness and death contribute to how individuals make cognitive and emotional meaning. Obviously, this will depend on the life stage of the dying person: When an elderly person dies, most people view it as more natural and inevitable than when a young person dies.

While they may fight mightily to survive, when they ultimately face the end, resilient people are able to do so with a measure of grace and dignity. This is captured in the following quote from Scott Nearing, whose goal was to live to the age of one hundred and who indeed died shortly after reaching his goal:

By many people death is considered an end. For others of us, death is a change; a good deal like the change from day to night—always thus far followed by another day, never the same twice, but a procession of days. I believe there is a revival, or survival, in some form. Our life goes on.

THE RESILIENT FAMILY

Applied to the family as a whole, resilience is reflected in shared beliefs in all of the above areas. If you think of the individual as having a personality, then you can see how a family also has a personality. That personality is what we mean by the *family culture*. It appears that resilience is part of some families' culture—in other words, some families as a whole are more resilient, whereas others are more fragile. At the bottom line, the members of a resilient family share a belief that despite the tragedy that lies ahead, as a whole the family will live on and thrive.

Individuals who have known families who have coped effectively with major illness and loss may be helped by looking to these families as role models.

✿ *Mark's and Arnold's Stories*

When Mark, age thirty-seven, was diagnosed with amyotrophic lateral sclerosis (ALS), he remembered how his grandfather had carried on his life as a farmer as long as possible after being diagnosed with lung cancer. He recalled how the family, friends, and the hands who worked the farm all pitched in to help during the final stages of his illness, when his strength was all but sapped. Mark determined to try to be "strong like Papa" and expressed appreciation at having such a strong role model.

Arnold, in contrast, had watched his father become increasingly angry and abusive toward his mother while he battled lung cancer for three years. When Arnold was diagnosed with pancreatic cancer at the age of forty-seven, he was terrified that he would become like his father and not be able to control himself. Fortunately, he sought counseling from his pastor—himself a cancer survivor—and was able to rise above the role model his father had presented.

How Resilient Is Your Family?

If you scour your memory, chances are you will be able to think of one or two people you have known who strike you as being particularly resilient. You may also be able to identify one or two people you've known who were psychologically fragile. Most people are not either extremely resilient or fragile; instead, their personality falls somewhere between these two extremes. The same is true for families.

You can use the following inventory to get a sense of just how resilient you (and your family) are. Answer each question as it applies to you, as you think it applies to your terminally ill family member, and as it applies to other members of your family. After you answer each question, you can total your score to come up with a *resilience index* for you and anyone else in your family. You can then look to see if there is any pattern of resilience (or fragility) that runs through your family.

RESILIENCE INVENTORY

Instructions: *Respond to each of the following questions in terms of how well it describes you, from 0 (not at all) to 5 (completely). When you are finished, total your scores.*

I believe that I was put here for a purpose	0 1 2 3 4 5
I believe in the saying "For every door that closes, another door opens"	0 1 2 3 4 5
My life has meaning, which motivates me to keep going even in the face of a crisis	0 1 2 3 4 5
I believe it's true that every cloud has a silver lining	0 1 2 3 4 5
I believe that every life crisis also presents us with opportunities	0 1 2 3 4 5
I am someone who is willing to take risks	0 1 2 3 4 5
I and my family can emerge from this crisis stronger and happier	0 1 2 3 4 5
I have always been a person who believed that I am the master of my own fate	0 1 2 3 4 5
There is something important to be learned from an experience with terminal illness	0 1 2 3 4 5
Surviving a crisis is a matter of hard work and perseverance, not luck	0 1 2 3 4 5

Total score: _____ = Resilience index

Take a look at your resilience index. How accurately do you think it describes *you* in terms of your true beliefs? Do you think you may have slanted your answers in one direction or another? In which direction: resilience or fragility?

Most people, if they take some time to reflect and answer the resiliency questions honestly, find that their resilience index falls somewhere in the middle range, between 20 and 40. There are, of course, exceptions: people who are truly very resilient. Conversely, there are people who fall at the opposite (low) extreme. These are people who will have the hardest time getting through a crisis like the one you and your family are now facing.

If your resilience index is above 40, consider yourself in pretty good shape to weather a crisis, to find meaning and opportunity in it, and to emerge stronger for having gone through it.

Now, take a look at any resilience indexes you may have calculated for other members of your family. The following questions are offered as food for thought:

- How resilient do you think your family is as a whole?

- Based on your knowledge of them, who are the most resilient members of your family? Conversely, who strike you as the most fragile? Where would you place yourself?

- How are the resilient family members reacting to the news? How are the least resilient family members reacting?

- What are the needs of the less-resilient family members right now?

- How can you work with the resilient ones in your family as you enter the first stages of this family crisis?

One example of an incredibly resilient family dealing with the terminal illness of a youngster is poignantly described by Laurie Strongin in her recent book entitled *Saving Henry.* For seven years, the entire extended family, including friends and many significant others, rallied around this family with their medical travails, pouring their hearts and souls into providing support and sharing caretaking. How this family navigated the five stages we describe is inspirational.

Building Resilience

What should you do if you discover that your own resilience index appears to fall somewhere below 20? Does this mean that you are in for hard times? The answer depends on whether you want to do something about it or not. If you feel helpless to change your outlook on life, then the coming months (and possibly years) may indeed be painful and highly stressful for you. They may take a toll on your emotional and physical health.

On the other hand, if you choose to do so, it is possible to work on changing the way you approach life in general and the current life crisis in particular to become more resilient. We offer some guidelines for doing this. What follows are two tried-and-true methods that psychologists have used to help people move from a less-resilient toward a more-resilient stance toward life.

SELF-TALK

Self-talk means that you must make a habit of making resilient statements to yourself—statements like those that appear in the resilience inventory. There are many ways that you can prompt yourself to challenge your nonresilient thinking. For example, you can purchase a weekly calendar and write one resilient statement at the top of each week. Then each day when you open the calendar, read that week's resilient statement to yourself. You can also type out or write all ten beliefs listed in the Resilience Inventory, and then tape them up—individually or as a group—in a place where you will see them every day. Begin each day by taking a moment to read one or all of the beliefs. Then take another minute or so to pause and reflect on them.

It may strike you as hard to believe, but self-talk has actually been found to be an effective method for changing thought patterns. The secret lies in the fact that most people are not *consciously* aware of their inner beliefs and how these beliefs affect them. Even resilient people more or less just act in resilient ways, without being aware of the underlying beliefs that motivate their behavior. Similarly, the nonresilient person may not be consciously aware that a tendency toward fragility—for example, to get easily discouraged—is actually based on an inner belief that perseverance in the face of adversity is useless. The resilient person, in contrast, inwardly believes that perseverance usually pays off. So, if you use the self-talk technique conscientiously for a period of time, you can expect your behavior to change.

COGNITIVE ROLE-PLAYING

A second effective method for changing beliefs (and, in turn, behavior) is called *cognitive role-playing.* This is just a fancy term for what boils down to imagining yourself in different situations and then imagining how you would react in each situation *depending on what beliefs you held.* Here is an example:

> Your spouse was scheduled today for an MRI of the spine to help determine if a disk problem is the cause of fairly intense lower back pain that started about a month ago. You have two children, ages six and ten. Your family enjoys a comfortable lifestyle, but that lifestyle depends on both you and your spouse working full-time. You have just left work and are on your way to pick up the children from their after-school day-care facility—a responsibility you and your spouse alternate. Your cell phone rings. You answer. It's your spouse, sounding decidedly upset. He (she) blurts out the news: "They found a tumor that may be malignant. I have to have a biopsy tomorrow morning."

There are two ways to respond to this situation, depending in part on how resilient you are. Naturally, it is appropriate to be alarmed at hearing this news. Beyond that, your initial reaction also depends on what you believe about life and life crises. Imagine yourself being in this situation and then imagine how you would react if you held one or both of the following *nonresilient* beliefs:

- If the tumor is malignant, it will be fatal. My family and my life will fall apart.

- Why is this happening to us?

- I'm cursed, doomed to suffer.

If you imagine having such beliefs in this kind of situation, chances are you feel scared and powerless and perhaps hopeless. You may experience an urge to run and hide somewhere.

Now, imagine being in this same situation, but this time try on the following beliefs for size and see how you react:

- This is serious, but even if it's malignant, there may be treatments.

- Whatever happens, I will be there to make sure my children are okay, and we will find a way to come out of this just fine.

- I need to let the most important people in my life know so that I can start counting on them right now for help and support.

How do you feel when you view this situation through the lens of resilient beliefs? Do you still feel as anxious? Does the situation seem hopeless? Do you feel like running away or standing your ground?

YOU CAN BE RESILIENT!

Believing that you cannot change nonresilient attitudes and doubting the power that a resilient personality has to affect behavior as well as health are in fact aspects of being psychologically fragile. Becoming more resilient, in turn, begins with facing and challenging your own pessimism. If you put some genuine effort into conducting these exercises, you *can* become a more resilient individual. This will benefit not only you, but others in your family as you navigate your way through the difficult times and challenges that death represents. And the time to begin is now.

✔ Shannon's Story

"I am one of five sisters in my family," Shannon explained, "and losing my 'baby sister' to breast cancer gave me the biggest scare of my life."

Shannon was now the youngest of four sisters, after her sister's passing. She had always felt as if she and Suzy were twins due to their close ages (they were born eighteen months apart). She described Suzy as a slight but strong and determined individual, who never gave up easily on any goal she set for herself. "She was my younger sister, but in some ways I looked up to her," Shannon explained.

Shannon said that she had a lot of support from friends during the difficult time of her sister's illness. That illness also served to bring the four remaining sisters together to help Suzy. Shannon remarked that Suzy's death seemed to be especially hard on her two oldest sisters. "Suzy's death made us all realize our own mortality," Shannon said, "but for some reason it hit my two oldest sisters hardest. I'm sure they had never imagined that they would be burying their baby sister."

Shannon felt that Suzy's death meant not only the loss of her younger sister but also a loss of part of herself. Shannon and Suzy had shared a room as children, and even as an adult, Shannon had always felt that when she looked at Suzy, she still saw the girl in her and believed that Suzy saw her in the same way. According to Shannon, the loss of Suzy meant the loss of that part of herself.

Suzy was divorced when she died and left three daughters.

Shannon did not have to worry about any financial issues related to her sister's death. Suzy's two oldest children were in their twenties by then. One had already finished college and had a good job. The next oldest was just about to start college. However, because she was their legal guardian and godmother, Shannon did find herself thinking on occasion about what would have happened had she had to become their guardian when they were younger. Fortunately, their father was still alive. He was a professional, and Shannon described him as "a great dad."

Shannon's major worry was about her young niece, who at fourteen would not have the benefit of a full-time mother around for some of the most important changes and events of her life. "I worry about her," Shannon said. "I worry about her dating—of making sure she meets the right kind of boys and avoids getting involved with the wrong ones. I worry that she will not feel good about herself. I even worry about her wedding day—whether it will be a happy time or a sad one because her mom won't be there. Thank goodness she has her faith and knows that her mother is looking down on her on every special day of her life."

Shannon went on to discuss how prayer and going to church was really helpful for her during her sister's illness and how church groups had been very supportive of both her and Suzy during such a painful time.

Shannon would like to know how best to support her niece without seeming like she is trying to be another mother to her and also without stepping on her brother-in-law's toes. She wants to be there for Suzy's children but also does not want to be intrusive. Shannon discussed how this will be especially important if her brother-in-law pursues a romantic relationship in the future.

Shannon and her sisters have been volunteering for breast cancer support organizations and planned to participate in the Avon Walk for Breast Cancer in honor of their sister. She thought it might be a good idea to suggest that family members consider volunteering time to a reputable organization that supports research related to the illness that killed their family member. Shannon finds the volunteer work therapeutic for herself and believes it might be helpful for others, but only when they feel ready to do it. "I couldn't have done it that first year after losing Suzy," she said, "but it helps me so much now. It gives me hope for my nieces, my own daughters, and perhaps someday their daughters."

Shannon thought it was most important to share her experience of how grieving can come on in waves separated by periods of relative peace, and that people should remember to be kind to themselves when the hard times hit. "It's such a long and painful process and it never goes away, but every day gets a little bit better."

Chapter Six

EARLY MEMORIES

What to Expect and What They Mean

One of Sigmund Freud's early followers was the psychiatrist Alfred Adler. Unlike Freud, who pretty much limited his work to adults, Adler had a keen interest in working with children. After breaking ties with Freud (having failed to sway his ideas on anything), Adler went on to establish the first child guidance clinics in Vienna.

Adler's interest in children (or, more properly, childhood) may have had its origins in several key experiences he'd had when young that he believed shaped his future. One was getting pneumonia at age five and overhearing the physician tell his father that Alfred was frail and therefore he doubted that the boy would survive. It was then, Alfred said, that he decided he wanted to become a doctor and help people recover from serious illnesses.

You could say that at that moment Alfred took a decided turn toward being resilient.

A second clear recollection that Alfred recalled was his father's frequent admonition to "not believe anything," by which the elder Adler meant challenging bald statements made by authorities, especially those statements that seemed to have no basis in common sense. As an adult, Adler was inclined to ask even a revered authority to justify a statement that was put forward as fact rather than simply accepting it blindly. Of course, many of psychoanalysis' assumptions about the human psyche, about the nature of mental illness, and about therapy were just such statements, and so Adler eventually came into conflict with his mentor.

One of the conclusions that Adler drew from working with children was the importance of early memories. He developed a habit of asking his patients to recall and share their earliest recollections. From Adler's perspective, a person's early memories held the key to what would eventually crystallize as their identity. In Adler's case, for example, his reaction to getting ill and being perceived as frail and later being thought of as unlikely to succeed (his father had been advised to take young Alfred out of school and apprentice him to a cobbler) was transformed into a driving desire to be strong and successful. Teddy Roosevelt, the American president, had a resilient personality that was forged by a similar set of circumstances.

Adler's work led to such commonly used phrases as the *inferiority complex* and the *superiority complex*. Fundamentally, he believed that the way an individual views his or her strengths and weaknesses, combined with significant early relationships, is the crucible from which identity emerges. A healthy identity, in turn, leads to a personality and an approach to life that is very much like the concept of resilience just discussed. It also leads to a personality characterized by self-confidence and self-esteem.

Crisis and Early Memories

It has been our observation that crises—including the crisis presented by terminal illness in a loved one—often have the effect of stirring up early memories, either consciously or in the form of dreams. Our early relationships shape us. Some of our earliest memories of these relationships can hold key insights into our identity: our sense of who we are and how we fit into the scheme of things. As part of this, early memories offer important insights into our place and role in the family, as well as our view of ourselves: whether we are strong or weak, smart or not so smart, talented or not talented, attractive or ugly, and so on. Understanding this can mark the launching point for taking charge of your role as the family moves into Stage 2 of the grief process.

✰ *Madelyn's Story*

Madelyn's parents had divorced when she was six. After that, she and her younger brother spent roughly 80 percent of their time with their mother and 20 percent with their father, who had taken a job one state and three hours away. Madelyn remembered that she had done well in school and never had behavioral problems. At the same time she had been an anxious child, rather shy and insecure, despite being pretty, smart, and artistic.

Her mother, who had worked only part-time before the divorce, took a full-time position and worked hard to get ahead and increase her salary. Meanwhile, like many children in her situation, Madelyn took on increased responsibility for looking after her brother, who was two years her junior. By the time Madelyn was ten, she was accustomed to being a latch-key child. She would get off the school bus, let herself into the house, and lock the door behind her. She would then finish her homework while listening to music and eating a snack. When she was finished, she would take a frozen meal of leftovers from the freezer and begin heating it up for the family's dinner. Sometimes she would heat up some tomato sauce from a jar, throw in some meatballs her mother had bought at the market, and put on a pot of water to boil for making pasta.

Madelyn missed her father terribly when her parents first divorced. She would manage to maintain her composure when he would visit but would break down and wail uncontrollably as soon as his car disappeared around the corner after he'd leave. On those nights, she would often cry herself to sleep.

Madelyn had a good relationship with her mother, whom she described as responsible and organized, though somewhat less affectionate and comforting than her father could be. There were also times when Madelyn's mother would confide in her—things like her thoughts about a man she might be interested in, or about whatever frustrations she was experiencing at work. Madelyn listened to these things and did not protest, though privately she had always felt a bit uncomfortable in the role of her mother's confidant.

Shortly after Madelyn turned twenty, her father called and told her that he had been diagnosed with prostate cancer. Though the news shocked and upset Madelyn, what surprised her even more about her own reaction was how in the following days her mood became marked by periods of intense depression followed by

periods of equally intense anger. She had never been a moody per-
son, and the change was striking, not only to her but to others.

At a face-to-face meeting with her father, Madelyn learned that
the cancer was more advanced than he had at first let on. He was
inclined, he told her, to undergo an aggressive treatment that
included radiation therapy and, most likely, surgery. Only then
could his condition and prognosis be reassessed.

At this meeting with her father, Madelyn described herself as
"holding it together," and she felt it had gone well. Then again, she
acknowledged that she had more or less been "holding it together"
since childhood.

Madelyn's mood swings continued as her father entered treat-
ment for his cancer. At that point, she decided to see a therapist to
try to figure out what was going on. She wanted to be supportive, and
she felt that the emotional roller coaster she was on could get in the
way of that.

It was in therapy that she was asked about her early memories
of her father. There were a few in particular that stuck out in her
mind:

- Her earliest memory was a vague one. Madelyn guessed she
  must have been a very young child, but what she remembered was being comforted by her father. She had an image
  of being in his arms, being rocked on a rocking chair, her
  head on his shoulder.

- Reading at night before bed was another early memory.
  Madelyn's father would lie beside her and go through their
  regular ritual in which he would ask her what book she

wanted him to read. She would almost always choose one of two or three books, all of which both of them had long ago memorized. When the book was finished, her father would kiss her on the forehead and say good night.

• Madelyn's third memory was of going to a park and being pushed by her father on the swings. She would call out "Higher, higher!" She could remember laughing very hard and feeling a thrill as she watched the landscape fly by. Every so often, if her level of excitement got too high, she would yell "Stop!" and her father would stop the swing by catching it. He'd then hold it back until she said "Let go!"

Madelyn could not figure out the significance of these early memories. She had not thought about any of these things for many years, but after learning about her father's diagnosis, she'd found these memories popping into her consciousness repeatedly. Her therapist suggested a couple of ways in which they could be relevant. The memories suggested, for example, that Madelyn's father had been a major source of comfort for her, probably starting when she was a toddler and he rocked her in his arms. Later on, he read bedtime stories to her. He was a source of fun (taking her to the swings) as well as a source of security (being able to stop the swing when she got anxious). It was evident that she was very special to him and that she basked in his love. Then, after the divorce, he was gone.

These early memories were in fact very significant for Madelyn. On the one hand, she was a young adult who was on track to become a successful adult. On the other hand, as successful as she was, she was often riddled with anxiety and self-doubt. This insecurity caused her to defer to others more than she thought she should and to not assert herself when her own desires or opinions differed from those of others. Similarly, Madelyn knew she was loved by both her parents. However, viewed from the perspective of a young girl, Madelyn had not only been loved but also abandoned by her father. She had long ago covered up the intense grief that she'd experienced at the time and never allowed herself to experience any anger over being abruptly left behind when her father moved away. These emotions were coming to the surface now that her father was faced with a potentially life-threatening diagnosis.

Madelyn expressed reluctance when her therapist suggested that she needed to address this unfinished business with her father. Eventually, though, with much support, she was able to have a conversation with her father about her feelings. To her relief, he was receptive; in fact, he had long harbored some guilt, not so much over his decision to divorce, but his decision to take that out-of-state job so quickly. He could well understand, he said, how Madelyn might feel not just sad, but angry. His worst fear, he confessed, was that his own actions might make his daughter unwilling to trust men and therefore deprive her of an opportunity to find a fulfilling relationship.

This father-daughter dialogue went on intermittently for a year as Madelyn's father underwent treatment and was ultimately declared in remission. They both knew, however, that because of the severity of the cancer, there was a significant chance that it could recur, either in the same place or in another organ. That said, their relationship was now stronger than it had ever been. In addition, Madelyn was finding that she was becoming a more assertive and less anxious and insecure individual in general. She was still the kind, thoughtful, and responsible person she had been since childhood; however, at the same time, it was as if Madelyn had found her voice, meaning that she was becoming better at standing up for what she wanted and did not want to do. She believed that this change would serve her better in the years ahead than the mostly accommodating person she had been until then.

Madelyn came to appreciate that her early memories held valuable information about how she had come to be the person she was. She also realized that, rather than sweeping them under the rug, letting such memories see the light of day and talking about them had played a role in allowing her to change. It was ironic, she said, that it took her father's illness for this to happen. "But like the saying goes," she said, "there's a silver lining inside every cloud."

Mining Early Memories for Insights

We will shortly be discussing the second stage of family grief, in which the family (or at least parts of it) typically comes together to cope with the crisis and to provide aid and support for the terminally ill loved one. Before we contemplate that, however, it is important to pause and reflect. It is not unusual for family members to report that they have experienced vivid dreams and long-repressed memories soon after learning that a family member has been diagnosed with a terminal illness. Some of these may be uncomfortable, and they may be tempted to ignore or even suppress such memories. As was true for Madelyn, however, such dreams and memories can hold many keys to better understanding family relationships. They can point to unresolved issues. They hold important clues to how you feel about yourself and how you relate to others. And they can hold clues to ways in which you and other family members may want to alter some aspects of your relationships as well as the roles you play in the family's functional structure.

When confronted with a crisis such as a terminal illness in one member, families will not only come together but will quickly *regress* into old, established roles, rules, and structures. These old roles, rules, and structures may have been more (or less) functional at the time they emerged. However, they may not be the roles or the structure that one or more individual family members would *choose* for themselves now, if they had that choice.

It goes without saying that an individual is not likely to change his or her role within the family if he or she is not aware of what that role is. Crisis makes it easy for all of us to slip into old patterns. In contrast, pausing and making ourselves open to early memories (either consciously or through dreams) can form the basis for changing our role within the family.

Read through the following list. The items may very well evoke one or more early memories of your family and your place within your family.

- What are your earliest recollections of your relationship with the family member who is now terminally ill? How do these memories make you feel: Happy? Comforted? Anxious? Unhappy? Angry?

- Try to sort out your early memories in chronological order, starting from the very earliest recollections. Taken together, these memories tell the story of your relationship with this family member. Did that relationship remain basically the same over time or did it change? If it changed, when did it change and in what ways?

✦ Do you believe that your early memories suggest that you were very important to this loved one or not so important?

✦ What early memories do you have of the other members of your primary family, including your parents, your siblings, and anyone else who lived with you while you were growing up? What are the best of these memories? What are the worst?

✦ Taken together, what story do your earliest memories have to tell? How does the story clarify your role in the family? Were you one of its main characters, a *star*, a member of the supporting cast, or someone who usually stood in the background?

✦ Do your earliest memories evoke any emotions that you would sooner repress? What are these emotions? Are they directed at any individual or at the family as a whole?

✦ Looking back, if you could have changed one thing about your family, what would that have been?

Maintain a Journal

If you haven't already done so, it can be a good idea to begin a personal journal, or diary, now. Your answers to the above questions can be your first entries in that journal. Add further memories to it as they come to mind as well as other thoughts you have as you move ahead. You may find that sharing your journal or diary at some point with other family members helps all of you get in touch with past experiences and feelings. Some individuals find it helpful to think in terms of *prediagnosis* versus *postdiagnosis*, meaning maintaining some perspective about how the diagnosis has affected you and your family. These insights will serve you well as you enter into the second stage of family grief.

✒ *Rebecca's Story*

Rebecca described her mother as her best friend and spoke about how losing her completely changed life as she knew it. "My mother lived down the street from me for my entire life," Rebecca said. "She always played a huge role in my daily life and my family's daily life."

Rebecca is a schoolteacher, and when her two daughters were toddlers, her mother would baby-sit them while she and her husband were at work. Later on, her mother's home became the daycare center that the girls went to before and after school. As a result, they were about as attached to their grandmother as they were to their mother.

Rebecca admitted that her mother spoiled her and her family. She did this by taking Rebecca shopping for clothes and out to lunch and by taking the girls for weekends so that Rebecca and her husband could get away by themselves. Twice she even paid for the entire family to go on vacation together.

Rebecca recognizes that she never really separated from her mother and that is why her death was so devastating to her. "It's hard for any woman to lose her mother," she said, "but my mother and I were especially close. I lived with her and Dad until I got married. Even then, Ian and I lived just up the road from them."

Rebecca's mother played a peacekeeping role in her marriage, sometimes defending Ian when she felt he was being ganged up on by his wife and daughters. She even bought him a male dog "so that he wouldn't be the only man in the house."

Rebecca's mother's death was so life altering for her that she reported being severely depressed. "For two years," she explained, "I didn't want to get out of bed in the morning and had to force myself to put one foot in front of the other. It seemed like I suddenly didn't know how to do anything without knowing I would see her at some point during the day. I don't think I was the best teacher for those two years."

Rebecca finally sought counseling through her church to help her to cope with the loss of her mother and the impact that it had on all of her other relationships. She also spoke with her physician and went on medication for six months, and only by a combination of the two did her spirits finally begin to lift.

Rebecca shared the following thoughts about her mother's illness and death, which she thought others might relate to:

- She wished she could have anticipated how her mother's illness and death would affect her relationship with her husband and daughters, especially with respect to her emotional and physical availability to them. She realized in retrospect that her grief not only affected her as a teacher, but as a mother and wife as well.

- She wished she had seen and appreciated more the peacekeeping force that her mother had been in her marriage, which saw some hard times in the year or so after her mother's death.

- It was only after her mother's death that Rebecca fully realized just how much she depended on her mother financially, especially considering that she did not receive much of an inheritance after her mother had to spend the last ten months of her life in a nursing home. This eventually put a financial strain on her own family because Rebecca continued to shop and spend after her mother's death.

- She had no idea how intensely lonely she would feel without her mother being available to her. She said that to this day she occasionally picks up the phone to call her mother, forgetting that her mother has passed away. If she had anticipated this, she would have devoted more time to cultivating friendships.

- Based on the above, she also wished that she had elected to go away to college (instead of commuting from home), and/or that she and Ian had bought a house a bit farther away, so that she could have had some time to separate from her mother earlier in her life.

- She wished that her mother's condition could have been diagnosed sooner so that she might have gotten more effective treatment or care that could have prolonged her life.

❧ STAGE 2 ❧

UNITY

We cannot suppose that death is the end of any adventure except that of the body.... There will be things yet to be done, and the stuff that we work on will be the utterly familiar and still mysterious and exciting stuff of ourselves.

—MARY AUSTIN

Chapter Seven

BUILDING SUPPORT NETWORKS

What one family member may see as a catastrophe—a diagnosis of terminal illness—another will perceive as a challenge to be confronted head-on. While one may feel overwhelmed and become paralyzed, another may begin to rally resources. Differences in psychological resilience, as discussed in chapter 5, may account in part for these different initial reactions in the crisis stage. The result can be confusion and even conflict among family members. A mother, for example, may be deciding about whether to participate in a clinical trial of a new, experimental treatment. One of her adult daughters may feel rather adamantly that she shouldn't do it, while a second daughter believes just as strongly that she should. Amid such potential disparities, as it enters the second stage of grief, the family is faced with the need to build a support network. One part of this network will be a medical team that will play the central role in the treatment of the terminally ill person. A second aspect of the support network will be made up of nonprofessionals who can be called on to help shore up the family as a whole as well as the ill family member. And the third part of the network will be the family itself.

First Step: Building a Team

One of the first tasks facing the family at this point is to begin considering all the options for medical treatment. These options will be dictated to a greater or lesser degree by the insurance plan that covers the ill family member. Persons over age sixty-five will be covered under the federal Medicare program. These individuals may have purchased a supplemental policy that might cover additional treatment options. Younger adults and children will be covered by a diverse array of insurance plans with variable levels of coverage, deductibles, and co-pays. Health insurance reform, which at the time of this writing is in its initial stages of implementation, may in the long run help mitigate these disparities in coverage.

The family as a whole should be aware of both the range and the limits of any insurance coverage that will be relied on in the months ahead. Like it or not, some consideration may have to be given to the possible costs of treatments that are not covered, especially surgeries and medications, which can be extremely costly. Some medications used in cancer treatment, for example, can cost thousands of dollars for a single dose. Not every insurance plan will cover such treatments. Moreover, it is advisable to have someone in the family be responsible for independently researching drugs and other treatments relative to their actual effectiveness as well as their appropriateness. Some much-touted drugs for treating cancer, for example, may extend life on average for as little as a few months despite their high cost and potential negative side effects. The patient and the family should take these realities into consideration when making decisions about treatment.

Many insurance plans require the patient to choose a *primary care physician*, or PCP, who then becomes the gatekeeper for referrals to specialists. Most often the PCP will refer the patient to a specialist within the patient's healthcare system. Not all specialists will be in this network. The family may decide it is important to seek one or more consultations with experts who are out of network. If the patient's insurance plan initially denies coverage of an out-of-network consultation, we strongly recommend appealing that decision. Many insurance plans will allow such outside consultations if their initial denial is challenged. However, the appeal process can be time consuming and taxing, and it can seem overwhelming to a patient who is already experiencing weakened vitality. In addition, many older people are accustomed to complying with whatever their personal physician (or insurance carrier) suggests. For this reason, it is again important for other family members to be prepared to be part of a *team*. The patient may need assistance from other family members to appeal a negative decision. The family, working as a team, is in the best position to assess medical information, make decisions, and advocate for a specific course of action.

❧ Jim's Story

A week after Jim, age fifty-six, had a routine physical, he told his wife, Marilyn, that the PSA test that was a part of the yearly exam had shown an elevated level and his doctor said he'd felt a small but hard lump on the prostate itself. The next day, Jim and Marilyn went to the local community hospital and met with the urologist to whom they'd been referred by Jim's primary care physician. The urologist ordered more tests. The results were positive for prostate cancer. The urologist then told Jim and Marilyn that he wanted to schedule surgery. Jim agreed, and surgery was scheduled for the following week.

Marilyn and Jim then told their oldest daughter about the diagnosis and treatment plan. She insisted that they postpone the surgery until they traveled to the nearest city with a cancer hospital—a two-and-a-half-hour drive. Jim's daughter wanted him to see an oncologist before deciding on any particular treatment. She explained to her father that a surgeon might be invested in surgery, whereas an oncologist is a generalist who might recommend alternative forms of treatment. While Jim was eager "to get this over with," his daughter's insistence and her subsequent recruitment of her two brothers to support her position motivated him to agree.

Jim enlisted the help of his primary care physician in setting up an appointment at the cancer center. While it turned out that the oncologist also recommended surgery, he suggested a regimen of radiation therapy in advance of surgery, to shrink the tumor. This approach, the oncologist explained, might result in fewer negative side effects from the surgery. After much discussion with his family, Jim decided to have the radiation treatment in the city and then decide where he wanted to have the surgery.

Sometimes it is not easy for the patient or the family to know exactly which specialist to consult, particularly if the illness crosses specializations. Marianne's situation offers an example.

✔ *Marianne's Story*

Marianne, age seventy, is a cancer survivor. She also currently has a cardiac condition. Because of symptoms such as urinary bleeding, her primary care physician referred her to a urologist, who found a polyp. He wanted to remove it, because he thought it might be cancerous—a surgery that involved general anesthesia.

Because Marianne also had symptoms that she referred to as "mental confusion," Marianne's daughter-in-law, a nurse, was concerned about the impact that general anesthesia might have on Marianne's cognitive processing. The cardiologist said that there was in fact a high level of risk. The urologist, however, refused to consider doing the procedure with anything but a general anesthesia. At the suggestion of Marianne's PCP, a third specialist—a neurologist— was called on to conduct a neurological evaluation. After the neurologist agreed with the cardiologist's assessment of the risk of general anesthesia, the daughter-in-law and Marianne's son were able to find a different urologist who was willing to perform a biopsy using a nerve block.

Jim's and Marianne's stories are good examples of how, as they enter into this stage of unity, most families come together as a team. That said, it is also true that almost all families have a skeleton or two in the closet as well as unresolved grudges, grievances, jealousies, and resentments. For some, these may be so emotionally intense that effective teamwork is impossible. For the majority, however, these issues will be put on the back burner in the interest of unity. These issues will reemerge, however, in later stages of family grief.

Meet the Payers

Health insurance companies are also known as third-party payers, meaning that they represent the go-between that connects the patient (the first party) with the doctor (the second party). Functioning in this third-party role, insurers increasingly are not only the source of payment to the healthcare system but also the gatekeeper that determines which medical services and procedures will be approved and paid for and which will not.

Most individuals do not read the fine print in their health insurance plans and are unaware of the definitive list of covered services. Rather, what most people focus on when deciding what insurance plan to sign up with are the overall cost of the plan and the out-of-pocket cost of co-pays for office visits and prescription medications. Many people falsely believe that all health insurance plans cover the same range of services.

Health insurers publish the list of services and procedures each of their plans cover as well as how much they will pay (versus how much the patient is expected to pay) for each. They also provide the list of healthcare providers who participate in their various plans, plus the ground rules for using specialists, for contesting denied benefits, and so on. This information is available in most cases through the Internet, by visiting the health insurer's website. It is our hope that health insurance reform will eventually level the playing field with respect to what is covered (at least minimally) by insurance policies and that the emergence of health insurance exchanges will make insurance more affordable for all.

It is very important and helpful if one family member takes responsibility for gathering the information about covered services, deductibles, and access to specialists. At least one person must peruse this material and become expert in it. It should also be made available to any other interested family members. This information will play a significant role in the decision-making process.

Negotiating with third-party payers can be both time consuming and very frustrating. Yet, in most cases, if someone persists, accommodations can usually be made. The patient may not be in a position to put this much energy into the process, which means that one or more members of the family team (sometimes in conjunction with the patient's PCP) needs to do so. The problem, we have found, is that families too often allow themselves to become passive and uninformed. They may be intimidated by the formal wording through which third parties sometimes couch their denials. As a result, they may not thoroughly investigate all the options available and not persist in the face of resistance from third-party payers.

Sometimes the patient and the family decide that it would be desirable to change providers and/or healthcare systems. This option, unfortunately, is typically available only to individuals who are insured through their employers via group policies. Moreover, changing plans is often only a yearly option. For example, if you learn of an experimental trial for which your loved one appears to be eligible, you may or may not be able to follow that route, depending on the insurance carrier. Or you may find, over time, that you are having difficulty relating to a particular doctor and so you want to make a change. Again, the patient and the family may or may not have an option to do so.

Although it may be tempting to think of changing insurance plans, once a terminal or potentially terminal diagnosis has been rendered, this may not be a practical option. Recently, insurers have been barred from refusing to extend coverage for such pre-existing conditions. However, they may insist on increasing premiums. At present, the route we recommend is for the family to become educated about the limitations of coverage and the process for appealing denials. This is true even if a decision to change insurers is made.

ESTABLISH A CHAIN OF COMMAND

Today, when a person is diagnosed with a terminal illness, there are usually a number of medical personnel involved in the treatment. How many and what kind of medical specialists will be involved depends in part on the complexity of the diagnosis and how the disease progresses. For Marilyn, for example, several diagnoses came into play; therefore, several specialists were involved.

We recommend that the family consciously think in terms of a *chain of command* for treatment decision-making purposes. Ultimately it is the patient—the terminally ill family member—who sits at the head of this chain. He or she, however, will also have one or more confidants (a spouse, an adult child, a parent, a close friend) whose opinions will weigh heavily in any decisions that are made. All families develop their own chains of command. This is usually not a conscious decision so much as a process that reflects *modeling*. In other words, when they form a family, a couple usually organizes it in a way that more or less models the structure of the families they were raised in.

A family's organization can definitely be altered, for example when the head of the family is the one who receives a terminal diagnosis. Most often, though, a family's first response to learning of a terminal illness in its midst will be to be somewhat rigid and resistant to changing the way things have always been. As a result, some family members will likely have more influence than others, at least initially, simply because they always have. This may not sit well with you if you perceive yourself as having less influence than some others (or less than you would like). You may feel jealous or resentful. Alternatively, if you happen to find yourself in a leadership role, you may feel burdened or resentful. As time goes on, some competition may emerge among family members who may want to play a greater role than they have when it comes to making important decisions. On the other side of the coin, some family members may want to be able to delegate some responsibilities to others. Such family dynamics are part and parcel of the new grief.

Understanding that these dynamics often begin to emerge in this stage of grief can be key to mitigating their effects. Putting words to your feelings can help your family shift roles somewhat and adjust. However, even if you encounter resistance right now, you may find some comfort in knowing that more opportunities for change will present themselves as your family moves into the later stages of grief.

From our perspective, there is no reason why all those family members who are truly invested can't be included somewhere in the chain of command. For example, one or two may be asked to become expert in the patient's health insurance plan, while others work on identifying specialists who can be consulted, and others still can research treatment options and their likely outcomes.

Another important consideration is managing the interactions of the various specialists: oncologist, surgeon, radiologist, and other healthcare providers. Which of these individuals is in charge? Is this the person whom the patient trusts the most and who will have the final word when it comes to determining medical treatment? On what, if any, issues do the doctors disagree when it comes to the best course of action? If more than one specialist is consulted and interviewed for a specific procedure, who will go with the patient to the appointments and what issues will be discussed? In that regard, here are some questions we recommend the patient take into consideration:

- What is the specialist's understanding of and experience with your particular disease?

- What are the specialist's specific recommendations for treatment?

- How well does the specialist explain these recommendations? Are there any areas of confusion?

- Does the specialist explain the pros and cons of each alternative, such as possible side effects? If the specialist offers only one treatment option, why is that?

- Does the specialist answer your questions and address your concerns in a way that you can understand?

- Do you feel confidence in this person? What is the climate like in the office?

- Do you feel that this person respects you and is interested in you as a person? Does the specialist appear to be attuned to your emotional state?

- Does the specialist know the other doctors involved in your case, so that they can collaborate effectively? For example, is one specialist affiliated with one hospital, whereas all others are affiliated with another?

- What does your accompanying family member(s) think of the specialist and his or her recommendations?

- Can the specialist suggest resources or provide sources of information about the diagnosis and its treatment?

IDENTIFYING COLLATERAL SUPPORTS

As the family moves into action as a group, it is important to look beyond the immediate family to identify people who are willing and able to be of assistance in one way or another. As the process of treatment moves ahead, the tasks that may need to be attended to can be myriad and range from those that are highly emotionally charged to the banal. They can include such things as getting to medical appointments for testing and treatment, doing food shopping, preparing meals, baby-sitting, and running errands. They can also include major decisions about treatment (or no treatment) as well as critical financial decisions. Some families tend to be rather stoic and resistant when it comes to reaching out to others, including in-laws, neighbors, friends, and community resources. They may seek to take on all of these responsibilities themselves. If the family is large enough, this may work. If the family is small, however, or if these responsibilities will have to be borne by adult children who have other family responsibilities, the added stress can be considerable. For that reason we advocate reaching out to collateral sources. Here is an example of one family member who did this.

✿ Ed and Mary's Story

While Ed, fifty-one, did not seem to be interested in discussing his diagnosis of tertiary pancreatic cancer with anyone in his family, his wife, Mary, forty-nine, felt overwhelmed by this sudden and frightening turn of events in her life. Their college-age children wanted to know if they should immediately return home. Mary suggested they wait until further information was available. Ed said he did not want them to come home; he wanted everything to go on exactly as it had before his diagnosis. He told Mary he wanted to take it one day at a time. And he did not want to put anyone out.

Ed had always been a stoic individual. Mary understood and respected this. Theirs was a family that had always kept largely to itself, remaining on the fringes of their community without any significant involvement. They lived in a suburb of a large Midwestern city, and aside from Ed's occasional business-related social functions, he and Mary did not go out much. They had a few close friends whom they saw occasionally. Up until Ed got ill, they found this life-

style completely satisfying, as they enjoyed each other's company very much.

Mary had returned to teaching second grade after her youngest son left for college and was still in transition from being a full-time mother and wife to balancing her family and professional activities. Because of the lifestyle she'd chosen to live, when Ed got sick, she really had no close confidants to whom she could talk. She had cordial but distant relationships with her two siblings and her parents, all of whom lived in different parts of the country.

About a month after Ed was diagnosed, Mary went online to learn more about pancreatic cancer. When she did, she discovered several websites that offered not only information but also support, in the form of forums and chat rooms, for people with terminal illness as well as their families.

While Ed said that he did not feel the need for online support, Mary did, and she joined two of these groups. She reported that they met her needs, and she looked forward to reconnecting, at least briefly, with each of her online support groups at the end of each day.

In today's world there are many opportunities for support, both through the Internet and face-to-face. About a year into Ed's illness, when Mary found her caretaking responsibilities increasing, she started a support group in her community specifically for caretakers—like herself—of terminally ill family members. When Ed died six months later, she continued her leadership of this group and networked with others to develop another online support group for caretakers. This was Mary's way of memorializing Ed's final struggles. She would tell you today that this experience changed her life profoundly. It enabled her to engage socially through these activities and find new meaning for her life. Several years later, she became a hospice volunteer and deepened her feelings of meaningful connections.

Many medical centers—metropolitan, suburban, and rural— provide support groups for both the terminally ill and their family members on site. We recommend that at least one member of the family contact the social worker at the hospital where the patient is being treated and explore what type of support groups or networks are available. In addition, an increasing number of communities have wellness centers that are located in churches, synagogues, or community centers. These often operate as drop-in centers that are open certain hours and are run by volunteers; they typically are places of support for family members as well as for people with illness.

As Ed and Mary's story shows, it can be vital to have sources of support outside of the family. The family that allows others to be of support is apt to be more resilient than the family who tries to deal with all the stress and do all the things that have to be done within the family. Fresh perspectives often lead to important insights. Others who have experienced the same type of illness and crisis can serve as role models and even as sources of advice. Mary, for example, said that she found it easier to talk to strangers online than to members of her church. For some reason, she felt less concerned about how those she interacted with online might view her and her family, and she found it easier to share her true feelings with strangers. She felt she learned a great deal from others' experiences, that this information helped inform the decisions that she and Ed had to make at different times.

As important as collateral sources of support can be, not everyone will be ready to reach out to these immediately. For example, it took some time for Mary to feel comfortable doing this. If she had felt pressured to do it sooner, she may well have dug her heels in instead. Her approach to seeking support first came via the Internet and only much later did she participate in and start a face-to-face support group.

Some families want to share their news with friends, but fear either distancing on the one hand or intrusiveness on the other.

✒ Betty's Story

Betty, who was diagnosed with Huntington's disease at the age of forty-nine, and her husband, Hal, decided to tell only a few close friends. Betty did not want her friends to call a lot to ask how she was doing, and she told that to the few intimate friends with whom she did share her diagnosis. "I do not want to become the disease," she explained. "I don't want people's sympathy. I just want us to continue living as we do as long as we can."

In Betty's case, there was an issue about genetic testing for her two children, but they would have to make their own decisions about that, she felt, with their spouses. At the time of her diagnosis, there were no grandchildren in the family. Most of Betty and Hal's friends respected the boundaries they requested. When one did not, Betty and Hal decided to screen their phone calls and not pick up the telephone when that particular friend called. Eventually, that friend got the message.

About a year after the diagnosis, Betty and Hal found support groups for Huntington's disease, and they decided to try one out. Then they learned that one of their children was also involved in a support group. In time, Betty, Hal, and their children all got involved in raising funds for research into the disease.

It is in times of crisis that we find out who our real friends and supports are and they are not necessarily whom we might have predicted them to be—just as our own reactions to the crisis are not necessarily what we expected. There are some friends and family members who just are unable, for a variety of reasons, to cope with terminal illness. It is almost as if they felt they could catch it, regardless of their level of education and awareness. In fact, some physicians distance themselves from friends who are terminally ill; they may rationalize that they deal with this in their everyday professional lives and cannot in their personal lives. This may be particularly disappointing to the family of people with terminal illness; we expect physicians to be compassionate, helpful, and supportive, forgetting that every human being has different issues and feelings about life and death.

Often people are not sure what they should or can expect from other family members and friends, and many fear being seen as dependent or demanding. One way to ensure that these lines are not crossed—and that you are not perceived as overly dependent or intrusive—is to take stock of your expectations. You can do this by taking some time to discuss your expectations with a trusted friend and get some frank feedback on how reasonable they might be. For example, if a terminally ill mother expected a daughter who was married with children to phone twice a day and to always be available, even during periods of remission, this may indeed be an unreasonable expectation. This mother might find herself feeling disappointed and angry if the daughter's attention wanes during noncrisis periods.

We shall have more to say about tapping into and using resources in chapter 8. This can be a complex, tricky, and frustrating experience as well. For now, suffice it to say that we encourage families not to be too proud to accept help when it is offered or even to seek it out from those they believe would be available and willing to help out now and then.

✍ Eliza's Story

Eliza's mother struggled with breast cancer for ten years before finally dying of its third appearance. Eliza remembers a constant feeling of unease during that entire period of time—as if her mother could disappear at any moment.

"We knew Mom was very sick and that she could pretty much die at any time. By the time she did die, I was in my mid-twenties, but Jane, my middle sister, had just turned eighteen, and Lauren, the youngest, was only fourteen. Those last few months especially were just awful for them."

Eliza discussed her role in the family, which for most of the ten years that her mother was battling cancer involved trying to be a caretaker for her younger sisters while also attending college, starting a career, and pursuing a relationship. Lauren developed an eating disorder after her mother's final bout with the cancer, and Eliza believes that her sister Jane's abuse of both alcohol and sleeping medications began then as well.

"I felt like I had to be the strong one for them, like a second mother, because our own mother was so sick. But I guess I didn't do such a great job . . . look where they are now."

Following her mother's death, Eliza's father pulled away from her and her sisters. He rather quickly remarried—a woman they uniformly disliked. He stopped trying to help his younger daughters, financially or emotionally. He and his second wife recently moved to another state, and he has pretty much dropped out of the picture. Eliza still feels like the responsibility to save her sisters remains on her shoulders, even though Jane is now nearly thirty and Lauren is in her mid-twenties. "They were just kids when Mom was going through her ordeal," she explained. "I felt like they didn't get a shot at being kids or teenagers. Mom was always sick and needed so much care. I hate what cancer did to our family." She sighed. "I'm so tired."

Eliza discussed missing her mother, but more than that she talked about how anxious it made her to feel obligated for helping her sisters to work out their problems. Eliza is an attorney and works long hours. She was recently divorced, and she believes that the situation with her sisters contributed in part to her husband's leaving her because she spent so much time trying to help them or clean up their messes.

Looking back on her experience, Eliza wanted to share the following with others:

- "Seek out all the supports that you can. Don't hesitate or worry about putting people out. Let them tell you if they feel put out. We were three girls whose mother was engaged in a long-term fight with cancer, and we definitely could have used more support."

- "Use the supports you find as resources to turn to after your loved one dies. We were left high and dry, first when our mother died and then when our father bailed out on us."

- "Begin to think about and prepare yourself for the significance of your eventual loss well before it actually happens."

- "Think about seeking counseling if you are a couple and one of you has a terminally ill parent."

Eliza sees two reasons for this: to keep channels of communication open, and to help the other spouse understand why his or her partner might withdraw after the death, as Eliza believes she did.

Chapter Eight

NAVIGATING THE MEDICAL AND SOCIAL SERVICES MAZES

As was said earlier, one of the first tasks facing families on receiving a diagnosis is to learn more about the illness or disorder that faces them. There are many ways to do this: by visiting websites, by talking to others who have experienced the disease, by contacting associations such as the American Cancer Society and other knowledgeable disease-specific organizations, and by asking questions of the medical team that is working with the patient. With respect to the last of these options, the family must be prepared to enter and then navigate its way through what we call the *medical maze*.

You'll Need a Point Person

In today's healthcare environment, assertive advocacy is necessary to successfully navigate the medical maze. Ironically, this maze owes its existence in part to a positive development: the emergence of an increasingly diverse and sophisticated armamentarium of medical treatments and technologies. Unfortunately, it also owes its existence to a fractured healthcare system that, despite recent efforts at reform, remains lacking in coordination and uniformity.

Many people—including a growing number of older and widowed men and women—are not in a position to fully comprehend the information they get from multiple sources, so as to understand the options they may have or weigh the potential ramifications of each of those options. Being able to turn to a knowledgeable family member for help with this is no small blessing. For that reason, we have recommended that the family designates one or two members as "point persons." Often this role emerges naturally. Firstborn children, for example, from an early age often play a role within the family that is much like that of a point person. They may look after younger siblings, help out more with household tasks, and generally be responsible. In contrast, in large families middle and youngest children typically do not move into such roles unless they are pressed to do so. During the unity stage, families usually fall into familiar patterns, so that oldest children may be looked to once again for leadership. Since time and experience often change us, not all family members may be equally comfortable being relegated to roles they once played. If this describes you, rest assured things do not have to remain this way forever. Initially, though, you should not be surprised if this is how your family reacts to crisis as it marshals its resources in a display of unity.

Regardless of whether they emerge spontaneously or are chosen by the family through consensus, it is the point person or persons' responsibility to become knowledgeable in the areas discussed in this chapter and to present information to the family as a whole for their edification and so the ill family member can make informed decisions about his or her treatment.

As you may expect, this is no small responsibility. There will likely be much information to sift through and many decisions to be made. However, if the decision-making process is shared, it can further unify (instead of possibly divide) the family. The point person or persons must therefore be prepared, in terms of time and energy, to take on this commitment. There may be family members who would like to play this role but either cannot do so or else need help doing so because of competing commitments and priorities. For example, a family member who once readily took on a leadership role may find herself having to cope with multiple responsibilities (children, a career, a house, a marriage) that require her to ration her time.

At this stage, the major focus is on the person with the disease, and the goal is to identify and rally resources to cope with that disease. Anxieties, tensions, and feelings of frustration—all of which can arise during the long period of time required to gather information, schedule appointments, and make decisions—can persist. At the same time, each individual family member's personal prior experiences with the healthcare system will color his or her view of the current situation. Those whose experiences have been largely positive will have one view. In contrast, those who have experienced frustration or disappointment will be viewing events through a different lens. It is important that families expect such differences and respect them as being based on experience. All views and opinions should be put on the table. Realizing that people can in fact have very different (and equally valid) perspectives based on their experiences forms the basis for working toward a consensus and building a base of support for how treatment will proceed.

By facilitating this process of gathering information, establishing respect for differing views, and opening communication, the family point person (or persons) can do a great deal to help reduce tensions. It allows family members to feel included while being able to carry on with the day-to-day responsibilities of their lives. This is especially important for family members who have their own families to tend to and jobs they cannot afford to be away from for significant periods of time. As information flows and as decisions are made, a measure of relief is felt by everyone.

Don't Wait for Them to Call You

If medical test results are not communicated to you and your family in what strikes you as a reasonable amount of time, do not assume that this means everything is okay. On the contrary, we advise families to be persistent in telephoning doctor and clinic offices to learn the test results. Do not worry about how you are perceived by office staff. Some people are leery of being persistent or assertive, thinking they are being rude or overly demanding. Keep in mind, however, that our healthcare system depends on *quantity* as much as it does on *quality*. While the family understandably feels that their crisis is a high priority, it is only one of many cases on the schedule of the doctors they are consulting with. It is not that medical professionals don't care; rather, efficiency demands that they have many patients to care for.

The family member with the diagnosis or the family's point person needs to feel some degree of control of the process. The patient may need to sign a form authorizing his or her doctor(s) to communicate with the point person(s). We advise asking if this is the case and then following up to obtain the appropriate authorization(s). We have found that establishing effective communication strategies from the outset will pay off in the long run. Some suggestions for talking with doctor and clinic offices include the following:

- "I'm very anxious about my test results and need to learn about them as soon as possible."

- "I would like to have my test results transmitted as soon as possible to Dr. _____ with whom I have an appointment on _____."

- "Can you tell me how I can get my test results as soon as possible?"

By using the pronoun *I* in all of your communications, you are taking responsibility for what you need and not implying that someone else is at fault in any way.

Seek Specialists and Get Second Opinions

Some people are reluctant to request a second medical opinion because they have a relationship with the physician who made the initial diagnosis, who is often their primary care physician (PCP). Or, it may be a specialist that the PCP referred them to. Some people have told us that they were reluctant to request a second opinion because they didn't want to hurt the doctor's feelings or create the impression that they believed the doctor was incompetent. In other words, the idea of seeking second (or third) opinions somehow becomes a loyalty issue.

Feeling loyal to a trusted physician is understandable, but it is not reason enough for the patient and the family to not pursue this option. After all, the doctor will get over any hurt feelings he or she may have, but the patient won't get over the disease without doing everything possible to obtain the most advanced, comprehensive treatment. No one would expect their PCP to perform open heart surgery. And even heart surgeons differ in the experience they have with various specific procedures.

The truth is that the vast majority of physicians—both PCPs and specialists—harbor no ill will toward patients who elect to pursue second or third opinions. On the contrary, they are taught in medical school to expect this and not to take it personally.

So the first step is to consult with specialists (preferably at least two of them) to obtain information on all possible treatment options, including each option's possible side effects and the statistics on outcome. Some physicians are reluctant to be completely open about these issues because they believe it is important to be upbeat and optimistic, even when a patient is facing a grave diagnosis. If for some reason the diagnosing physician appears hesitant to fully disclose in response to your requests for more information or balks at giving a referral for a second opinion, you have sufficient reason to be more insistent. If the doctor still resists making a referral, the names of other specialists can be obtained through word of mouth—for example, through a support group or by accessing websites such as that of the American Medical Association (www.ama-assn.org). Most insurance companies also have websites that list participating providers by specialty. Ultimately, the family can work effectively only with a medical team that is open to other opinions and transparent when it comes to sharing information.

WHOM TO SEE, WHAT TO ASK

It is important to seek specialists who have experience with the specific disease or condition that was diagnosed. For example, if the family member has been diagnosed with uterine cancer, she needs to consult an *oncological gynecologist* who has treated a large number of these cases as opposed to a general gynecologist who may not have specialized knowledge and skill.

Another important consideration is coordination of care. This is the chain-of-command issue again. Just as the family needs to establish a chain of command regarding how decisions are made, so it must be with the patient's medical team. In other words, there must be a *medical* chain of command that parallels the family's. Together the patient and the family need to decide which of the doctors who are on the medical team will be at the head of this chain. If the diagnosis is cancer, for example, it may make sense to have the oncologist be the one in charge, even if surgery and radiation are also parts of the overall treatment plan.

The doctor who is to coordinate the treatment plan must be the medical point person, the individual to whom all test results and recommendations are forwarded. It is this physician's responsibility to digest the information—which can be vast and complex—and help the patient make treatment decisions. This includes determining if and when additional medical specialists need to be brought in. In that event, the patient and the family's point person(s) should be prepared to ask questions such as the following:

• What are the available treatments for this illness?

• Are there any clinical trials? How do we find out about them?

• Where is the best place to receive these treatments?

• What exactly is entailed in each treatment?

• What are the pros and the cons of each treatment: prognosis, side effects, length of treatment, and so on?

• What statistics are available about the efficacy of each option?

• *What* do you recommend? *Why* do you recommend this course of treatment?

• How much time do you think we can reasonably take before making this decision?

In some situations there will be little controversy about treatment options because the strong consensus is that there is only one that is possible and reasonable. In that case, the only decision to be made is whether to pursue that treatment option versus no treatment at all. The latter is in fact an option that is occasionally chosen—for example, by an individual whose prognosis is exceptionally poor and whose quality of life for his or her remaining days would not be improved (and could even be worsened) by the treatment. Although family members may urge otherwise, they must remember that the patient is ultimately at the top of the chain of command and has the right to refuse treatment. Extending life briefly at the cost of its quality is a very real issue today. While many family members and physicians may lobby for this option, it ultimately is the patient's choice to make, and this choice must be respected. We also believe that it is important that the patient have a trusted friend, family member, or counselor with whom they can talk frankly about treatment options, including the option to refuse a particular treatment.

In most situations today, there will be treatment alternatives, ranging from most aggressive to least aggressive. Each will be associated with different statistical outcomes, along with different potential side effects. Each of these options must be assessed not just in terms of the nature of the disease but also in the context of the family's circumstances and the patient's wishes. Like it or not, finances may be a necessary consideration. And here again, a patient's decision to not pursue a costly, uncovered treatment that offers marginal benefits and a high likelihood of negative side effects needs to be respected, as the patient is likely thinking of the welfare of the family as a whole when making such a decision. It is up to the patient (along with the designated family point person) to check out what the patient's insurance policy will (and will not) cover. Keep in mind that all insurance plans include an appeals process, in the event you do decide to pursue an uncovered option.

If the cost of travel to obtain an evaluation by an out-of-state specialist is an issue, there are some organizations that will help provide or cover the cost of travel for individuals who have a substantiated need. In addition, the American Cancer Society operates a number of Hope Lodges that are located in or near medical center areas across the country. These lodges provide free residence for cancer patients (regardless of income level). The point is that if family members research carefully, they will be surprised at the amount of information and support resources that are actually available. Depending on their attitude about asking for help, some families may need to work on swallowing their pride to avail themselves of this help. The bottom line is that family members must be willing to ask themselves: What is more important here: our pride or getting the help we need to confront this illness head-on?

🌿 Jeannette's Story

Jeannette, age fifty, was diagnosed with an advanced noninvasive breast cancer. She lives in a major metropolitan area and has good health insurance and, therefore, had no trouble consulting with three oncologists at three different medical centers. One recommended a mastectomy, even though she tested negatively for the genetic type of breast cancer; one recommended a lumpectomy; and the third suggested she begin with a lumpectomy and, depending on the lab results, undergo further surgery and/or radiation treatments if necessary.

The mother of three teenage children and married to a man who was recently laid off from a lucrative long-term job due to a dramatic downturn in business, Jeanette was anxious about how long she could afford to take off from work for her recovery. She had a limited amount of paid sick leave, and though she would not lose her job, she would be forced to take an unpaid leave if she were to be out longer than two weeks.

It took several weeks of agonizing over the pros and cons—often using her husband, as well as two close friends, as sounding boards—before Jeanette finally opted for the third alternative. The

next decision was where to have the surgery and by whom. Jeanette
elected to go with the first medical center she had consulted.

Two weeks later, after more tests, Jeanette received news that the
margins that defined her cancer were no longer clear. This meant that
she would need to have a mastectomy, followed by several radiation
treatments. She felt as if she were back to square one and had to repeat
the whole decision-making process. At this point her husband was
unable to provide much in the way of support. He had fallen into a
depression over being unemployed despite a strong résumé and was
worried that between his unemployment and Jeannette's illness they
might lose their home to foreclosure.

Fortunately, one of Jeanette's friends was able to step up and recommend that they go together to talk to a social worker at The Wellness Community. This is a nonprofit organization that provides professional programs of education, support, and hope. It can be accessed via the Internet at www.thewellnesscommunity .org. This support enabled Jeanette to obtain the necessary resources to coordinate her treatment plan in such a way that she could schedule her surgery and recovery in an optimal manner. She ended up needing only an additional week off from work. Meanwhile, her husband was able to secure at least temporary work through a temp agency specializing in highly skilled workers. Though certainly not out of the woods, things were not looking nearly as bleak for Jeanette and her family as they had been.

POST-HOSPITAL CARE

In today's world, patients are discharged from hospitals very quickly after procedures, including major surgeries. Home healthcare is often recommended in lieu of longer hospital stays. Services such as follow-up nursing care by visiting nurses and physical therapy can be provided and are highly recommended. Basically our advice is this: Say yes to every form of post-hospital care that is available to you and covered by insurance. Most of these services will be paid for by insurance plans, simply because they are much less costly than hospital-based treatment. When arranging and coordinating continuing care, we recommend that you take nothing for granted and follow up on every aspect of your insurance plan. If in doubt, call the customer service number (usually listed on the back of your insurance card) and ask about all post-hospital services that are covered and how you can arrange to get them. In some cases, a doctor must request them. Don't be shy to ask a doctor to do this (and don't assume the doctor will think of it on his or her own).

Unfortunately, some families initially resist or outrightly reject the notion of home-based care. They believe that they can manage everything themselves. That decision often proves to be a bad one. It may work for a short period of time, but unless the family happens to include a nurse (and perhaps a physical therapist), the patient's medical needs will soon prove overwhelming. The reason is simple: The trend toward early release means that patients are discharged with much less healing than would be the case if they had remained in the hospital longer. Consider, for instance, heart surgery. Not so long ago patients who underwent bypass surgery could expect to remain in the hospital for several weeks. While they were there, nurses would monitor them and change their dressings regularly, and physical therapists would get them up and moving and on the road to recovery. Today such patients may be discharged as soon as three days after surgery. Obviously, there is a big difference between a body that has been healing in a hospital for four weeks versus one that has been healing for four days.

In addition to taking advantage of any and all available post-hospital care, we highly recommend looking into community resources, such as "dial-a-ride" programs. Eligibility for such services often has to be determined by the agency. Many such agencies are at least partially subsidized by the community and so can offer either free or low-cost services. Usually a family member has to obtain and fill out an application, submit it, and follow up on it. This can be well worth the effort, however, as it spares family members having to take extra time out of potentially busy schedules in order to drive the patient to treatments and medical follow-up appointments.

Hospital social workers can often provide phone numbers to community programs, including Meals on Wheels (which will deliver precooked meals to housebound individuals). Local senior centers and local government offices also often have such information. These personnel typically are only too happy to assist.

When a member of the family has special needs, such as a developmental disability, it may be necessary to seek additional services so the family can temporarily focus on the ill individual. Here again there are public- and private-sector resources that are available for such emergencies, even if families have never needed them before. The first step is to identify what resources may be available in your area (talk to your doctors, ask at local government offices, and check the yellow pages). For children with developmental disabilities such as autism, the school system and individual organizations—Autism Speaks (www.autismspeaks .com) is one—can point families in the right direction for finding support services. Other organizations, such as the American Cancer Society, also have websites that direct families to available resources. When eight-year-old Danny, for example, was diagnosed with a brain cancer whose treatment would require a lengthy hospital stay, his parents were able to tap into resources that allowed them to hire a trained early childhood intervention worker to live-in three days a week and care for their two other children so that they could spend more time at the hospital with Danny.

ACCEPT REGRESSION

As you can tell from reading this chapter, Stage 2 in the family grief process can be very complex and stressful. Many individuals have told us that at this point they felt as if the expectation were to drop everything and pitch in, meaning letting go of other priorities and responsibilities. That is usually not practical; only in unusual cases is a family member in a position to drop everything else in his or her life.

We've already alluded to the fact that at this stage you may find the members of your family returning to roles they played years ago. This regression is normal, and you should expect it. Even though the family as a whole has moved past the crisis stage, each member should also expect to experience some of the emotions that initially washed over them, at least occasionally. The stages of family grief are not separated by sharp lines; rather, they reflect the different issues that families will be focused on as a terminal illness progresses. Just because the overall focus shifts, however, does not mean that individuals cannot sometimes regress to an earlier stage in the family grieving process. Carly's story, which concludes this chapter, illustrates how a person can experience earlier emotions and reactions over and over again and how difficult it can be for some people to move on.

It is a mistake to try to discourage family members from regressing. For example, a family member who has been doing a lot to pitch in may wake up one morning, turn to their partner, and say, "I can't believe this is really happening! I don't think I can face _____ today!" Rather than responding in a way that communicates that this person should be beyond such thoughts or feelings, it is better to validate them as a normal part of the grief process. A kind word of sympathy—"I can understand how you would feel that way"—can go a long way in such circumstances.

Family members should expect to occasionally experience intense anxiety, sadness, or even anger at this stage. If these periodic regressions are viewed from the perspective that they are normal and expected, they will be less upsetting to all involved. If, on the other hand, the family responds to a regressive episode by trying to talk the family member out of it (or somehow scolding him), that will only make that family member feel ashamed and, sooner or later, angry. Grief is an ongoing *process*, not a one-time *event*. Therefore, it is not reasonable to expect any family member to simply get over it or move on.

Periods of regression can be particularly difficult if you are a family member who has assumed the role of a point person. In that case, you are likely to feel guilty, especially if what you are feeling is a desire to get away from the burden. The emotions experienced at these times can drain energy that is needed to take care of business in this second stage. It is precisely for this reason that our earlier recommendation was that, if possible, there be more than one point person. That way one can step up when the other is being weighed down by some intense feelings. It can also be helpful if the family point persons keep records that others can refer to if they need a break from their duties.

Keep Records

Everyone we have talked to has reported that they have found it extremely helpful to begin keeping a record of all medical contacts, test results, and so on. These men and women say that the sheer amount of information that must be processed during this stage can be overwhelming. Moreover, without a written record, it is easy to forget information. John, for example, told the story of how he managed transportation issues.

✔ John's Story

John mentioned how he had spent weeks (and hours of time) arranging for a community service to transport his wife to her chemotherapy treatments. He had already used up the lion's share of his personal time and wanted to save some so as to be home for a week or so after she underwent surgery. When the van did not show up on the first day it was supposed to, John immediately called the social service agency. The person he spoke to said they had no record of his wife's approval for this service, much less being scheduled for pickup.

Fortunately John had taken the time to keep records of all of his and his wife's interactions with the medical and social services systems. After driving his wife to that day's appointment he returned home and looked under T for transportation in the accordion file he was using. There he found a copy of the application he had filled out,

along with a copy of the approval letter he had gotten. He then called
the agency back, asked to speak to a supervisor, and persisted until
after fifteen minutes, he was told that his wife's paperwork had been
misfiled. John got an apology, and after that there were no snags in
his wife's transportation.

John's records consisted of a series of manila folders that he kept in an accordion file whose pockets were alphabetized. He had files for:

*   *Medical team:* each doctor on his wife's treatment team by name. This included not only names and contact information but the notes that John took at each meeting with each doctor.

*   *Medical test results:* from blood work to the results of an MRI. These were arranged by date.

*   *Insurance:* including information on the insurance policy that covered John and his wife and the list of covered services, co-pays, and so on.

*   *Medications:* records of all medications ordered, by whom and when, along with receipts for co-pays.

*   *Support services:* filed alphabetically, so transportation services were under 'T', visiting nurse services were under V, and so on.

*   *Internet resources:* websites that provided information about diagnoses and treatment, as well as the web addresses (URLs) of support groups.

We have included a description of John's record-keeping system because it impressed us as simple yet comprehensive. It was a system that others could refer to and use with little confusion in his absence. Finally, it relieved John of the stress of having to keep all this information either in his head or written down but kept in different places where it could be lost.

Whatever system the family's point person uses, we urge him or her to maintain it and let other family members know of its existence.

✍ Carly's Story

"My fiancé, Sean, was twenty-eight when he died," Carly said. "We had ten years together, but it should have been a lifetime."

Carly felt so lucky that freshman year in college when she met Sean. They seemed to click from the moment they met. They had so many interests in common, and their temperaments and senses of humor were perfectly matched. "I felt so lucky that I met the love of my life so soon," she said. "All of my friends were having dating disasters, and I had found the man I wanted to spend my life with."

Sean was diagnosed at age twenty-six and was ill for sixteen months before succumbing to the cancer that had spread through his organs. According to Carly, "It was horrible. I felt like someone was playing a cruel joke on me. I had it all, and then I was going to lose it. We loved each other. We rarely fought. It just seemed so unfair."

Through it all Carly felt that she had to present a positive face to her friends and family, but most of all to Sean. They went to his doctors' appointments together. She knew objectively that he might not survive very long, but all the while she was convinced that she would have more time with her fiancé.

While Sean was receiving chemotherapy, he lost seventy pounds. Six feet tall, in the end he weighed the same as Carly, who is five feet two. "I couldn't believe how skinny he was. It was so scary. I tried everything," she explained, "to get him to eat and keep food down. But he just couldn't."

At some point, one of Sean's friends suggested that he try marijuana as a way of reducing what had become chronic nausea and discomfort. He did and found that it greatly helped both the nausea and the physical discomfort. Unfortunately, in the state where Sean and Carly lived, he was unable to legally obtain marijuana to help with his symptoms. So Carly began to obtain it for him illegally.

"I was scared to do it," Carly confessed. "I mean, I was never into drugs, but I had to help Sean. It seemed like the only thing that did help him. I didn't use it myself. Lucky for us, Sean had a friend who smoked pot occasionally, and he provided me with a small but steady supply. Sean was afraid to have this friend deliver the stuff to the house, though. He wasn't so worried about himself but about what might happen to me if the police ever followed his friend and arrested him at our place. So I met Sean's friend every couple of weeks and picked up the pot."

"Until then I had been feeling helpless," Carly explained. "I could change his sheets, help to clean him, and clean up after him when he was sick. But none of that actually made him feel better. The meds they gave him just made him feel sick. The marijuana was the only thing that actually helped."

Carly left her job as a paralegal to care for Sean, not wanting to miss a moment with him. The apartment they were renting was not too expensive. Carly had always been a saver, and between her savings and a small income she was able to bring in by doing some work for the law firm using her home computer, they were able to make ends meet, if barely. She recalled being torn by all sorts of different emotions. "I thought I would have my whole life with him and that I was so lucky. Part of me felt like I was being punished for thinking I had it all. I'm not a particularly religious person, but there were times when I would find myself being angry at God and having conversations with him in my head."

Carly said she did not know how to manage after Sean died. She had dedicated the entire last year of his life to taking care of him, and she felt that she had no purpose after he died. "Sean was everything to me, he was my whole life and then he was gone and I had nothing. I will never be able to love again like that; there will be no one else in the world so perfect for me."

Carly's family and friends have tried to get her to start dating again, but she feels that she isn't ready for it. To Carly, Sean's death felt like the end of her youth. It's been two years, and she is still having a hard time coping. She has found some satisfaction and a focus by joining a group that is trying to get medical marijuana legalized federally.

At first Carly did not believe that she would ever love again. Even now she isn't sure that there is anything anyone could have told her to prepare for this loss. She said that "the pain was so great, the loss so shocking, that I don't think there is anything I could have heard that would have prepared me."

Carly recently joined a bereavement group that was offered through her town's social service department. She says she was not ready for it right after Sean died, but that she would encourage people to pursue some sort of support or counseling "once the worst of the pain has subsided." She told us that she still has down days, but admits that these are now outnumbered by good ones.

At first inclined to keep her experience to herself, she is now open, even eager, to meet more people in her age range who have experienced a similar loss of a spouse or partner to a terminal illness. She has also found some support through online communities and has begun to form a bond with two women whose experiences closely mirror her own.

Chapter Nine

TAKING CARE OF BUSINESS

FINANCES, WILLS, TRUSTS, ETC.

I had not imagined all the legal forms that follow the death of a spouse. Death certificates—tax papers, conversations with lawyers and accountants . . . Money is just money and I have not paid as much attention to it as I should have. This is my error. I tend to wait for rescue by a shining knight. Not this time.

—ANNE ROIPHE, *EPILOGUE: A MEMOIR*

✒ Marsha's Story

Marsha, age fifty-two, was in her business office when the call came. Her husband of twenty-eight years, Tim, had suffered a heart attack—his second in as many years—while walking up a flight of stairs where he worked. This one was massive and proved to be fatal: Tim was pronounced dead shortly after arriving in an emergency room.

To her surprise, Marsha's first response was anger: Since his first attack, Tim had not lost weight, despite doctor's recommendations; nor had he consistently followed up with treatment for his hypertension, which had been poorly controlled for years. His doctor had warned them that Tim was "a walking time bomb." He had been told that he was at high risk for a second heart attack, and his doctor had wanted him to come in regularly for blood pressure checks. But Tim was always too busy to follow up. He didn't exercise, and he'd get angry at Marsha if she tried to prepare healthful meals. He was stubborn; he ignored warnings—and now he was dead. On one level, Marsha had expected this, ever since the first attack, and she'd thought about it regularly since then. She knew it was likely that Tim would go before she did. She'd even imagined what it would be like to be a widow—where she might live, things she might want to do.

In her usual efficient manner, Marsha went through the motions of calling her adult children and other kin, telling them the news and following up on the funeral arrangements she'd already made in anticipation of this day. Throughout that period, though, and for the following several weeks, Marsha said that she felt that she more or less "stood on the outside, watching life go by." It was like living in a haze. At times, conversations around her seemed muffled, as if there were a curtain separating her from those who were speaking, either to her or each other. She was pretty much unable to eat or sleep.

It was only as the haze began to melt away that the anger that Marsha held in her gut gradually gave way to deep sadness and pain, and even then only when she was alone. Several weeks later, Tim and Marsha's attorney called and suggested that she come in to talk. He sounded somber.

During that meeting Marsha learned that Tim had taken out a large line of credit and had tapped into their savings in an effort to help his business, which was suffering. He'd done all this without telling Marsha. Hearing this did not make Marsha mad—it made her feel nothing at all. She left the attorney's office in shock.

Tim had worked with and confided in this attorney for years, but Marsha had met him only once, a few years earlier, to sign their wills. Now, according to the attorney, as they met for a second time a few days later, the goal suddenly had shifted: from preserving assets to avoiding having to sell the house in order to pay off Tim's debts. He had a life insurance policy, but it would not be enough. As if that weren't bad enough, the real estate market was currently severely depressed, and even if she did sell the house, there was no way that Marsha would be able to sell it for what it would have been worth even a few years earlier.

These circumstances fueled Marsha's feelings of betrayal. It shook her sense of who she was, what kind of man Tim had been, and what their marriage had meant. She found she felt alternately desperate and furious, and did not know to whom to turn. Fortunately, the attorney had a sense of ethics, and although he could have left Marsha to deal with her dilemma on her own, he did not do so. Instead he saw Marsha through her financial crisis. He explained that, while perhaps painful, the issue of Tim's business debts might be dealt with through a bankruptcy filing. Since the business was not jointly owned with Marsha, and because Tim had taken out the line of credit using only his name, the attorney advised Marsha that her main financial loss might be limited to the savings that Tim had spent. The attorney also advised Marsha to have friends or family immediately try to sell any and all of Tim's office furnishings, computers, and so on via the Internet and keep the money. This was his only suggestion for recapturing some of the money Tim had lost on the business, which was ten years old and had never before turned a loss.

On a cloudy Sunday in the early fall, Marsha drove to the ceme-tery. She stood in front of a marble wall that housed Tim's ashes behind a six- by six-inch brass plate with his name etched into it, and vented her anger out loud. "I screamed at him," she said. "Stood there and screamed at him. I didn't care if anyone was around to hear me. Then I cried. I cried all the way home."

Marsha cried for about six hours after she got home, until she was drained. Then she fell asleep on the couch in her clothes.

Marsha eventually returned to see a therapist she'd worked with several years earlier, and together they worked on strategies for sal-vaging what Marsha could of her previous lifestyle as well as work-ing through her grief and feelings of betrayal. As angry as she was, Marsha eventually came to realize that she'd been wrong to abdi-cate all of the family's financial burdens and responsibilities to Tim. He had not intended to die and leave her in debt. His business had been successful before and no doubt he expected it to survive the financial downturn and to return to profitability again. Beyond that, Marsha knew that Tim most likely felt it would only upset Mar-sha to tell her that he'd taken out a line of credit and used up half of their savings. It was necessary for Marsha to forgive herself for not having been more involved in these financial issues, and not just be angry at him for keeping it secret.

Unfortunately, Marsha's is not a unique story. Since our culture shuns discussion of death, many families are totally unprepared for it when one member gets a terminal diagnosis. The news there-fore crashes through their denial, sending the family into a crisis state as described earlier. Moreover, our cultural phobia of death is what keeps many families from planning for this eventuality.

Even when someone has received a terminal diagnosis, preparing for death is often avoided because of the same denial. Marsha knew that her husband's health was precarious and that he was at risk. Surely Tim knew that as well, though he apparently chose to avoid facing it. He was not diagnosed with a terminal illness in the usual sense, yet Tim most definitely had a life-threatening condition. Given that reality, it would have been a good idea for him and Marsha to accept the possibility of death (while not being necessarily preoccupied with it) and to begin careful planning while he was still healthy. Neither of them did that.

A mother told us about how she had waited until she had established her career before marrying and having children. Now, at age forty-five, she and her husband, who was ten years her senior, had a five-year-old daughter and a three-year-old son. All were healthy. Nevertheless, this woman made sure that she and her husband consulted with an attorney and made out detailed wills, including establishing a guardianship as well as a trustee to manage their assets in the interests of the children in the event of their death. They made sure that each of them had adequate life insurance policies, and so on.

This couple did these things not because either of them expected to die or develop a terminal illness anytime soon; rather, they did it because it made them feel that their children's futures would be more secure if something *did* happen to one or both of them. This may be the ideal. However, it is still possible to do these things after a terminal illness has been diagnosed—or, as in Tim's case, after a person knows full well that he or she has a life-threatening condition.

Styles of Responsibility

Some people like to joke that there are only two compulsory things in life: death, and taxes. So it is that even during the crisis that a terminal illness creates, bills and taxes need to be paid. If that task has been assigned to the person who is now ill, it may be time for someone else in the family to step in and take over that responsibility or at least assist with it.

Most couples have their own idiosyncratic systems for paying the bills and managing the household finances. As the family enters this second stage of the grief process, this may be a good time to consider options that more than one family member can understand and use. Such options include using online banking and automatic payment of some bills, keeping detailed (or not so detailed) written records, and using a software package such as Quicken.

It turns out that people also often differ in their attitudes about paying bills. Some like to pay the full amount immediately on receipt of a bill, whereas others like to pay the full amount but prefer to hold payment until three or four days before it is due to maximize any interest they may earn on the money. Then there are those who are accustomed to sending partial payments. A third alternative is the budget plan, in which a fixed payment is made every month—for example, for electricity or heating oil—with any outstanding balance (or credit) being settled once a year. Finally, some people are fairly disorganized when it comes to paying bills and don't seem to be bothered by the occasional late-payment fine.

Whoever it is that steps up to the plate to assist with bill paying and budgeting needs to be cognizant of the way things have been handled in the past. Each of us has a comfort zone with respect to how money is managed. It can cause extra and needless stress to insist on changing things drastically and forcing the ill family member out of his or her routine. It is recommended that the newly anointed family financial manager(s) take the time to sit down with the ill family member and discuss the whole issue of bills, including taxes. When possible, it is probably best to use a system that this person is comfortable with. The exception to this might be those who are truly disorganized bill payers, in which case it is probably not reasonable to continue the pattern.

Assessing the Insurance Safety Net

There are two forms of insurance that need to be checked out as soon as possible after a terminal diagnosis has been rendered. This is especially true if the person receiving the diagnosis is of working age and is currently employed. The types of insurance are *life* insurance and *disability* insurance.

Short-term disability insurance is designed to replace lost income for a specified period of time, usually no longer than three to six months. In the event the policyholder becomes injured or ill and is unable to continue working, this form of insurance usually kicks in as soon as a doctor certifies the disability. It often yields benefits as high as the individual's usual paycheck. Short-term disability can be a strong safety net in cases such as surgery or injury. When faced with a terminal illness, however, short-term disability benefits are likely to run out long before the individual either achieves a state of remission or dies.

Long-term disability insurance, in contrast, usually takes

effect anywhere from sixty to ninety days after an individual is disabled. Long-term disability policies typically pay a portion of the individual's former salary, in the range of 50 to 60 percent. However, unlike short-term disability policies, long-term disability benefits may be payable for years. Many (but not all) employers offer their employees the opportunity to buy into group short- and long-term disability policies.

In addition to these personal policies, individuals may be eligible for disability payments through Social Security. This, however, can be a long and complex process. Many people elect to pay an attorney who is experienced at applying for these benefits, as opposed to doing it themselves.

Additional sources of money that may be available to the family at this time include savings accounts, trust funds, and deferred compensation accounts. Having someone in the family take responsibility for researching these assets and keeping tabs on available financial resources is very helpful, for that will give the family some sense of just what kind of safety net it has.

For obvious reasons, it is not possible to obtain meaningful life insurance after a terminal diagnosis has been rendered. That is why we encourage all family members reading this book and who are currently healthy (or at least not terminally ill) to consult with a financial adviser. The purpose of this consultation should be to review your assets and determine how much life insurance you should obtain. Factors such as whether you have any young children or dependent adults to provide for as well as outstanding debts should be considered. Life insurance is a form of safety net that complements disability insurance and that can go a long way toward relieving the stress on your entire family in the event you find yourself faced with a terminal illness.

Adding an Attorney to the Team

A terminal illness provides individuals and families with an opportunity to plan, which sudden death does not. One of the most important things for the family to consider as it marshals its resources in the unity stage is to hire an attorney with experience in estate planning. This attorney then becomes part of the team, alongside the family and the medical team.

The role of the attorney is to advise the patient on how best to use whatever financial safety net is available, to plan for the payment of debts and the disbursement and management of assets in the event of death. Usually a terminally ill person will include a spouse in the process, if there is one. If there are any adult children, it may be a good idea to at least sound them out on any plan before it is finalized, as Eleanor's story shows.

✔ *Eleanor's Story*

When Eleanor, a sixty-four-year-old widow, was diagnosed with pancreatic cancer, she was concerned about her thirty-year-old son, Jake, who had never been able to hold down a job, stay out of debt, or maintain a relationship for longer than a year. She decided to discuss her intentions about estate planning with her two older sons, both of whom were married with children and financially stable. She told them she was thinking of leaving the family home to Jake and arranging for a trust that would pay him a monthly stipend. That way, she said, Jake would not become a burden to his brothers. She based this on her belief that Jake was unlikely to ever be self-reliant or financially secure on his own.

Eleanor's other two sons protested. For obvious reasons, they felt this plan was not fair. They were being penalized, they said, because they were responsible. In that meeting both admitted that they had long harbored resentments toward Jake, whom they saw as being indulged and protected by Eleanor. As a result, they felt that Jake had never been taught to take responsibility for himself. Eleanor's plan, they argued, would only perpetuate that.

When Eleanor resisted her sons' arguments, the tensions in this family quickly became so intense that Eleanor's physician referred her to a counselor who specialized in mediation, and who agreed to meet with Eleanor and all three of her sons. It took several sessions for them to vent their feelings and thoughts, all of which were intensified by the impending loss of Eleanor. Finally, though, the mediator was able to help them arrive at what they all came to accept as a fair resolution. The negotiated agreement was for Eleanor's house to be sold after her death, for the estate to be divided equally, and for Jake's share only to be put in a trust administered by the family lawyer. Jake was also referred for vocational counseling and individual therapy, at Eleanor's expense, with the goal of becoming a more responsible adult.

Most families work with an attorney to meet the following objectives:

- To manage the ill person's medical treatment within the limits that they can control, including finances and treatment options.

- To transfer assets to family members in a way that the ill family member deems most appropriate and fair, either before or after death.

- To control the manner in which assets will be distributed— for example, instantly versus over a period of time.

- To minimize any taxes that must be paid as a result of any disbursements.

Neither of us is an attorney, but following our own advice, we have sought counsel from qualified attorneys to help us present this summary of the most important legal issues that need to be addressed while there is time to address them. The attorneys we consulted were unanimous with respect to one piece of advice: *If at all possible, do not wait until the terminally ill family member is hospitalized and perhaps too ill to participate to begin working on a plan.* In other words, start work on the plan as quickly as possible after the diagnosis has been rendered.

The rest of this chapter focuses on issues that you are well advised to turn your attention to in this second stage of the grief process.

Managing Medical Treatment

To manage a serious and possibly terminal illness, the individual should have the following documents drawn up, copied, and kept in separate locations known and available to at least *two* family members.

POWER OF ATTORNEY

Power of attorney is a document that grants either the ill person's partner or another designated person the authority to have access to bank accounts and other sources of funds to make payments on debts, file and pay taxes, run a business if necessary, and apply for benefits such as Social Security disability.

To be legal, a power of attorney must be initiated while the individual is deemed to be mentally competent by a doctor. Therefore, this needs to be done as soon as possible. Moreover, the power of attorney that is signed should be of the durable variety. A durable power of attorney continues to be effective after the individual who grants it (the "grantor") becomes incapacitated, whereas a simple power of attorney terminates if and when the grantor is deemed incompetent.

A *durable healthcare power of attorney* appoints a healthcare representative to make medical decisions as he or she sees fit. Spouses often assign each other this right and responsibility, but it can also be an adult child, a sibling, or even a trusted friend. Investing a person with such authority is not a decision to be taken lightly, but it can provide the terminally ill person with a sense that their care will be as they would want it to be in the event they become incapacitated. For example, if an individual decides that he does not want to spend his final days in an unconscious state in a hospital or nursing home, he can make that known via a document drawn up by his attorney, signed, and given to the person with designated power of attorney. That person can then order that the patient be brought home, or that certain interventions not be used.

Another way to appoint a person the ill family member wants to pass authority to in the event they become incapacitated is to have the attorney draw up what is known as a *springing power of attorney*. This power of attorney specifically becomes effective only when a third party, such as the patient's primary care physician, declares that the patient is incapacitated and not competent to make such decisions. The combination of a durable power of attorney, a medical power of attorney, and a springing power of attorney is the best insurance that any decisions made will be consistent with what the terminal family member would want.

🌿 Max's Story

When Max, sixty-two, lost his fifty-nine-year-old wife, Jan, unexpectedly to a heart attack, he felt totally adrift for the better part of a year. He was not in good health himself, having been diagnosed with emphysema and having already suffered one heart attack. Because of his own frail health, he had always expected to be the first one to go, and he had never given a moment's thought to what he would do or what life would be like if he were to be widowed.

Max and Jan had a will, and here again Max had always expected everything they had to go to Jan. They talked about how she might sell their house after a year or so and move into one of those over-fifty condominium complexes that seemed to be springing up wherever they looked or else into an assisted living center, depending on how old and healthy she was at the time.

Now Max found himself confronted by a totally unexpected set of challenges. Though not having a formal terminal diagnosis such as end-stage cancer, Max was nevertheless fully aware that his health was continuing to deteriorate. He had relatively little stamina, and even that was waning. He had recently gotten a rechargeable, battery-operated cart that he used to navigate through the local shopping mall. It was easily disassembled and stored in the trunk of his car. And about a year before Jan died, they'd had an elevator chair installed in the house so Max could ride to the second floor if he felt too weak to climb the stairs.

Max's greatest fear was that he would become incapacitated. He and Jan had three sons. All were grown, but the truth was that only one of them was responsible enough to be trusted to make decisions with a level head and not with just his own self-interest in mind. Max truly loved all of his sons, but he knew that he needed to seriously consider putting someone in charge in case he could no longer fulfill the role of money manager that had always been his.

Max had been a successful contractor, and as a result, the family had considerable assets. He also had four grandchildren. They had been the apple of Jan's eye, and Max knew that she would have wanted them to be taken care of even more so than their sons.

Max ended up taking the advice of his personal physician and consulted an attorney who specialized in estate planning. That attorney walked Max through all of the legal issues and helped him develop a plan that included most of the elements discussed in this chapter. Max then met with the responsible son, who was designated as executor of his will, and who was also granted power of attorney, both financially and medically, and went over his plan.

Perhaps most important of all, Max also had a long talk with his son. A few months earlier he'd visited his best friend after that friend was admitted to a hospital when the cancer that was killing him had proliferated in his chest and brain. Max hadn't liked what he saw. It broke his heart to see his buddy lying in that bed, hooked up to all those tubes and monitors. His eyes were open, but he was just staring out into space, his face expressionless. "They were keeping him alive," Max said. "But for what?"

Max explained to his son that, should he become incapacitated, he would not want his son to authorize medical interventions that were unlikely to significantly improve his overall quality of life. He did not, for example, wish his son to authorize any procedure that would most likely leave Max still incapacitated. "I do not wish to be kept alive just for the sake of being kept alive," he explained. Nor did he want his son to authorize treatments that would extend his life only marginally.

Next, Max set up a trust, with the attorney as trustee, to manage his and Jan's remaining assets according to guidelines that Max laid down. The family assets were to be managed in such a way that a certain amount of money would be distributed to all three sons twice a year. Additional assets were set aside, however, for the future benefit of the grandchildren. These assets could be used, for example, to pay for college or other educational expenses, unexpected medical expenses, and so on. When the youngest grandchild reached age twenty-five, any remaining assets were to be distributed equally among them and Max's three sons.

Lastly, Max brought his sons together for a meeting and explained the arrangements he'd made. He repeated the instructions he'd given his executor son. He did not ask anyone's approval, and did not allow himself to react when one son clearly looked unhappy. For his part, however, Max was quite satisfied.

ADVANCED MEDICAL DIRECTIVE AND LIVING WILL

An *advanced medical directive* is a document that allows a person designated by the patient the right to make medical decisions and to have access to medical records. This allows, for example, a spouse (or one of the family point persons) the right to authorize (or refuse) medical treatments, to be consulted by physicians as they consider treatment alternatives, to have priority access to the patient, and to authorize release of the patient's body from a hospital at the time of death. Some attorneys recommend that a separate document be signed authorizing the patient's spouse or a designated other to see what would otherwise be considered protected health information.

A *living will* allows the terminally ill to be on record as to whether they wish medical personnel to apply "heroic measures" to keep them alive if the alternative is death if these measures are not applied. A living will can also direct that a do not resuscitate (DNR) order be placed in the patient's medical chart. In that event, the patient is not resuscitated if his or her heart stops beating.

Without directives such as the living will and the advanced medical directive in place, there is no telling what frustrations the family may encounter, adding to the upheaval that is encountered in Stage 3 of the family grief process. We look to Max, described above, as a good role model in this regard. The people we choose to make medical decisions for us in the event we are not able to make those decisions for ourselves need to be clear about just how far we would want to go. Would we, for example, prefer life over death if that life were in a vegetative state? Or if we were not able to recognize even friends and family we'd known for years and years?

Estate Planning

Estate planning includes designating how personal assets are controlled and what happens to them when that person dies. Again, as stressful as death by terminal illness may be, it does at least allow for planning that too often is left undone when a person's death is sudden. Some of the most important things to consider when talking with an attorney about estate planning are discussed in the following sections.

THE WILL

The purpose of a will is fairly straightforward: It is designed to transfer property upon the death of the person who draws up the will. While the individual is alive, any and all property named in the will remains his or her personal property. Most often the beneficiaries of a will are spouses, children, and other relatives, although anyone (or any organization) can be named a beneficiary. Wills dispose of such property as homes, stocks, other personal property such as cars, boats, and bank accounts. A will appoints an individual, known as an *executor*, to stand in for the deceased person and to distribute property according to the deceased's wishes.

Wills are important for everyone. However, whereas all property owned by a married couple automatically reverts to the survivor in the event that one of them dies, that is not the case for couples who are cohabiting but not either married or living in a recognized civil union. In that case, the absence of a will leaves the deceased partner *intestate*, which means that any property they own may be claimed by blood relatives.

TRUSTS

Trusts are legal tools that can be used for two purposes. The first is to avoid having to go through a probate process when the grantor of the trust dies. In terms of what we are talking about here, the grantor would be the terminally ill family member (and perhaps his or her spouse if they form the trust as a couple). A second reason for forming a trust is to control the disposition of personal or family assets after the death of the grantor.

Max, whose story we just related, was happy to use a will and an executor to distribute some of his possessions, to sell others, and to pay outstanding bills after his death. However, he was not comfortable simply distributing all of the financial assets that he and his wife had accumulated in one fell swoop. Therefore, he elected to create a *trust*. This involved transferring many of these assets into a fund that was controlled by a *trustee* of Max's choice. The trustee in turn is authorized to manage these assets, which are then used for specific purposes as defined in the trust document. In Max's case, this included future educational costs for any of his grandchildren—a goal that had been important to both him and his wife. The trustee can be a family member or it can be an outside person. Many people choose to pay an attorney or a professional financial adviser—as Max did—to function as trustee for the duration of the trust.

Trusts are not for everyone. But they can and should be considered if the ill family member believes that controlling the distribution of personal assets after death would be in the best interests of everyone concerned. This may be the case if one or more potential beneficiaries has special needs and/or has limited mental capacity, such as those with chronic severe mental illnesses or cognitive limitations due to traumatic brain injury or mental retardation. It is not only possible but advisable to consider establishing what is known as a "special needs trust" for such individuals. Again, an attorney knowledgeable in this area is the best resource to consult with regarding such trusts.

CASH AVAILABILITY

✒ *Nora's Story*

Nora's husband, Jim, died so many years after his initial diagnosis of colon cancer that they had almost forgotten that he was terminally ill. He was undergoing treatment when he died, but Nora was not prepared for it. At Jim's death, all cash income from his retirement and Social Security ceased, and Nora was left without any access to sufficient cash for the next six weeks. She had to borrow money from friends to pay the mortgage and other bills. Whatever they had in savings was in Jim's name, and Nora did not have a pension of her own to fall back on.

From Nora we learn that it's critical to make arrangements to have access to cash in emergency situations.

THE LETTER OF INTENT

In addition to a will, over the course of time it is a good idea for the terminally ill person to write a letter detailing the disposition of personal items, such as Grandma's wedding band or a favorite piece of art. If these specific bequests are clearly written down, it will prevent family tension and resentments arising from misunderstandings or family manipulation. Such letters of intent can also be written with the assistance of an attorney so as to avoid any misreading later on.

FAMILY BUSINESSES

Family businesses are notoriously complex affairs, from both a psychological and a legal perspective. Typically, such businesses are started and built by one or two ambitious and hardworking family members. If they are successful, the business may eventually come to employ not only outsiders but other family members. If the business founder then becomes terminally ill, the family's crisis is further complicated.

We strongly recommend that a terminally ill person who plays a central role in a family business include an attorney on the team he or she is working with early on so as to be of help in determining the future of the business and the future roles of all family members who may depend on that business. In not a few cases, we have found it equally useful to bring an experienced family therapist onboard as well. In the unity stage of grief, the family will usually focus on pulling together and compensating as needed for the loss of the ill person. As they move into Stage 3, however, they can expect many issues to arise. These issues will be discussed in greater detail in chapters 10 to 13.

BLENDED FAMILIES

Blended families can face issues just about as thorny as those faced by a family business when one of the parents is diagnosed as terminally ill. A blended family is one in which one or both spouses have children from a previous marriage. Again, a family therapist can be an invaluable asset to a blended family as it faces the potential of losing one of the parents.

The spouses in a blended family will want to provide for one another and for both sets of children. Clearly, issues of jealousy, entitlement, and insecurity can arise in the children, in the spouses, or both. The issue of *competing loyalties* is endemic to blended families: Whose children are more important, those who are mine biologically or those who are mine via marriage?

Some couples who contemplate marrying and forming a blended family elect to try to circumvent potential future conflicts by negotiating a *prenuptial agreement*. These agreements usually specify what assets each partner brings into the marriage and which both agree will remain their personal assets, to be distributed on their death (or divorce) as they choose. If such an agreement is in place, we recommend that all children eighteen years and older be advised that it exists, even if the spouses decide jointly not to disclose the details of the agreement.

✿ Becky's Story

Becky's first husband, Curt, was diagnosed with amyotrophic lateral sclerosis (ALS) after they'd been married for twelve years and had two children, a son and a daughter, who were ten and eight at the time. Becky worked part-time for as long as she could while also continuing to raise the children and take care of Curt.

Curt proved to be an angry, depressed patient who did not suffer his illness with any degree of grace. Becky described him this way: "Curt was not a happy-go-lucky, optimistic type of person to begin with. But when he started showing symptoms, he became even more irritable and negative. He was negative not just about himself but about me, the kids, and life in general. He felt sorry for himself. He was angry that this was happening to him—like it should be happening to anyone else but him. He was constantly critical of me and increasingly intolerant and critical of the children. After he got the formal diagnosis of ALS, he became so nasty that I tried to keep the kids away from him as much as possible."

Curt died a mere eighteen months after being diagnosed, and Becky believed that his negative attitude and depression had contributed to his quick deterioration. Indeed, Curt did not strike us as a particularly *resilient* individual. To Becky, it also seemed like the process had lasted much longer than eighteen months. "It seemed like Curt was sick for years," she said. No doubt Curt's personality had colored Becky's experience as well.

After Curt's death, Becky decided to keep the house they'd lived in and rent it out. She and the children moved in with her parents, who owned a large old farmhouse that had plenty of room for them. Becky's parents helped watch the children while Becky went back to work. An accountant by training, she had a skill that was marketable and was able to command a decent salary.

Becky didn't date or even socialize much for the next three years. By then, both children were old enough not to need baby-sitters. They were both responsible children who did well in school, had friends, and pursued outside activities.

Becky met Dave shortly after her younger child went off to college. At first Dave seemed to be the opposite of Curt: outgoing, happy, and on top of the world. He was a teacher, liked his work, and got along with her children.

Becky noticed two things about Dave, however, that made her feel uneasy. First, he didn't seem to have any friends, and he rarely talked about or saw his family, despite the fact that they did not live very far away. She knew others, though, who weren't especially close to their families, so she more or less ignored that.

The thing that bothered Becky more about Dave was that he never invited her to his place. He would take her out to eat, or to the movies, or for a walk, but they would always return to her place afterward. Finally, after several months of this, she decided to confront the issue head-on. At that point it seemed that they were headed for a commitment, and she just needed to put this concern to rest. So one evening she just came out and told Dave that it was important for her to see where he lived.

"He grimaced," Becky said. "In fact, if I close my eyes, I can still see that grimace on his face. But then he shrugged and said okay. I remember his saying that he hadn't had time to clean house lately and that it was messy. I told him I didn't care, that I wasn't afraid of messy."

What Becky saw when she entered Dave's house was well beyond anything she had imagined on the drive over. "There's no other way to say it," she explained. "It was a hovel. A total disaster. Piles of things were everywhere. It was like he hadn't thrown anything out in years. In some rooms you literally had to walk down a narrow aisle through the piles. There were books, magazines, furniture, cardboard boxes, clothing, tools—anything you could imagine—scattered and piled up everywhere."

Becky said that her initial, gut reaction to what she saw was to turn and run. But she didn't. In fact, rather than seeing this as a harbinger of things to come, Becky wrote it off, just as she'd written off Dave's social isolation. Six months later they moved into a rented house together.

In retrospect Becky realized her mistake. She'd been so emotionally battered by her experience with Curt that she'd been willing to ignore virtually everything just because Dave struck her as upbeat and happy. As she later learned, however, he was only this way as long as everything went his way. If things didn't go his way—if he wanted one thing and she wanted another, for example, he quickly got testy.

In relatively short order, the house that Dave and Becky were renting began to resemble the house he'd lived in before. Moreover, she found that Dave did not want her touching anything that was "his." "He'd get bent out of shape if I tried to clean up one of his messes," she explained.

Becky compensated for this by more or less dividing the house into Dave's space versus Becky's space and strictly enforcing the boundaries that separated the two. A second good decision she made came when Dave began to pressure her to buy a house together. He did not, however, mention marriage. Becky found herself feeling grateful for that. By that time she had pretty much ruled marriage out.

Becky could not say just why it was she stayed with Dave. Her best guess was that it was simple inertia—it was just easier to stay than to go. A close friend, however, suggested that Becky had become so accustomed to negativity and unpleasant living conditions with Curt that she didn't know things could be better. In any case, Becky told Dave she'd decided to move ahead with his plan to buy a house, but only if he agreed to sign a document that she had an attorney draw up. This document stated that Becky had brought prior assets into the relationship—her former house—and that Dave would have to quit any claim he might make to any part of those assets. In addition, Dave would have to agree that in the event of Becky's death, her interest in the house they jointly owned would go not to Dave, as co-owner, but rather to Becky's two children. She had an individual will drawn up and appointed a trusted friend as its exec-utor. Dave hemmed and hawed over Becky's conditions for the better part of a month, but when she stuck to her guns and refused to relent, he eventually agreed and signed the necessary documents.

Regardless of how you may feel about Becky's relationship with Dave, hers is a good example of the kind of planning that is often useful when two individuals who have children from prior marriages or relationships contemplate making a commitment to their relationship. While Becky recognized that her commitment to Dave was less than wholehearted, she also recognized that joint ownership of a home represented a degree of commitment. Having grieved the loss of a husband, Becky had learned something from that experience and took action ahead of time to take care of business.

GAY AND LESBIAN FAMILIES

✒ *Marguerite's Story*

When Marguerite received a terminal diagnosis at the age of thirty-six, she realized that her partner, Debbie, might find herself in uncharted legal territory with respect to the custody of their seven-year-old son, Nick. Marguerite had given birth to Nick with the aid of an anonymous sperm donor; Debbie had undergone gynecological surgery in her twenties that had eliminated her ability to conceive. Debbie applied for and was approved as Nick's second adoptive parent.

Marguerite and Debbie had been together twelve years. After Nick was born, Debbie left her position as a photographer for a large urban newspaper to stay home with Nick. She continued to do some freelance work from a home office, and occasionally on weekends she would take a job shooting a wedding or anniversary celebration.

Marguerite's family did not accept her sexual orientation, and they'd had no contact with her for more than a decade. Marguerite had sent them a birth announcement, but she never received a response.

Debbie's family, in contrast, was warm, loving, and accepting of her and Marguerite as a couple, and they actively participated in their grandson's life. Whereas Marguerite and Debbie had been married in a state where gay marriage was legal, it was not legal in the state where they now resided. Debbie had not proceeded with another adoption application. She was not even sure if that would be legal in their state.

Marguerite and Debbie did not want to relocate because they had excellent healthcare benefits and close relationships with a circle of friends and Debbie's family. Adamant that she never wanted her family to have anything to do with Nick's upbringing, Marguerite sought counsel from several state and national gay rights' organizations. Eventually, she was referred to an attorney who proceeded to make sure that Nick would be entrusted to Debbie in the event of Marguerite's death.

It was also important to Marguerite that Debbie be given healthcare power of attorney and durable power of attorney, and that she be named as the executor of her will. One thing that this attorney did chide them on was the fact that they had not taken these legal steps years earlier, when Nick was born.

Many nontraditional families are particularly sensitive to societal and cultural oppression. It is important that they have an attorney draw up the necessary legal documents to protect themselves, each other, and their children from the types of disasters that can occur if their affairs are not in order. There have been cases in which the biological parent's family is named guardian or custodian regardless of the nature of the relationship.

Making Critical Information Accessible

Stage 2 is the time to begin organized, written record-keeping. Independent of whether a terminal diagnosis leads to remission or to death, this is a time for increased transparency. This task may represent a challenge for those families whose culture values privacy. Some parents, for example, prefer to keep their financial status to themselves, feeling that it is none of their children's business, even if those children are grown. By the same token, some adult siblings may prefer to not share financial information at all or to share it only in general terms with one another. In normal circumstances, these personal preferences may not present a problem. When confronted with what has the potential to become a financial disaster, however, it is more important that the family as a whole understand what kind of financial resources are available so as to inform the decision-making process. We have heard too many horror stories of families who found themselves blindsided by what amounted to catastrophic medical bills not covered by insurance, by mortgages, and by other bills that could not be paid as a result of an unanticipated loss of income.

Among the items of information that need to be available, at least to selected family members, are the following:

- A list of all medical and legal professionals involved with your family: names, telephone numbers, mailing addresses, and e-mail addresses.

- A continuously updated list of all medications and medical appointments.

- The names and telephone numbers of service providers for the house: lawn service, auto service, plumber, electrician, handymen, cleaners, etc.

- A list of all life and health insurance policies: identification numbers, customer service numbers, and agent names and telephone numbers.

- Computer passwords for online bank access, ongoing accounts and services (for security reasons, this information may be restricted to just one or two family members).

- Real estate and income tax records.

- Credit card and debit card numbers and online passwords (may be limited to one or two persons).

- Copies of all wills, trusts, living wills, powers of attorney, and so on: the originals should be on file with the attorney who prepared them.

- Birth certificates and marriage certificates.

All important papers should be organized and easily accessible to those who may need this information. That includes spouses and any family member(s) who have power of attorney. Of course, they can be kept in a home safe or locked fire-resistant box.

While many people are reluctant to collect this information even after being diagnosed with a terminal illness, more and more people are taking the initiative to gather critical information and make it accessible to executors or trustees or those with power of attorney.

✒ Lindsey's Story

Lindsey is twenty-six and single. She said that she was never particularly close to her grandmother, Amanda, who lived in the United Kingdom for most of the time that Lindsey was growing up in the United States. When Lindsey was ten, however, and after her grandfather died, her grandmother left England and came to stay with them because both Lindsey's mother and grandmother were only children. With the help of friends and an attorney, Lindsey's mother was able to obtain a green card and find employment for Lindsey's grandmother. Although Amanda didn't earn a lot of money, she was able to help with some of the family's modest expenses.

Amanda was diagnosed with breast cancer when Lindsey was fifteen. She underwent aggressive treatment, and her cancer went into remission. Three years later, the cancer reappeared, this time in Amanda's lungs. A second round of treatment ensued, but the cancer had already metastasized, and Amanda died a little less than a year later. Throughout this time, neither Lindsey nor her three siblings had any insight into how much money came into the family or where it went. Even when Lindsey was eighteen and legally an adult, her mother never discussed issues such as savings accounts and insurance policies.

According to Lindsey, even though it is well known that breast cancer runs in families and that she and her mother were thus at

some risk, there has never been even a single mother-daughter con-
versation about what Lindsey should do in the event that her mother
got seriously ill or died. Lindsey spoke about how difficult it had
been for her mother, who was a single working mother and some-
times had to take time off of work (without pay) to take care of
Amanda. Lindsey's impression was that her mother was also not
especially close to Amanda, but felt obligated to take care of her.

Lindsey said she did not really feel terribly sad when she was
first told about her grandmother's relapse. Indeed, her demeanor
did not suggest any intense emotions when she spoke about it, or
about Amanda's death. If anything, one could detect a trace of anger
in her voice. "Everyone's grandparents die," she explained. "It wasn't
that hard or strange for me. Maybe that's because we were never
that close. I mean, my grandmother wasn't mean or anything,
but neither was she particularly affectionate. She was kind of an
aloof, emotionally cool person. She never showed that much interest
in me."

What does worry Lindsey, though, is the thought that her
mom could get sick like her grandmother had. She is aware that
because breast cancer runs in families, she, her mother, and her
older sister were all at risk. As she spoke about this, Lindsey's
demeanor changed noticeably and her expression reflected a defi-
nite sense of worry.

Lindsey felt bad for her mother. "My mom had to put her life on hold
twice in order to take care of my grandmother. For years all she did
was work, take care of Grandma and us kids, and keep house. She
had no time for friends, no time for herself. I did feel resentful,
because it was like I lost my mother to my grandmother. Also there

were long periods of time when our family lived from week to week, from paycheck to paycheck. If I ever have a daughter, I wouldn't want her to have the feelings that I have if I have to go through the same thing with my mother."

Lindsey had watched as her mother had to help Amanda emotionally, physically, and financially despite having to raise four children. Though her mother is currently healthy, Lindsey fears that someday she may have to be the caregiver for her mother because her siblings have all moved far away. "What if I had to do that on my own?" she asked. "It was so hard for my mom, and it would be so hard for me."

Lindsey still is not aware if her mother has a will, or what her wishes would be if she were to suddenly die. She does not know if her mother has any life insurance or what benefits her health insurance covers. She does not know how much money, if any, her mother might have in bank accounts or what kind of retirement benefits she might be entitled to other than Social Security, which she will be eligible for in four years.

Lindsey said that it would be a relief if she could talk with her mother about all of the above issues. She sees no purpose in venting her resentments about Amanda and has no desire to do so; on the other hand, it would do a lot to ease her anxieties, she says, if she knew the details of her mother's finances. Her story is the perfect example of why it is good to have greater as opposed to lesser transparency on these issues. Lindsey's mother does not have a terminal diagnosis, but the risk factors alone in this family would seem to warrant more openness, both about finances and about breast cancer. Like many children—even adult children—Lindsey hesitates to initiate this discussion. She has taken her mother's silence as indication that her mother does not wish to talk about these things. For that reason, we encourage parents to take the initiative. This can be done at any time, but it certainly should be done after a family member receives a terminal diagnosis.

🖋 *Patrick's Story*

Patrick lost his mother to breast cancer when he was four years old, and his father to a brain tumor recently. He is now twenty-three.

"People ask me all the time if I'm okay," Patrick said. "Sometimes they start to cry when I tell them my story. I don't feel sorry for myself, though. This is my life, and I think I've just come to accept it. I had two great parents and now they are gone. Some people have both parents alive and don't get the love in a whole lifetime that I got in a short time."

Patrick talked about how being an orphan at such a relatively young age does make him feel vulnerable at times, as well as sad. At the same time, he expressed tremendous admiration for his older sister, Amy, whom he described as his "second mom."

"I'm so lucky to have such an amazing sister. And my extended family, too. Our uncles and aunts have really been here for us." He smiled as he thought about it. "Amy and I both knew my dad well, and that connection we shared makes me feel like part of him is still with us."

Patrick talked about how not having his mother alive, for example, for his and Amy's high school graduations or for her wedding two years earlier, was very sad for both of them, but he took comfort in the belief that his mom would have been very pleased with their choices and proud of their accomplishments. She had been trained as a teacher and had been a very good one up until her career was cut short.

"*I miss my dad," Patrick said. "I was just laid off from my job when he died, and I knew he'd know just what to say and what I should do. Times like that—when I find myself in a tight spot—make me really miss my dad. I don't really remember my mom that much, but Amy has told me stories about her. She was nine when Mom passed away.*"

Patrick feels that it is important to him that his sister lives a healthy lifestyle and gets regular checkups due to her potentially increased risks of having cancer. "I want to take care of myself too," Patrick explained. "I don't want either Amy or I to be alone the way my dad was after my mom died. I want to be there for her always, and I want her there for me."

Besides taking care of his physical health, and despite the fact that he is healthy, Patrick was adamant about making a will and making sure that Amy knows everything about his insurance and savings, has power of attorney, and so on. "One thing life has taught me is that you can't live with your head in the sand," he said. "You should always talk about these things to those who are closest to you. I don't get why people don't take care of that. It's so irresponsible!"

Patrick said that his father was extremely careful to keep him and his sister informed on a regular basis about the state of his finances. He also wrote out his funeral plans and specified how he wanted his end-of-life care to be managed. Patrick and Amy were given powers of attorney to see to it that their father's wishes were followed. They took this as a sign of love on their father's part. Patrick expressed respect and relief that his father had taken pains to be so organized. He understood very well that his father did this so that his children would not have to worry about finding information or deciding what to do at the same time that they were coping with their grief.

"My dad had to deal with everything plus taking care of two little kids after my mom died," Patrick explained, "and he didn't want us to have to deal with any of that. I guess I would advise adult children to talk to their parents and ask about their plans and desires should anything happen. Like I said, one thing my life has taught me is that you never know what will happen and life isn't fair. People need to know what their parents want so they can honor their wishes."

❧ STAGE 3 ❧

UPHEAVAL

Here begins the open sea. Here begins the glorious adventure, the only one abreast with human curiosity, the only one that soars as high as its highest longing. Let us accustom ourselves to regard death as a form of life we do not yet understand; let us look upon it with the same eye that looks upon birth; and soon our mind will be accompanied to the steps of the tomb with the same glad expectation as greets a birth.

—MAURICE MAETERLINCK

Chapter Ten

CHRONIC ILLNESS, EMOTIONS, AND FAMILY DYNAMICS

Even as the family pulls together in the unity stage there will usually be some initial signs that reflect the underlying upheaval that prolonged terminal illness creates. Lindsey's account, told in the last chapter, of the effect that her grandmother's two bouts with cancer had on her family, is a testament to the upheaval that is part of the new grief. Just living with the uncertainty that is associated with a terminal diagnosis is stressful, not only for the patient but for the entire family. Beyond that there are the actual lifestyle changes it creates. Loved ones may have willingly altered their own lives and shifted priorities to pitch in and accommodate the needs of the ill family member. Despite their willingness to do these things, the unity stage inevitably leads to stresses and tensions within the family because:

- Lifestyles can get skewed and out of balance as a consequence of added responsibilities. Established routines become disrupted, and new ones may have to be added. Priorities may have to be realigned and the time devoted to them reapportioned. The impact of these changes may not be very noticeable (or bothersome) at first, but eventually it can't be ignored.

- Former family roles are often re-created, and issues that may have been buried long ago begin to rear their heads again. For example, as mentioned earlier, people find themselves falling back into old family roles, such as mediator or problem solver, that they thought they'd shed long ago.

What to Expect

The person with the illness may, over time, want to reclaim, at least temporarily, responsibilities that have been reassigned to others; alternatively, he or she may resist taking on previous responsibilities even in a period of remission. The patient's autonomy and dignity are major priorities, but changing circumstances may necessitate collaboration among all adult members of the family about who can and will do what, and for how long. Expect the situation to be fluid. Also, expect everyone to experience fluctuating moods as well as periodic changes of attitude—from a willing and eager helper to a resentful and reluctant helper, for example. Tensions can become particularly voluble during periods of remission, when it seems as if everything is back to normal and at least some family members want a respite from any added responsibilities they have taken on.

Family dynamics will dictate how the family—as individuals and as a unit—copes with the situation. By family dynamics we mean the way a family functions, including the unwritten rules it lives by and the roles that different family members play, including their responsibilities. Some family members, for example, are accustomed to playing the role of mediator or peacemaker; others are organizers. Our impression has been that the strains in the family system that are caused by terminal illness first show up in the form of *emotions* that family members may feel uncomfortable acknowledging. Anger, resentment, and jealousy are the most common ones. Family members may feel guilty about having such feelings in a time of crisis and may try to suppress them. But our experience is that such feelings are normal and to be expected, and our advice is that you can try to suppress your feelings, but in the end you can't help feeling as you do. Try as you may, these feelings will occasionally erupt. As dismaying as this may be, it is actually a potentially healthy thing for the family as a whole because it gives everyone an opportunity to face reality— the stresses on the family—and to create new family dynamics that meet changing circumstances.

It is not unusual for the stress created by chronic or terminal illness to manifest in impatience—with the person who is ill, with fellow caregivers, and with professionals. At this point everyone's attentiveness is stretched and their reserves of energy are depleted; therefore, everyone is vulnerable to losing patience.

✒ Michael's Story

"My mother had always been sick as long as I could remember," Michael explained. "When I was little, I was always afraid that I would wake up one morning and that she would be dead. That's why I could never go to bed or fall asleep if I felt there was any kind of bad feeling between us. I had to go through an elaborate ritual with her every night. It involved kissing each other three times and repeating certain prayers. That's the only way I could get to sleep."

Michael's mother had been in and out of remission his whole life. In the end, her cancer spread to her brain and other vital organs. Her eventual death, at fifty-six, was extremely difficult for Michael and his two brothers, but it was his father, Ben, whom Michael found himself worrying about after he didn't have his mother to worry about anymore.

After his wife's death, Ben poured all of his energy into work. He put so much time into his job as a financial adviser that he had very little life outside of that. And that seemed fine with him. His sons were all grown by then and two of them were married with children and lived far away. Michael was the youngest, also married, but not yet a father.

Michael was aware that his father's health was not the best. "He doesn't exercise at all," Michael explained, "and he doesn't have a particularly healthy diet. And probably worst of all, he smokes."

According to Michael, Ben's only social outlet was a weekly poker game that he'd been part of for years. However, despite how long they'd known one another, as far as Michael could tell, these men never saw one another outside of the poker game. Ben spent the bulk of the little free time he had alone in a one-bedroom condo in an over-fifty community that he'd purchased about two years after

Michael's mother's death. He did not complain; still, Michael worried about him and made it a point to visit him at least once a week on his way home from work.

Although Ben showed no interest at all in dating, Michael worried that he might somehow meet and get involved with a gold digger. It was actually Michael's wife, Stephanie, who first voiced this concern. She argued that Ben was vulnerable. "Some young gold digger could come along, seduce him, and then clean him out," she'd told Michael more than once. Michael countered that as far as he was aware, his father had never dated anyone other than his mother. Stephanie persisted, however, bringing up this issue periodically. In her opinion, the fact that Ben didn't date made him that much more vulnerable to being taken advantage of. In time, her anxiety seemed to infect Michael as well.

When Michael's father was diagnosed with chronic obstructive pulmonary disease (COPD), Michael's level of anxiety rose. He found himself re-experiencing the fears he'd had about waking up to find that his mother had died—only this time it would be his father. He increased his after-work visits to his father to three times a week, and he made a point of calling him at least briefly every day. That seemed enough to quell his anxiety, at least for the moment. However, Stephanie was not happy that her husband was spending that much time with his father, thereby altering their own routines considerably.

Things went along this way for approximately a year. During that time, Michael and Stephanie began talking seriously about having a child and buying a house. They had good credit ratings and some (but not enough) money saved for a down payment, and they agreed that they would work together to cut back on expenses so as to add to it. In the meantime they decided to discontinue using birth control. The one issue that Stephanie brought up—and repeatedly—during these talks was Michael's relationship with his father. She let Michael know that while she was trying to be tolerant and understanding of all the time he was spending with his father, she was not happy about it. Furthermore, she would definitely resent it and resist if she got pregnant, at which point she would want Michael to be home more.

Six months later Stephanie was not yet pregnant, and Michael's anxiety had gotten noticeably worse. He had developed intermittent insomnia and had taken to using a sleeping pill to help him fall asleep almost every other night. Even then he would sometimes wake up at 3 A.M. and be unable to get back to sleep.

While he had never before had any negative thoughts or feelings about his brothers, Michael now found himself feeling angry at times over the fact that they lived farther away and took little responsibility for their father. On their weekly phone calls to Michael they would inquire about Ben's health, but there really wasn't much to say other than that he was in a process of slow but steady decline. Michael asked his brothers to call their father on a regular basis, but for them, regular contact apparently meant no more than a weekly phone call.

At that point, Stephanie, feeling frustrated about not being pregnant, about Michael's involvement and preoccupation with his father, and about Michael's anxiety and insomnia, began making comments to the effect that Michael seemed more interested in his father than he was in their marriage and that this made her wonder what his priorities were. What would happen, she asked him once, if she did get pregnant? Would Michael be there for her as much as he was there for his father? Would his anxiety and insomnia disable him as a husband and father?

Michael also found himself receiving significant pressure from Stephanie to find out what his father was planning to do with respect to his will. Since they were saving to buy a house, she said, she thought it would be fair to ask if her father-in-law might be thinking of leaving them some money when he passed away. She asked Michael to find out if Ben was contemplating creating any kind of trust for his grandchildren, and if so, if he would make a provision for any children that she and Michael might have after his death.

These conversations were very uncomfortable for Michael. He thought Stephanie was being highly insensitive in thinking about money. Although her concerns were perhaps legitimate, he did not want to be the one to have to initiate a conversation with Ben about money. So he didn't. Unfortunately, this reticence on Michael's part only annoyed Stephanie all the more and increased the tension between them.

Both Stephanie's jealousy and Michael's emerging irritation with his brothers were signs that they had moved into this third stage of family grief: *upheaval*. It wouldn't be surprising if one or both of them felt guilty about harboring such feelings. However, being a normal (and expected) part of the grief process, there is no justification for such guilt. Rather these emotions are the natural result of the stresses and strains that a prolonged grief process places on families.

Nora offers another example.

✂ Nora's Story

Nora, forty-six, was the oldest of four children and the only daughter of Helen and Charlie. When Helen was diagnosed, at the age of seventy, with lung cancer, Nora, who lived in a neighboring state, immediately went to spend time with her parents. This meant having to use ten of the twenty-five personal days she had accrued in her job as a pediatric nurse.

Nora had always been the caretaker in the family. As a teen, for example, she had often been required to come home from school and look after her younger brothers and start dinner, instead of visiting with friends. That being the family's history, it was pretty much assumed by everyone in the family that Nora would now once again take charge and be the helpful one. Her brothers expressed concern, of course, but neither they nor their wives offered any type of concrete help.

Nora believed that her youngest brother had always been her mother's favorite, and she had long harbored some simmering resentment about this. He struck her as the least responsible of the four children. He was never the one, for instance, to offer to host parties or family get-togethers but seemed content to go along for a free ride. As much as this irritated Nora on one level, on another level she'd always thought it was not worth confronting him.

As was the pattern, Nora was primarily responsible for helping her parents navigate Helen's illness. She found herself pretty much alone in the process of helping her parents consider treatment options. And she had to single-handedly contend with her father, who was being especially difficult during this time. Charlie was a stubborn man. He refused to consider moving into a one-floor residence, which would have eliminated the need for Helen to negotiate stairs. He refused despite the fact that they rented an apartment in a senior complex where such a switch would have been possible. He even argued vociferously against bringing in a visiting nurse or other home care personnel, arguing that he could take care of Helen's needs (which he clearly could not).

For the next couple of months, Nora tried her best to remain on good behavior, despite her growing discomfort. No longer able to take time off, she commuted dutifully each weekend to be with and take care of her parents. It was about a two-hour drive, and to save on gas money she stayed overnight, leaving her husband to take care of their two high-school-age children. During the week, when Nora was back home (and at work in the hospital), Charlie taxied Helen to and from doctor appointments and helped as much as he could around the house. He had never been much for cooking and cleaning, though, so Nora could not be sure how well her parents were actually doing when she wasn't there.

Though they sympathized with her and wanted to be supportive, Nora's husband and children eventually began to resent Nora's continued absences. They began pressuring her to get her parents to bring in more help and to request help from her youngest brother, who like them lived a couple of hours away from Nora's parents.

It was only when Nora came down with the flu, and her doctor told her she was suffering from exhaustion, that she finally called her younger brother. Her sister-in-law answered the call, and Nora asked if she or her brother could help out that weekend with Helen and Charlie. Her sister-in-law said that she and Nora's brother had plans to take their son to his team's hockey game that weekend. He was on a travel team, and they made it a point to go to all of his games. These plans had been made well in advance, she said, so they would not be able to spend that weekend taking care of Helen and Charlie.

Nora, finally finding her voice in this matter, spoke up and suggested that either her sister-in-law or her brother go to the game,

and that the other one drive over and help out with Helen and Char-
lie. The sister-in-law bristled. The hockey game, she replied testily,
was not a vacation but an important family activity that they were
not willing to miss.

After she hung up, Nora broke into tears. In the past, she had always
enjoyed her caretaking role and found it personally rewarding, but
now she felt worn out and angry. She was worried that it was damag-
ing her own family. And she was angry at her brothers and their wives,
at her parents for depending on her so much for so long, at her father
for being so stubborn, and at herself for not setting better limits.

At that point, in a follow-up meeting with her doctor, Nora was
referred to a support group, which helped her begin the process of sort-
ing out the intense feelings that she was experiencing (and which she
felt guilty about).

When it became clear, about three months later, that Helen could
not tolerate the radiation treatment she was receiving, end-of-life issues
moved to the forefront of everyone's thinking. At that point Nora felt that
she was beginning to understand not only why she had felt so angry but
that her feelings were normal and to be expected and that she was not a
bad person for feeling them. She realized that if she accepted her feel-
ings (instead of trying to banish them), they could point the way toward
some changes she might be wise to make in her life.

Embracing Upheaval

Many family members experience guilt about certain emotions,
particularly anger and resentment that they may experience

when someone is diagnosed with a terminal illness. Sometimes this anger and resentment is diverted elsewhere: onto the medical system, for example, or some aspect of the social services system. One family appeared to direct all their frustration and anger at the local dial-a-ride service for not being prompt, when in fact they were frustrated and angry over the fact that the terminally ill family member was stubbornly resisting what seemed like a reasonable medical treatment plan and would complain bitterly when the van was even ten minutes late.

It is understandable that people might feel shame and guilt about harboring negative feelings at a time when another family member is suffering. As we shall see when discussing Stage 4 grief, such emotions actually represent opportunities to take stock of family roles, allow long-unresolved issues that may be contributing to alienation and jealousy to surface, and set the stage for family renewal. Our strong advice, then, is for families to expect upheaval and to embrace it, not to run from it. A good place to begin is by taking stock of how your family's dynamics have been affected by your loved one's terminal illness.

Putting Everyone in the Picture

This stage of upheaval does not refer exclusively to the family members of the person with the terminal diagnosis. Rather, the upheaval we are speaking of here applies equally to the family member who is fighting a dire illness. Even if he or she tries to resist it, the patient's place and role in the family inevitably will also be altered. It is important, therefore, that the person with the illness try to be clear about what he or she wants and expects from others. Knowing what is expected of them affords loved ones the opportunity to gauge how much they are able to take on and how their lives may be affected. They can start thinking about how these expectations can be met and by whom. This can go a long way toward ameliorating family turmoil.

Being clear about expectations can be particularly difficult for people who are used to being self-reliant, who are used to being in control, or who have been the family caretaker. For these people, asking for what they need may not seem natural. One mother of two young children was so accustomed to having her life revolve around them that when she was scheduled to begin chemotherapy for breast cancer, she just assumed that she would be driving herself there and be back in time to meet them at the school bus stop!

Some ill people are reticent to clearly state what they'd like from others because they fear that they will be asking too much. Others may feel threatened that someone is tying to wrest control from them. And others may harbor a belief that if family members really cared, they would know what to do without being asked. Such individuals may never stop to think how difficult it might be for another family member to read their mind and know what they really mean when they say, "I'm not feeling so well today." Does that mean that they just need some time to rest, does it mean that someone should contact the doctor, or does it mean that someone should dial 911?

If you are the ill family member and are struggling with your illness, we encourage you to do your best to communicate as clearly and straightforwardly as possible what works for you and what you want, such as:

- Do you want someone to be with you all the time at the hospital or treatment center?

- Do you prefer being alone for your treatments and having people drop in for short visits?

- Can you say no when someone wants to do something that you really do not want them to do for you?

- Are you willing and able to ask someone to do something for you or help you do it?

- Are you willing to accept the fact that your own role in the family needs to change and that you will need the help of others?

Here are some further guidelines that ill family members can use to make their feelings and expectations clear to the entire family:

- *Don't be stoic.* Practice articulating what you are feeling out loud: "I'm feeling frustrated," "I'm scared," "I'm sad," "I am feeling angry."

- *Connect the dots.* Make the connection between *what* you are feeling and *why* you are feeling that way: "I feel _____ when you _____ , because _____." (Example: "I feel hurt when you go off and watch TV by yourself because it makes me feel like you don't want to be with me.")

- *Take responsibility for your own ambivalence and resistance.* Don't be afraid to admit it if you don't like relying on people, feel you are being a burden, or have a hard time giving up control.

Assessing the Impact of Terminal Illness

Many if not most family members sincerely want to be of help in this time of crisis, even though the crisis itself may go on for months or years. As we know, however, not all family members will be equally involved. Those who are most involved may do their best to avoid thinking about the upheaval that terminal illness creates in their own lives or they may minimize it in the interest of being helpful. However, the emotions that can erupt—both within themselves and within their own families—attest to the reality of upheaval. To avoid having these emotions fester and grow into larger issues, we recommend taking the time to contemplate how this family crisis has affected you in each of the following areas.

ROUTINES

Routines make up the fabric of daily life. Almost everyone's lifestyle is organized into a series of routines that are repeated time and again. For working people, these routines may be different during the week from what they are on weekends. For couples with children (and single parents), these routines tend to be even more complex and crowded. Routines, in turn, are typically tied into responsibilities: getting to work on time, getting the children dressed and ready for the school bus, and so on. People whose lives are less tied to routines tend to be either retired or intentionally footloose.

If you are like most people, disruptions in your daily routines create stress. That's because such changes often mean that something either does not get done or someone else has to do it. As a simple example, consider two working parents with two elementary-age schoolchildren. Chances are their daily routine starts off by getting up in the morning and showering, shaving, and dressing. Then they wake up the children; feed them breakfast; and supervise washing up, brushing teeth, and getting dressed. Meanwhile, they eat breakfast themselves. They also have to make and pack a school lunch. Then they have to get the children to the bus stop and wait for the school bus to arrive, before heading off to work. And this is just the morning schedule!

Now, imagine that the father of one of those parents is diagnosed with a terminal illness and requires lots of help and support. How will those added responsibilities affect that parent's day-to-day life? Where and how will he or she fit in the added responsibilities? How many added responsibilities will the other parent need to take on? How will that family's daily routines be affected? And, as time goes on, what emotions do you imagine these changes in lifestyle, routines, and responsibilities are likely to evoke?

RELATIONSHIPS

Relationships that are most often affected by prolonged illness in a family member include marriage and parent-child relationships. The most common effect is a dilution in the quality of these relationships as each person's time is now divided between these relationships and the needs of their ill loved one. Needless to say, if the ill person happens to be the parent of young children, the terminal illness itself and its treatment will have a profound effect on the parent-child as well as the marital relationship.

Initially, spouses and children will be tolerant of the impact that terminal illness in a relative has on their own family life. They will want to be supportive of both the ill family member and their own spouse or parent. If asked, children will often deny feeling lonely, resentful, or jealous. Spouses will be quick to express their support in a noncomplaining manner.

But is it reasonable to expect children and spouses to continue to remain neutral about the loss in the quality of their relationship with a parent or partner who has chosen to take on the kinds of added responsibilities that terminal illness entails? The honest answer is no, it is not reasonable. On the contrary, rather than attempting to maintain a veneer of unambivalent support, it is more realistic to expect ambivalence and reaction as time wears on.

TRADITIONS

If routines constitute the fabric of daily family life, then traditions bond the extended family. Think for a moment about the traditions that your family of origin (your own parents, siblings, and relatives) observed. What occasions were these traditions tied to? What did these traditions entail? Were they primarily organized by one person and held in the same place or was this responsibility somehow rotated among family members? Finally, as a child how did you feel about these traditions? Did you look forward to them?

Children in particular but also adults look forward to observing and participating in family traditions. They are a means through which we can experience being part of a larger whole, a valued member of a special group: the family.

Sometimes families choose to forego traditions when a key

family member becomes terminally ill. While others in the family may express a willingness to do this, it is not reasonable to expect that such a decision will have no impact. For example, here is one New England couple's story.

✍ *Nora and John's Story*

Nora and John were used to celebrating Christmas by having a breakfast together with their two children after opening presents beneath the tree and then traveling to Nora's parents' home for dinner, where the children would play with their cousins. John's parents, who were retired in Florida, would mail their presents in advance and speak with everyone by phone on Christmas morning. That had become another part of the family's Christmas tradition. When Nora's father was diagnosed with prostate cancer just before Thanksgiving, she and John went along with her mother's decision to forego the annual Christmas dinner, at least for that year. The problem was, neither Nora nor John put much thought into coming up with an alternative tradition.

That Christmas could have turned out to be a disappointing one to all involved. However, Nora and John's children, who were eight and six, while understanding that Grandpa was ill, nevertheless reacted strongly when they were told—a week before Christmas—that they would not be going to their grandparents' house for Christmas dinner. They joined forces and insisted that their parents continue the tradition. They were adamant. It was not enough, they said, for their family to have dinner alone. They wanted their parents to prepare the exact same meal that their grandparents prepared every Christmas and invite the same relatives to join them, including all their cousins and their grandparents. Then they offered to help.

As shocked as Nora and John were by the intensity of their children's reactions and as reluctant as they were to take on the responsibility of this family tradition, they quickly understood just how important it was to their children. They contacted the rest of the family, and arrangements were made for dividing up responsibilities for cooking. And so that Christmas, the family tradition lived on. It was agreed among Nora, her sister, and her brother that they would take turns in the future, rotating the family's Christmas tradition among them.

Nora and John's children not only experienced firsthand the upheaval that a family crisis such as terminal illness creates, but gave a voice to it. As we shall see in the next chapter, that constitutes a healthy way for families to successfully negotiate this third stage of family grief.

⚘ *Morgan*

Morgan's father, Adam, passed away from congestive heart failure in 2007 and was morbidly obese at the time of his death. Her father had qualified as morbidly obese for the last fifteen years of his life, and his doctors had repeatedly pleaded with him to pursue weight loss surgery (gastric bypass). His family, including Morgan, had also begged him to take better care of himself, to eat well, to exercise, and generally to find a reason to live.

Morgan's mother divorced Adam five years before his death because she could no longer stand to live with a man who took so little care of himself and cared so little for her or his family that he would let himself deteriorate that way.

Morgan's father had been a dentist and had served in the navy. Before Adam gained weight, she had always been intensely proud of him. "*He was always so handsome and smart,*" *she said.* "*As a young kid, I always wanted to show him off to my friends. As a teen, I dreamed of him walking me down the aisle on my wedding day.*" *Then she frowned.* "*But that all changed. He got worse and worse. He wouldn't reach out for help, and he wouldn't do what we pleaded for him to do. He couldn't even come to my wedding because he was too big at that point. He saw me and my sisters maybe twice in the last couple of years of his life. And he only met my daughter once.*"

Adam pulled away from the family, and Morgan doesn't know why he let that happen. She related how she, her sisters, and her mother all felt so helpless to do anything for Adam. She remembered how depressed her mother became after realizing that Adam would never take the necessary steps to take care of his health. After the divorce, her depression lifted somewhat, though from Morgan's perspective, her mother was permanently affected by Adam's slow demise.

Morgan repeatedly used the word abandoned *in describing her father's death and how he "allowed" himself to die. Morgan, her sisters, and mother called Adam's death "a slow suicide." This brought on an additional level of shame to the family, as they are Irish Catholic and see suicide as a sin.*

"*We know he didn't really kill himself,*" *Morgan explained,* "*but that's how it feels to us. He didn't want to be here anymore, so he just let himself go.*"

Morgan said she felt very angry with her father for allowing his health to slowly but steadily deteriorate. And at the time of his death, she'd felt that it signified Adam's lack of love for her and her family. She did not know for certain if Adam suffered from depression but said that she wouldn't be surprised if he had. "*I don't know why he would be so depressed that he'd just allow himself to die,*" *Morgan said,* "*but I just can't think of another explanation.*"

Morgan still asks herself these questions:

- Could she and her sisters or her mother have forced her father to get surgery? She never knew enough about what his doctors recommended to feel like she had a grasp on the situation.

- How will she cope with the feelings of guilt she still sometimes experiences over the idea that her father died a slow suicide?

- How she can explain Adam's death to her daughter when she grows up?

- How can she find a way to talk to her sisters and mother about her feelings? She's sure they feel much as she does, but they've never really talked about it openly.

- Will she ever be able to let go of her feelings and accept her father's death?

- How can she cope with the relief she sometimes feels now that she does not have to deal with Adam's health issues and all the frustration that entailed?

- Her husband, who is only forty-two, recently had a minor stroke, which Morgan believes was stress related. She is worried that he will become depressed like her father did, and she would like to know what she can do to prevent that.

It is understandable that Morgan would harbor such questions. It is also not that surprising that she kept her feelings pretty much to herself and that she felt guilty. As we've said, such silence, though typical, can be toxic to individuals and the family as a whole. The remedy, we strongly believe, is for family members to validate their feelings and allow them to see the light of day. In Morgan's case, that would mean finding family members or trusted others with whom to share her feelings and ask her questions. This may be true for you as well.

Chapter Eleven

BREAKING THE SILENCE

COMMUNICATING ABOUT UPHEAVAL

The following story is a typical example of what can happen if family members are unable to communicate about the upheaval that prolonged illness creates in the family's dynamics.

✐ Mason's Story

Mason lost his grandmother to Alzheimer's disease. He fondly recalled his relationship with her: "My grandmother practically raised me when I was small and both of my parents were working. She taught me everything I know about cooking, gardening, and music. My grandmother was my link to my Swiss family, and when I lost her, I also lost that connection."

Mason's grandmother played a very important role in his life. In fact, he described feeling closer to her than to either of his parents, in part because she had been his primary caretaker and in part because they appreciated similar things such as art, music, and European history. Losing his grandmother, therefore, signified a loss of culture, connection, and sensitivity in Mason's life. In contrast to her, he described his family as all-American. "In some ways, I've never felt that I fit in with the rest of my family as well as I fit in with my Swiss grandmother," he explained.

His grandmother's illness frightened young Mason. He was eleven when she was first diagnosed and fifteen when she died. He felt that his family not only did not explain her illness to him in an adult manner but avoided talking about it. As a result, he could not fully understand why she sometimes could not remember who he was or why she eventually had to live in what he thought was a hospital but was actually a nursing home. "I was old enough to understand this," he said, "but I don't think my parents believed that. So I was left in the dark."

Mason also remembers that there was a great family strife throughout the time of his grandmother's illness. He now knows that this was due to financial strains that his grandmother's caretaking needs placed on the family. Not only was she less and less able to take care of him but she also needed more and more assistance, which the family could ill afford to pay for. At the time, however, all Mason knew was that his father and uncle (who owned his own business and was considered successful) did not get along. Indeed, the two did not speak for several years after Mason's grandmother's death. He still does not know the details of what the issues were, as the family never talks about it, but he strongly suspects it had something to do with paying for his grandmother's care.

Mason said that his father was devastated after his grandmother passed away, and so his mother spent a great deal of her time comforting him. His mother and grandmother never got along, and he recalled his mother making occasional comments about what a burden her mother-in-law had become. Mason believed that his mother was actually relieved to have her husband all to herself again and to be free of the expense of her mother-in-law's care. "It's true, though I feel a little guilty even saying that," said Mason.

These many years later, Mason still feels a tremendous loss because of his grandmother's passing. He also admits to harboring some lingering resentments over the way his family handled the whole matter of his grandmother's illness and death.

As a result, he has some very specific and strong recommendations to families:

- Parents should know that children need to understand what is happening when a family member becomes terminally ill so that it is not such a scary process for them. Mason thought he could have handled more information than his parents were willing to give him. We have already addressed this issue, but Mason's strong feelings in this regard only reinforce our advice: to begin talking to children soon after the crisis begins.

- Parents should not avoid talking to even very young children about what death means. If his parents had talked with him about death, Mason believes, his grandmother's illness and death might not have been quite so traumatic for him.

- Families need to support kids so that they don't feel alone after losing a significant family member. In Mason's case, he felt that neither he nor any of his cousins got much attention from the adults in the family. "They seemed to be focused on themselves," he said.

* "Don't keep conflicts such a secret." Mason was quite firm in this belief. He believed he could also have understood if his father and uncle had conflict over paying for his grandmother's care. The way they handled it, however, led to longstanding resentments but little understanding.

Mason's father's maternal aunt has been very ill for a year now, and he sees history repeating itself. His father now spends a lot of time with his great-aunt, and his mother once again appears jealous. But, once again no one is talking. Mason doesn't know how to broach the issue with his mother. On the one hand, he can understand how she might feel neglected; on the other hand, he believes that jealousy in a time of crisis is inappropriate. He wishes he could recommend a support group to his mother, but he doesn't know of one for people in her position. Perhaps he could find a counselor she could talk to about her feelings.

Finding Your Voice

What is most striking about Mason's story is the lack of communication within his family. First his grandmother and now his great-aunt fell victim to terminal illness, and in both instances, the upheaval that it created was borne in silence. The result? Unaddressed (and unresolved) marital unhappiness, alienation between brothers, and a child who was left to deal with his grief alone. And as vocal as Mason was about what he thought should be done, it seems that he himself had still not been able to find his voice and speak his mind; instead he was looking for a support group or a therapist to help him solve the problem. Our response to him was: better late than never. And so we encouraged him to pursue both of these options.

There are reasons families have difficulty communicating honestly about the upheaval they are experiencing, and the first of these has to do with guilt and shame. Most family members feel obligated to help out in a time of crisis. Even if the result of this helping is a seriously disrupted family life, financial hardship, or marital stress, they may very well feel that it would be inappropriate to express their discomfort or to complain. We have heard variations on the following explanations for not speaking out many times.

It would be selfish to complain. Many family members have told us that regardless of how put out they may feel or how much of a burden having to care for a terminally ill family member has placed on them, they would either feel selfish or fear that they would be perceived as being selfish if they were to complain. One wife said, "We have very little family life or marital life anymore. My mother-in-law has been in and out of remission twice in the past two years. It has cost us money, but more important, it has eaten up so much of our time, especially my husband's time. He's worn down. For me to complain would only make him feel worse. Besides, what would it accomplish?"

In this instance, the woman would feel ashamed of herself if she were to put a voice to how she felt—to how chronic, terminal illness had impacted her family. So she opted to suffer in silence.

Speaking up is useless. The second reason families don't communicate honestly in the upheaval stage has to do with a sense of hopelessness.

🖎 *Marissa's Story*

"Nobody asked for this to happen," said the father of twenty-nine-year-old Marissa, who'd recently been diagnosed with leukemia. She had a five-year-old son, Tyler, and had divorced a year earlier. Although she'd been employed as a teacher, Marissa now had little choice but to move in with her parents. Her ex-husband, who'd turned out to be addicted to cocaine and gambling, had moved to another state and in any case was not in a position to help out. Marissa also had two older brothers. They were both married, had families of their own, and lived some distance away.

Marissa's father, Rob, had recently taken advantage of an early retirement incentive program and had been looking forward to turning a lifelong interest in antiques into a part-time restoration business. Her mother, Gretchen, a nurse, was still two years away from retirement. Gretchen liked her work in an intensive care unit but also found it tiring. The upshot was that Marissa and her son moved back in with Rob and Gretchen. Gretchen continued to work, while Rob stayed home with Marissa and Tyler.

Having Marissa and Tyler at home was not something that Rob resisted. Quite to the contrary, he'd been the first to suggest it—insisted on it, in fact. That this would mean considerable added expense to him and Gretchen, not to mention the impact on their lifestyle, was not something they would ever complain about. They'd already discussed the possibility that, depending on how Marissa's treatment went, Gretchen might have to keep working. In addition, Rob knew he would be doing a lot of childcare for the foreseeable future.

Privately, Rob admitted that his and Gretchen's plans—his antique restoration venture and extensive travel—had to be put on hold. A year after Marissa had moved in, she was still in treatment and struggling to beat her cancer. Tyler had started kindergarten, Gretchen was still working, and Rob's antiques business was yet to get started. Despite all of this, neither Rob nor Gretchen apparently felt free to bring up the issue, even between themselves.

Finally, Rob and Gretchen decided to try out a support group that was recommended to them by one of the nurses who worked at the clinic where Marissa went for treatment. It was only there that Rob felt he could crack the door that sealed his true feelings, and he did so only after he heard other parents express their pain and frustrations. As much as he loved his daughter—and would willingly take on her disease if that would free her to live her life with Tyler—he neverthe-less sometimes felt sad that the things he'd hoped to be doing now had to be put on indefinite hold. Then Gretchen expressed similar sentiments and asked Rob why he'd never spoken about it but instead had put up a cover story of not being bothered at all. The reasons, he explained, were two: first, he thought it would be selfish of him to complain, given the travails that Marissa was going through, and second, he didn't believe it would make any difference. "We're stuck with the situation," he explained. "So why complain about it?"

Why, indeed, complain about it? Simply because the thoughts and feelings that Rob was having were normal. Marissa's illness was creating a great deal of upheaval in Rob and Gretchen's life. To acknowledge that upheaval did not mean that they loved her any less. One effect of Rob's decision to keep his thoughts and feelings secret was that his wife, who'd sometimes had similar thoughts and feelings, felt alone with them and ashamed of what she felt.

Another reason to be able to talk about the upheaval in your life is that it puts you in a position to do something about it. In the case of Rob and Gretchen, that might mean finding a way that they could still do some traveling while not abandoning either their daughter or their grandson.

Complaining would hurt my pride. The third common reason people hesitate to talk about the upheaval in their lives is pride. In the case of Mason, described earlier, it is possible that pride stood in the way of his father and uncle being able to talk about the financial stress that Mason's grandmother's illness had created. Some people have told us, in effect: "Yes, I'm hurting financially as a result of having to deal with terminal illness, but it would hurt my pride to have to admit it."

Again, what is to be gained by keeping silent in the face of upheaval? Nothing. In fact, silence only perpetuates (or exacerbates) the misery. Silence closes the door on potential solutions. It becomes a breeding ground for resentment. The only way out of this trap is for family members to find their voice. This may mean taking the risk of sounding selfish, of confronting feelings of help-lessness or hopelessness, or of swallowing one's pride. The alternative, though, is to risk doing long-term damage to marriages and families.

Guidelines for Talking About Upheaval

Given the fact that most people are ambivalent—for all the reasons just discussed—about talking openly about the upheaval in their lives, the question is how to go about it. The stories we've related illustrate why, despite the fact that silence may represent the path of least resistance, not talking about such issues may very well make matters worse in the long run. Here are some suggestions that may help you talk about upheaval.

Make it normal. The first and perhaps most important rule about talking about the upheaval that a loved one's terminal illness has caused in your own life is to understand that this is a normal part of the family grief process. In a word, it is to be *expected*.

Don't wait long. It can be a lot easier to talk about upheaval if you start talking about it sooner rather than later. Holding in feelings such as anxiety, resentment, or frustration will only allow them to fester, so that when they finally do come out, they are much more intense than you might want them to be. On the other hand, it is easier (and less threatening to others) if you acknowledge how coping with terminal illness is affecting your life. Even making simple comments like "It's getting harder to keep up with housekeeping than it was before mother got sick," can introduce the idea of upheaval in a way that undermines any taboo surrounding it. It opens the door to other family members who may be feeling a similar burden.

Take responsibility for your own upheaval. People have told us that one of the things they would fear if someone in the family began talking about the upheaval in their lives is that this would somehow become "a blame game," as Sharon put it.

✹ Sharon's Story

Sharon was hesitant to talk about the upheaval in her life because she thought her two younger siblings might get defensive. As the oldest child, she had always been the most responsible one anyway. As her parents got older, for example, she took over most of the family traditions. Now her parents were in their eighties and had limited stamina. When her father was diagnosed with liver cancer, it was more or less assumed by all that Sharon would be the one to do the heavy lifting when it came to caretaking responsibilities. When their father was told he could no longer drive, everyone assumed Sharon would take on that task because their mother had stopped driving many years earlier. For Sharon, this meant providing transportation for medical appointments and treatments, food shopping, and other errands.

After four months of taking care of her parents, Sharon was feeling tired and not a little resentful toward her siblings for not helping out more. She had sought informal counseling from a female pastor who knew of her situation, to try to work through some longstanding ambivalence she had about her father. It seemed that, although he could be a benevolent and generous man at times, her father had always taken very little responsibility as a parent and was more inclined to take care of his own needs before he took care of others. Moreover, Sharon had long suspected that her father had had an extramarital affair that he and her mother had covered up. Even at age ten, Sharon noticed that her parents' marriage had cooled off and that the coolness had lingered for years.

Sharon found the pastor to be a useful, nonjudgmental sounding board for her feelings. After a while, she began to see that whatever had transpired in her parents' marriage, it was between them. They could have separated, but they chose not to. So while there may not have been a great deal of romantic passion, there was nevertheless something between them that kept them together.

Sharon's pastor also helped her accept her feelings now that she was caught up in the upheaval caused by her father's diagnosis. But the pastor also pointed out that as resentful as Sharon might feel, she alone was responsible for her present role. It was unreasonable to expect her younger siblings to change old patterns, if they were not even aware how Sharon was feeling and that she wanted some help and relief.

This last insight proved to be powerful for Sharon. Rather than going back to the family and blasting her siblings for laziness, she simply began talking about the burden she was feeling and how difficult she was finding it to simultaneously take care of her parents, her own children, and her own marriage. And she started speaking up and asking for help.

Identify areas where help is needed. The last thing to do is to as straightforwardly as possible let other family members know the areas in which you could use some help to reduce the upheaval in your own life. Following up on Sharon's story, she opted to voice her feelings by saying, "It would be great if someone could pitch in with the grocery shopping for Mom and Dad every other week. That would help me catch up on my own shopping and housework." In time, her strategy began to work. With her pastor, plus a support group she'd joined, serving as encouraging coaches, she practiced in her mind asking one or another of her siblings for some simple, concrete help. She also practiced how she would respond if she encountered any reluctance on their part to help. As it turned out, she encountered very little resistance. One of her siblings even commented, "I've spoken to my wife several times about helping out, but to tell the truth, I was always under the impression that you preferred to do it all yourself."

In the next chapter we move further into the upheaval stage of family grief, which has the power to unearth memories that many of us may have kept buried for years—memories not unlike the ones that Sharon sought counseling for. For now our message is that you are much better off learning to give a voice to any upheaval you are experiencing.

❦ Emilie

"I had just lost my mom," Emilie explained, "and then my dad went into the hospital with pneumonia. My daughter was due to have her baby the next day, and I just felt so overwhelmed. I felt like I couldn't be there for everyone, but that I had to be."

Emilie and her mother had been best friends. They were extremely close, and her parents had always played an important role in her life as well as in the lives of her two daughters. They all lived in the same town, less than a mile away from each other. And Emilie, her husband, daughters, and parents had even rented adjoining cottages on a lake for the same two weeks in July for many years.

"When my mom got sick, I wanted to do everything I could for her," said Emilie. "At first it was just keeping an eye on her and spending more time with her, but eventually it turned into changing her diapers and feeding her. It was like having another baby."

Emilie's mother was diagnosed with Alzheimer's disease eleven years earlier, and she had lived much longer than her doctors thought she would. Emilie said that her mother's illness was extremely hard on her, but worse on her father, who had always been very devoted to his wife.

"I'm so scared," Emilie explained, "that my dad is going to die of a broken heart now. He's been in and out of the hospital with pneumonia and other respiratory infections for the past year. I don't want to be an orphan; I don't know how I'll handle it."

Emilie has a younger brother who lives in the same town as she and her parents, but she has borne the brunt of the caretaking work. She feels lucky that her parents had good insurance plus enough money to pay for treatment for both of them, and that she had (and has) some help so that she was not solely responsible for taking care of either her mother or her father. However, Emilie nevertheless discussed feeling "daughter's guilt"—the persistent thought that she, and she alone had to take care of her mother.

"We wanted to involve Mom in my girls' weddings," said Emilie, "but to be honest, she could be so embarrassing, making racist remarks out loud. And she had to be watched continually. I felt so awful for my mother, but I just couldn't put the girls through that. So both times we ended up having someone stay with Mom and take care of her at home instead of having her at the wedding. I knew that was best for the girls, but it also broke my heart because I'd always imagined Mom being there, and so had they."

Emilie is coping with her grief over losing her mom, but she also feels guilt, due in part to the sense of relief her mother's death brought. During her mother's illness, Emilie often prayed for an end to the pain and misery, and she welcomed death because she knew it would end her mother's suffering. "At the end she wasn't my mom anymore. I knew her so well, and I know she would have hated to have anyone see her like that. It was not just losing her, but losing her one piece at a time."

There is a part of Emilie that is relieved to no longer have to be a caretaker for her mother (although she did so willingly). Still, she doesn't know what to do with her own free time now. She believes her marriage is good but acknowledges that she may have taken it for granted and wants to do more things with her husband.

Emilie does not know how her relationship with her brother will unfold in the future because she realizes that she harbors some resentment over his relative lack of involvement in their mother's (and now their father's) end-of-life issues. She's spoken to her minister about her feelings. The minister also knows Emilie's brother, and she is thinking about taking him up on his offer to meet with the two of them.

Chapter Twelve

THE BEST OF TIMES AND THE WORST OF TIMES

Revisiting the Past

Like Ebenezer Scrooge in Charles Dickens's *A Christmas Carol*, during the long night that is terminal illness, families may find themselves confronted by many unpleasant ghosts before dawn arrives. However, just as Dickens's story has a happy ending, so can the process of family grief.

The truth be known, many people have told us that if they hesitated to roll up their sleeves and help out, even at the crisis stage, the main reason had to do with resentments they'd been harboring, often for years. These resentments are clearly linked to past events and experiences. The child who felt unloved (or less favored), for example, or the sibling who felt left out, exploited, or abused may either balk when the time comes to pitch in and help the family in its time of need or do less than he or she could.

A decision to opt out, regardless of whether it is made consciously or unconsciously, while understandable, can have serious negative consequences in the long run. Family members who choose to stand back may find themselves saddled with guilt for being negligent at a time of need. Moreover, they may find themselves regretting having passed up an opportunity to address, and possibly resolve, longstanding grievances. For these reasons, we advocate facing the past and confronting whatever issues it raises. The first step of that process is to bring the skeletons out of the closet.

Your Family Photo Biography

To paraphrase, a single photo is worth a thousand words. This is especially true when it comes to unearthing long-buried family issues. Some people might ask, Why bother unearthing such issues? Why not just leave them buried? The answer is this: If leaving them buried were a guarantee that they would not emerge to color the family's dynamics, that approach might make sense. But the fact is that these issues *will* emerge, and they will affect the way the family responds to the crisis of terminal or life-threatening illness. To prevent them from poisoning the waters, it is better to identify and face unresolved grievances now and to try to really put them to rest, instead of sweeping them under the carpet. That's where the idea of a *family photo biography* comes in.

To complete this exercise you will first need to assemble (if possible) a collection of family photos that spans as many years as possible. This collection should include the following:

- Photos of yourself and your own family if you have one.

- Photos of the ill loved one.

- Photos that show you, the ill family member, and other immediate family members, such as brothers and sisters. Try to get a mix of photos that are old and relatively recent.

- Photos that show your own family plus extended family members (uncles, aunts, grandparents, cousins). Again, try to find some photos that are old and others that are newer.

After you've accumulated your collection of photos, clear a large tabletop and arrange your photos as follows:

Starting at the top with the oldest photos you have, arrange your photos into piles in descending order, from past (top) to present (bottom). This is your *time line*. For example, if you have photos of your own parents when they were young and dating (or marriage photos) put these at the top of the tabletop. This is the *beginning* of your family photo biography.

Next, arrange all your other photos into piles that show you, any siblings you have, your parents, and extended family in descending order so that the newest photos are at the bottom.

Finally, if you have a family of your own—partner, children— place any photos you have of you as a family at the very bottom of the time line.

Now spread out all of your photos so you can take them all in. *Voila:* This is your family photo biography.

EXPLORING YOUR PHOTO BIOGRAPHY

Photo biographies like the one you have created almost always stir up memories and emotions. They can be especially powerful, though, when a family is in the midst of the grief process. They can be so powerful, in fact, that people who are repressing particularly painful memories may prefer to avoid creating a photo biography altogether.

For most people, however, the photo biography is something akin to an archaeological dig. Indeed, one man compared it to unearthing and exploring an ancient city.

⚹ Jon's Story

"There are all these emotional nooks and crannies, and long-forgotten memories that get stirred up," said Jon when describing the photo biography that lay spread out before him on his dining room table. A recent photo of him, his wife, Sharon, and their two daughters anchored the bottom of the biography. Above this were photos of his parents and his two brothers, extending back in time from six months ago (his parents' anniversary celebration) to when he and his brothers were toddlers. Jon's father had been diagnosed with bladder cancer three months earlier. Already he looked much thinner and older than he did in a picture that was barely six months old.

Jon's photo biography included several photos taken on Christmas mornings when he, his brother, and his sister were young. It had been a tradition of sorts for their father to snap a picture of the three of them, dressed in pajamas, sitting beneath a huge tree and surrounded by presents. There were also photos of the family on various vacations. There were photos of Jon's brother and sister, who both were older than he, at their respective weddings. There were also photos of Jon's own children being held by his parents at his children's first birthday parties. And so on.

Extending out from either side of the center of Jon's time line were photos that showed Jon's brother and sister and their families, as well as relatives on both his father's and his mother's side. There were aunts and uncles, two great-uncles, a great-aunt, and numerous cousins, nieces, and nephews. He'd placed these photos in his "family photo tree" as he called it, in the correct chronological places. For example, photos of his father's brother when he was young were placed alongside photos of Jon's father as a youth. The table was full.

Looking at this photo biography, Sharon remarked that it gave her a better sense of just where her husband had come from, and where he fit in within his family. "I can see traits in Jon and know where they came from, as well as who seems to be inheriting them," she explained, referring to their two daughters. "I think our youngest has a personality most like Jon's older niece. They also look somewhat alike."

In contemplating the photos before him, Jon made the following observations:

- His sister, Jane, who was the oldest, had played a role as a sort of third parent to Jon and his brother when they were young, and he felt that she'd slipped back into that role immediately when Jon's father was diagnosed.

• As a child, Jon had more or less accepted his sister's authority, despite sometimes resenting and resisting it. Today, as
helpful as it was in ways, Jon no longer wanted his sister to
be the one in charge, making the important decisions with
his parents but largely leaving Jon and his brother out of the
process.

• The older photos stirred up Jon's childhood jealousy of his
brother, Ted, who'd been an outstanding athlete right
through high school. He was surprised not only that the
jealousy was still in him but how intense it was, especially
since Jon was much more financially successful than his
brother. Jon felt that his father had always favored Ted. For
example, he always showered Ted with praise for his athletic accomplishments. Jon even felt that a cousin, who was
his brother's age and similarly athletic, got more attention
from his father than Jon did. "I thought I'd put those feelings
to rest years ago," Jon commented. "I mean, I get along with
my brother now, though we don't see one another very often.
I wonder if that's why." Jon said the fact that he'd never ver-
balized his feelings to either his father or his brother now
bothered him, and he thought he needed to talk at least to
his brother about it, to clear the air.

The family photo biography is not merely a vehicle for getting
in touch with old resentments or jealousies. Rather, its usefulness
lies in its ability to identify issues that can now be at least
addressed, if not totally resolved. There is nothing, for example,
that Jon could do now about the past. On the other hand, as an
adult he did not have to accept a passive role with respect to his

father's care. And he even had an opportunity, by talking with his brother—and perhaps with his father—to put a voice to his feelings and see how these two important men in his life would respond.

As the family moves into Stage 4 grief, *resolution*, having a sense of what the important issues are, with respect to each person's role in the family, any changes they might want to make in that role, and any unresolved issues they feel it would be wise to address, is vital. Without that insight, family members are apt to be experiencing a lot of emotions, but they will have no sense of direction for what needs to be addressed or what changes they want to make.

GUIDELINES FOR EXPLORING YOUR PHOTO BIOGRAPHY

We recommend that you peruse your photo biography along with someone you know well and trust. This may be your spouse, a close friend, a sibling, or even a therapist. As you do, think about the following:

- What emotions come up when you look at photos that include you and the ill family member?

- As you look at the photos from past to present, do your feelings change? What experiences might be associated with any such changes?

- If you have siblings, what are your feelings about them? Have those feelings changed over time, and if so, how have they changed and why?

- Do you have any regrets as you contemplate the photos that tell the story of your life and your family's life? Conversely, what periods of time do you feel best about?

- Who in these photos do you feel closest to? Who do you feel the most distant from?

- Are there any faces here that you feel jealous of? Resentful or angry toward? If so, who, and why?

- If you could change anything about your relationship with the ill family member, what would that change be?

- How comfortable are you with the role you have tended to play in your family? If you could change your role in your family, how would you change it?

The Family Tree

Those for whom it is not feasible to create a family photo biography can substitute a simple family tree. It is constructed in much the same way, but in place of photos, the family tree uses brief *written descriptions* of each family member. Here is how to do it:

1. Purchase a package of lined index cards.

2. On each card write down the name of a family member. For each person, write down two or three of your most vivid memories of your *experiences* with him or her. Also write out a brief description of that person's *personality*. Try to use as many adjectives as possible: happy, sad, energetic, passive, quick-tempered, mellow, hardworking, lazy.

3. Using a red marker, draw a frame around the edge of the card for the ill family member. If any of your family members are deceased, draw a black border around their index card.

4. Organize your cards using the scheme described for the family photo biography earlier in this chapter, moving from past (top) to present (bottom), using a large enough surface such as a tabletop.

Once you have constructed your family tree, take some time to look it over, following the instructions in "Guidelines for Exploring Your Photo Biography," described earlier.

✿ Dave and Holly's Story

Dave found himself feeling very depressed after his mother, Lily, was diagnosed with an aggressive and advanced form of leukemia. He shared his feelings with his younger sister, Holly, who then confided that she was not feeling depressed so much as angry at Lily. "I know I shouldn't be feeling that way," she told Dave. "I mean, it feels like I'm being mean. But I can't help it. There are moments when I feel absolutely furious with her."

The history of Dave and Holly's family, which was revealed through both a photo biography and a family tree, shed light on their feelings. They had a sibling, Harry, who was the middle child and who was developmentally disabled. Not only had Harry taken up the lion's share of Dave and Holly's parents' time and attention while they were growing up, but it was clear to them that for some reason Lily had been ashamed of Harry. They felt that throughout their growing years she had not only devoted an inordinate amount of time to Harry, but she had also worked hard to make him more or less invisible to others. It had been apparent, for example, from as far back as they could remember, that Holly and Dave were not to talk about Harry to anyone outside of their immediate family. If either of them did have friends over—which was seldom—Lily would generally keep Harry out of sight. And she would often leave Harry with a sitter when they had to go to family events and holiday dinners.

Neither Holly nor Dave was ever able to fully comprehend the reasons for their mother's shame, and they'd never brought it up directly. However, both brother and sister were keenly aware that their mother expected both of them to be what Holly called "flawless children." And both had risen to the occasion. Both did well in school, and neither had ever gotten into a stitch of trouble. As Dave put it, "With Holly and me it was always good news—nothing but good news."

As a teenager, Dave experienced occasional bouts of depression. In addition, he had a tendency to be obsessive and compulsive. His daily routine was marked by numerous rituals that served to channel and release his anxiety (over having to be perfect). He said prayers ritualistically, and he could not get to sleep until his entire collection of toy soldiers was neatly stowed away. Socially, he was insecure and shy. And although he had a strapping, muscular frame, Dave's anxiety got in the way of being able to perform well athletically.

After their mother's diagnosis, Holly confided in her brother that as a teen she'd gone through a period when she was bulimic, alternately starving, then binging on junk food, and then forcing herself to vomit so as not to gain weight ("and ruin my perfect figure"). This was news to Dave. Furthermore, he learned that not only had his sister endured this bout with bulimia, but that she'd done so without ever revealing it to either parent. Why? Again, because it would have meant being imperfect.

On hearing Holly's story, Dave shared his own. When he was sixteen, he said, he felt so depressed that he'd even thought of suicide. The depression weighed on him. No matter how many rituals he tried, he could not get it to lift. Then, in desperation, he went to his mother. "I told her I was the unhappiest person I knew," he said. "I told her that I thought there was something terribly wrong with me and that I needed help."

"What happened?" asked Holly.

"Her face turned to stone," Dave replied. "Then she gave me this really angry look. And then she said that no child of hers needed any help, and that I'd damned well better snap out of it."

Needless to say, these siblings were carrying around a lot of what is sometimes called psychological baggage or unfinished business. Much of this was directed at Lily, but some of it was directed at their father, who had worked two jobs and was pretty much what Dave called a "nonentity" as a parent. Whereas Holly was angry at her mother, Dave's anger—which he only rarely allowed himself to experience, even as a child—had to do with his belief that his father's passivity had less to do with his work schedule and more to do with the fact that Lily was the dominant personality in the family. "I just saw Dad as not wanting to get my mother upset. I never saw him challenge her, even once."

Both Dave and Holly grew up, got married, and had children. For many years their feelings about the unresolved family issues were largely suppressed. The family got together for holidays, and even if they weren't the happiest of occasions, everyone—especially Holly and Dave—did his or her best to get along. Harry, who received federal financial assistance due to his cognitive limitations and who lived in a subsidized apartment, was usually picked up and brought along by either Dave or Holly. Harry had a job (and a job coach to help him) as well as help at home with things like cooking and housework. Both Dave's and Holly's children had developed a fondness for Harry, and they felt the feelings were mutual.

Despite the intense emotions that lay simmering in the background, both Holly and Dave came together in unity in response to the crisis of their mother's illness. Falling back into their roles as good children, they did not complain but volunteered to assist both parents in any way they could. They found their father to be totally open to such help and grateful for it. Lily, on the other hand, persisted in her old stubborn and dominant ways. She got along poorly with her doctors, declining several tests they wanted done and refusing to take medications they believed could at least slow if not arrest her disease. And when it became apparent that Lily needed more care than her husband and children could provide, she bitterly fought the idea of going to a nursing home.

As time wore on, both Holly and Dave began to show symptoms typical of the upheaval stage of family grief. Holly's anger toward her mother began to manifest in the form of irritability, impatience, and sarcasm, directed at both parents. She felt guilty when this happened, but as she told Dave, she could not seem to stop herself. Meanwhile, Dave found himself gradually sinking back into the kind of depression that had dogged him throughout his teen years.

The family photo biography was the vehicle that allowed Dave and Holly to get in touch with the source of their feelings and to identify the family dynamics that had affected them so much as youths.

They came to realize that they needed to work together to change those dynamics.

We will be addressing the process of resolution in part 4 of the book. For now, what is important to know is that Dave and Holly worked together, with the help of a counselor, to change the old family dynamics and take control of the situation, even when that meant opposing their mother. Their father continued to hesitate to confront or oppose his wife, and when that happened, the children intervened, eventually succeeding in placing Lily in a skilled nursing facility that could provide the safety and care she needed.

Making Friends with the Past

One of the themes associated with this third stage of family grief is the idea of *embracing* upheaval instead of running from it or resisting it. There is no denying that the new grief, as we are describing in this book, has the potential to create a great deal of upheaval in families. As time passes, grief can affect every aspect of family life and significantly alter the family's dynamics. It can be very uncomfortable indeed. Yet it is that very discomfort that can set the stage for resolution and renewal.

There is a saying that goes something like this: Every crisis creates opportunities. And so it is with family grief. As disruptive as the terminal illness of a loved one can be, it also presents the family with an opportunity. Embracing upheaval affords us the chance to tie up loose ends and resolve issues that may have remained buried for many years. The story of Dave and Holly is a good example of how crises can lead to positive change. However, change is likely to happen only if we have the courage to accept upheaval and look it in the face. We hope this chapter has encouraged you to do so.

✒ Connor's Story

"Mike was my little brother," said Connor, "and he was only eighteen when he died. He just died, and I don't know how to deal with it at times. I mean, I used to have to worry about him all the time. The whole family did. It was like we were always on call. Now I'm an only child, and I don't have to worry about him anymore. But now I miss worrying about him."

Connor, who is now twenty-five, explained how, when he was younger, he was embarrassed by the symptoms of his brother's disease: cerebral palsy. "But I always loved him," he added. However, he also felt that his brother's care was always more important to his parents than were his own needs. "I was always the healthy son," he said. "So I didn't need much attention. I think there were times when I resented it. At the same time, I think I felt a little guilty being the healthy son."

"I didn't know how to tell my friends about Mike when I was younger—I mean, how to explain his condition. But the older I got, the more involved I got in his life and the less uncomfortable I was having friends over to the house. In fact, my friends were very friendly to Mike. They all came to his room at the assisted living facility where he lived to help us celebrate Mike's eighteenth birthday last year. I don't tell new people I meet about my brother, though. It's just too personal and painful, at least right now."

Connor talked about how Mike had been moved from the assisted living facility, where he'd lived for two years, to a hospital six weeks before his death. He described how he and his parents were at Mike's bedside twenty-four hours a day, staying with him in shifts. He said it was initially too difficult to allow anyone else to be at his brother's bedside during that time. However, after three weeks of nonstop bedside monitoring, Connor and his parents were exhausted. At that point they decided to hire someone from the assisted living facility to come to the hospital from midnight until six in the morning. Connor explained that as exhausting as the caretaking was, it had been even more difficult to ask for help with Mike because Connor knew that their time together would be limited and he wanted to have as much involvement with him as he could.

Connor said that he understood why his parents had sent Mike to live in the assisted living facility; but he also commented that that had meant they all took on an added burden because none of them felt comfortable leaving him alone for long—they were just too accustomed to having him around. So Connor's parents made it a point to visit Mike for several hours every Saturday and Sunday so that he wouldn't feel lonely. And at least one of the three of them would stop by to visit him just about every day during the week. "I usually visited him at least twice a week and once on the weekend," Connor explained.

"After Mike went to the assisted living facility, we never had a normal family life," Connor said. "Life pretty much revolved around Mike. That bothered me at times, but I never felt that it would be right to complain."

Mike's death was very recent, and Connor is still grieving and having a difficult time coming to terms with the loss of his brother. However, he has been thinking about it a lot and wanted to pass

along the following to others who may find themselves in a similar
situation:

- It isn't unusual to experience "survivor's guilt" (Connor's
  words), referring to the nagging guilt he'd felt over the fact
  that Mike was born with his illness while Connor was completely healthy. "But don't let that become a burden," he
  advised. "You still will have to face issues and overcome
  obstacles of your own. Life offers us no guarantees. 'There
  but for the grace of God go I,' as the saying goes. So there's
  really no reason to feel guilty."

- Don't be too shy to ask for some attention for yourself. "That
  isn't being greedy," Connor said. "If I had just asked for some
  attention now and then from my parents, I believe I would
  have gotten it. They were just distracted by Mike's obvious
  needs, and I held back from asking."

- While he said that his own grief is terrible, Connor believes
  that part of his struggle is coping with his parents' grief. "I
  don't think they will ever get over Mike's death," he said.
  "And at times it seems like I've lost them as well as Mike.
  Last week I asked if we could all see a grief counselor
  together, and they agreed. I think that might help us a lot."

*Connor ended up cleaning out Mike's room in the assisted living
facility because his parents were still too overwhelmed with grief to
even contemplate doing it. He noted how this was a very difficult but
also a very intimate experience. Initially, he'd thought about asking*

his girlfriend to help him, but then decided against it. "It's hard to describe the feelings I had going through Mike's things, deciding what to keep, what to give away, and what to just throw away. I actually felt very close to him while I was doing it. I'm glad I decided to do it alone."

Connor decided to keep one of Mike's sweaters and a Western belt with a silver buckle as mementos. "I have the sweater in a drawer," he said. "It would fit me, but I still haven't worn it. I don't know if I ever will. I do wear the belt occasionally, though," he added with a smile.

"Mike liked to draw," Connor said, "I loved it when I discovered some old drawings he'd done, stuffed into the back of one of his dresser drawers. It was like finding a treasure." He bought a portfolio to keep Mike's drawings in. He plans on sharing them with his children someday.

Chapter Thirteen

UNDERSTANDING AMBIVALENCE

No discussion of the third stage of family grief would be complete without addressing one of its more uncomfortable aspects. By that we are referring to the *ambivalence* that loved ones—as well as the terminally ill—may sometimes experience in response to the whole process of life extension that has been made possible by medical advances.

Accepting Ambivalence

The ambivalence that family members and loved ones can experience as a terminal illness and its treatment drag on is normal. Nevertheless, it can cause people to feel guilty. In response, they may attempt to suppress their ambivalence. It may strike them as unseemly to have such thoughts and feelings—as if they were somehow betraying their loved one. As a result, they don't talk about it. Ironically, the terminally ill family member may very well also experience periodic ambivalence about going on. He or she too may hesitate to reveal any such ambivalence about ongoing treatment for fear of seeming ungrateful for all the help he or she is receiving. The bottom line is that ambivalence is something that is an inevitable aspect of the new grief.

✿ Marion's Story

Marion, seventy-two, has been suffering from emphysema for ten years. A heavy smoker since she was twelve, she continued to smoke intermittently for several years after her diagnosis. She has undergone lung surgery twice and has been susceptible to respiratory infections and pneumonia for the past four years. She has suffered severe reactions from her treatments and is confined to a wheelchair. She requires oxygen 90 percent of her waking and sleeping hours.

Marion's husband, Todd, recently suffered a severe stroke that resulted, among other things, in partial body paralysis and compromised vision. His doctors feel that without further treatment, Todd might have no more than six months to live. He is, nevertheless, refusing any such treatment. Formerly Marion's primary caretaker, Todd is no longer able to assume these responsibilities. It is doubtful that he will ever leave the nursing home he is currently in. He had been scheduled for a hip replacement before his stroke, but that has now been postponed indefinitely.

Marion and Todd have a daughter who lives a thousand miles away, and a son who lives five hundred miles away. Both want to help, but the distance, work, and the responsibilities of their own families place severe restrictions on how much they are able to do themselves. Marion has always been stubborn and independent. She's had trouble getting along with home healthcare aides. She is refusing to move out of the house that she and Todd have lived in for forty years, despite the fact that she is now confined to living in the finished basement, which includes a den, a kitchenette, and a bathroom. If one were to read Marion's behavior, she is clearly stating that she too does not want further treatment but has instead chosen to live out whatever remaining days she has at home.

Todd has communicated clearly to both children that he does not want any measures taken to prolong his life. Despite the effects of his stroke, his doctors feel that he remains competent to make that decision. He confided in his son that he is tired after years of conflict-ridden caretaking, has had friends who "lingered on longer than they should have," and feels that he is "ready to go whenever my number comes up." With the help of the family lawyer, Todd has signed the necessary documents to ensure that his wishes are respected. He has also specified how he wants his funeral and burial to proceed.

Both children acknowledge feeling some anger and resentment toward Marion, whom they feel brought her illness on herself. They believe that the caretaking she has required has ruined their father's golden years. They had always assumed, though, that Marion would predecease Todd. Now they have to accept the fact that both parents have decided against prolonging life and the distinct possibility that their father will die first, leaving the responsibility for their mother to them.

The son has accepted the role of healthcare proxy for Todd. He has informed the doctors of his father's wishes about no further treatment. He and his sister have also agreed that they will not oppose Marion's insistence on staying at home, unless things get to the point where she can no longer take care of her basic needs.

Ambivalence about when to stop or refuse treatment and wishing that the ordeal of terminal illness be over are in fact common for all family members. Marion's children were understandably ambivalent about the fact that she lived on despite severe limitations, and that her refusal to accept care had placed such a burden on their father. They were, however, able to admit these feelings to one another. Acknowledging and talking about it eased their guilt.

Accepting and sharing ambivalence has the potential to relieve a lot of pain. Such honesty also creates a very special intimacy. Medical personnel are focused on treating or curing the illness and staving off death, and so they often do not consider these kinds of contextual issues. Indeed, their role on the team that is caring for the terminally ill family member should probably not extend that far. The person in the best position to determine what is an acceptable quality of life can be only the patient, unless he or she is suffering from clinical depression or dementia and is unable to make this determination. Many of the miracle treatments that have emerged in recent years not only extend life but can have pernicious side effects that perhaps only those closest to the patient experience. One of these, so-called *chemo brain*, refers to the effects that chemotherapy can have on cognitive functioning, including memory and organization. Bills may not get paid, appointments may go unmet, the patient may get lost driving to a familiar location, and so on. Often the patient himself or herself is not fully aware of these deficits. In this case, those who have primary responsibility for the patient need to make others aware that the deficits exist and ask for additional help as needed.

✤ *Timothy's Story*

Timothy, who is eighty-three, recently underwent triple bypass surgery. While the surgery was successful, his recovery has been slow, due not only to his age but to the fact that he has been on dialysis for the past three years. His hearing is very poor, even with hearing aids. Overall, his health has been in a slow but steady decline for several years. Once a vigorous man whose favorite activity was taking three or four walks a day, he now needs a cane at minimum and often a walker to move from room to room. He and his wife, Laura, have lived for the past fifteen years in a retirement condominium that offers services such as groceries delivered to the door, weekly cleaning, and chaperoned activities, all of which they have historically taken advantage of. Since his surgery, however, Timothy has declined to participate in these activities.

Timothy and Laura have two sons, both married with grown children of their own. One lives in another state, while the other, Richard, lives only one town over—ten minutes by car. Like many in the so-called sandwich generation, Richard has long had responsibilities for both his own children and his parents.

One day, when he was driving his mother home from a visit after Timothy's heart surgery, Laura talked to Richard about how draining it was to take care of his father. "He does very little for himself now," she explained. "He gets easily irritated. He's very impatient, and he takes out all of his frustrations on me." Richard thought she sounded weary. "I decided to take a chance," he said, "and ask Mom if she had any mixed feelings about Dad going through this last surgery. She just sighed. There was this moment of silence. Then she said something to the effect that you can't live forever and that at some point quality of life may be the determining factor in whether someone wants to live or die. I definitely got the impression that she— maybe Dad too—had thought about it and was ready for one of them to go."

Two weeks after this brief conversation, Richard's father asked him to come over for about an hour to go over some financial issues. They'd done this every couple of years ever since Timothy turned seventy. The routine was always the same: Timothy, who was completely lucid despite his physical limitations and who had also always been a highly organized person, kept meticulous records detailing everything from his and Laura's burial arrangements to the income they derived from their investment portfolio.

However, when Richard and Timothy met this time, Richard sensed a difference in his father. Again, they went through all the records. Timothy explained to Richard that his greatest concern was that Laura be comfortable after he died. He wanted Richard to know where everything was located—checkbooks, certificates of deposit, savings bonds—so that he could help Laura access them. He also had a ledger that listed all of their bills and when they were paid.

After they finished this review, Timothy asked Laura to sit down with them. They then went over their will with Richard, including their living wills and the powers of attorney they'd assigned to him. They reaffirmed that he was to be the executor of their will, and they reviewed the terms of a trust they'd created for the future benefit of their grandchildren. Although Richard found all of this to be somewhat emotionally draining, he kept his feelings to himself. When all was done, Timothy turned to him, smiled, and said, "Good, now I'm ready to go."

It might be a mistake to conclude that Timothy actually wanted to die, or that Laura wanted him to. Rather, what their story reveals is the normal *ambivalence* that people can experience when modern medical treatments extend life while at the same time they reduce its quality. What Timothy was saying to his son was an acknowledgment of that fact, combined with an assertion that he was not afraid of death. Similarly, Laura was acknowledging that her husband's life was becoming progressively narrower over time, and that they both were aware of it.

When Jackie Onassis refused further cancer treatment because her reactions to the treatment were worse than the disease itself, her family and friends rallied to her side and ensured that her last few weeks would be as positive and comfortable as possible. When we see people's suffering, we not only empathize with their pain but can respect how worn out they become from expending the energy to stay alive. There is no right or wrong in these cases. It is ultimately a personal decision that every person who is diagnosed with a terminal illness must make.

Ambivalence: Pervasive and Normal

In Timothy's story, the spouse of someone who was experiencing a slow but steady decline in quality of life expressed her ambivalence about it. In addition, she had the courage to be honest about the burden she found herself carrying. As a terminal illness wears on (and may even enter periods of remission), many if not all family members who have rallied to help out may find themselves feeling drained, and they may experience some mixed feelings. In turn, they may find themselves feeling guilty, as in Christopher's story.

🌿 *Christopher's Story*

"Steve had a lump the size of a large mosquito bite on his collar bone that didn't go away for six months," explained Christopher, age thirty-two. "Being gay, I think he was afraid that it might be HIV/ AIDS. So he didn't want to face what it was, and he left it go for six months. By then it had grown to the size of a golf ball. When some friends and I finally dragged him to the doctor and they did some tests, none of us expected it would turn out to be advanced non-Hodgkin's lymphoma."

Christopher had lived with Steve—along with three cats—in a two-bedroom apartment that they rented in a house in a suburb of Boston. They'd been partners for a little less than a year when Steve was diagnosed. He was immediately admitted to the hospital for treatment (chemotherapy and surgery). Christopher's first reaction was to feel helpless. "I didn't know what to do," he said.

Christopher invited Steve's parents to come and stay with him during Steve's treatment, and they ended up living in Christopher's apartment during Steve's treatment both in and out of the hospital.

"I moved in with my own parents in Burlington so Steve and his parents could use what had been our space," Christopher explained. "I brought the cats with me. I also had to get rid of my plants and made sure the apartment was immaculate, because Steve was so fragile, physically. I didn't know where else to go or what else to do.

I really wanted to help. But Steve was unable to pay his half of the rent, and things started getting really tight. I felt uncomfortable asking his parents for money, but otherwise we'd have had to give up the apartment. Then where would Steve have gone?"

Christopher picked up the responsibility for taking Steve to and from treatments after Steve's parents had to leave to go back to work. He also made dinners, did the wash, and cleaned the apartment. He was happy to be there for his partner, but he also felt put out at times due to the time it took up, to not being able to have his cats at home with him, and because he still had to worry about how he would pay the bills while Steve was still unable to pay rent. "I feel so guilty that I ever had those feelings," Christopher said. "I mean, I wish that I had just been more selfless, but it wasn't that way. I got annoyed. I was scared, and now I wish that I had felt differently."

Christopher was clearly involved with some extremely difficult times with Steve. At first it appeared that Steve was going to make a full recovery. He even got back to work. But after about six months, his health began to spiral downward again. He had no energy, and then he started losing weight. Not long thereafter, it was discovered that Steve's cancer had returned. "It spread," Christopher said. "I believe it was actually another kind of cancer."

Christopher described how, as Steve deteriorated, he would have to clean him up, change his sheets, and make sure that he was taking his medication. "It had never occurred to me that I would be in this position, and I sure never thought it would be with a partner who was only thirty-two. It was hard for me, but when I was feeling sorry for myself, I should have only been thinking about Steve."

Christopher sometimes wonders how he would feel if he had to go through something like this with a member of his immediate family, like one of his four siblings, or a parent. He wonders if it would be different or whether he would feel the same kind of frustration and resentment that he felt with Steve.

Christopher feels like part of him disappeared when Steve died. "It's funny. You put so much of yourself into it that you begin to resent it. Then it's suddenly gone, and it's like there's a vacuum, a hole, in your life."

After Steve's death, Christopher began to take his own health more seriously. He admitted that he has become "kind of paranoid" about any lumps or bumps on his body, but he feels that "it's better to be safe than sorry."

In retrospect, Christopher has some strong feelings about his ordeal. "I'm so mad at Steve for waiting so long to go to the doctor," he said. "I'm mad that we had to drag him in there, and then it was too late. I am just so mad at him!"

Christopher misses Steve terribly and feels like he wants to move after living in the house where he was when Steve got sick. He hopes that younger people—like Steve—will realize that they are vulnerable to becoming sick and will take care of themselves. "I learned a lot about myself during that time. I miss Steve so much, and I am upset still that he didn't take care of himself from the beginning."

Christopher's ambivalence had to do in part with the financial crisis that Steve's illness created, and partly to the burden his friend's illness placed on him. When he first noticed the lump on Steve's collarbone, and after Steve was first diagnosed, he could recall no such ambivalence. He did feel somewhat helpless, but he resolved that by springing into action and helping out. In time, however, he moved into the upheaval stage of family grief, at which time he became open to other emotions, notably anxiety along with some resentment and self-pity. Like many people, he felt guilty about having such thoughts—as if to worry about paying the rent is somehow inappropriate when a loved one is terminally ill! Yet in our experience such thoughts and feelings are perfectly appropriate; indeed, they are to be expected. Terminal illness notwithstanding, life goes on. Bills have to be paid. We need to show up for work or lose our jobs. And caretaking can be a burden to even the most loving and devoted family members.

Approaching Resolution

The next stage of family grief, resolution, concerns an opportunity that terminal illness creates. It might strike you as odd to refer to terminal illness as an opportunity, yet it is true. Terminal illness, unlike sudden and unexpected death, allows the family a chance to unearth and address buried issues, communicate more honestly than they may have in the past, and restructure the family dynamics.

❧ STAGE 4 ❧

RESOLUTION

If the dead be truly dead, why should they still be walking in my heart?

—WINNENAP, SHOSHONE MEDICINE MAN

Chapter Fourteen

CARETAKING AND SELF-CARE

The material discussed in part 3 about the upheaval stage is the foundation for the family to move into the fourth stage of the new grief: resolution. Without the knowledge gained from embracing the upheaval created by the terminal illness of a loved one, resolution would not be possible. Sadly, many families avoid facing that very upheaval. They experience it, of course; they just don't want to openly acknowledge it or talk about it. The result is a plethora of loose ends and unfinished business that have the potential to cause permanent fractures in the family's solidarity. It also increases the likelihood that one or more family members will get burned out as a consequence of bearing too much of the load. In contrast, a willingness to face and assess the upheaval caused by this family crisis opens the door to eventual family renewal.

A good place to begin the process of resolution is by taking stock of just how much upheaval has occurred in your life. Then, you need to begin taking steps toward establishing a healthy *balance*, particularly between caretaking and self-care. By *self*-care we mean yourself as an individual but also your own immediate family (partner and children) if you have one.

While everyone in the family shares the stresses associated with caretaking, the primary caretaker is most often an adult living with the ill family member. This primary caretaker often sacrifices his or her own needs, goals, and autonomy to preserve family stability and provide care.

✔ Katharine's Story

Katharine, age fifty-two, was the primary caretaker of her husband, Matthew, age fifty-four, who had been diagnosed with esophageal cancer. Matthew had undergone several experimental treatments, and everyone outside of his immediate family thought he was doing great—as did he. Only Katharine and their two college-age children were aware of the cognitive and emotional impairments that were a side effect of these treatments. Even Matthew's doctors were so focused on curing the cancer that they seemed to pay little attention to Katharine's reports of Matthew's increasing irritability, flawed decision making, and inattentiveness.

At times, Katharine was ashamed about the resentment she felt over the lack of support she got from other family members, such as Matthew's siblings, or even an acknowledgment by anyone else of exactly what she was living with. Of course, she was partly responsible for this, as she was reticent to tell people in detail just how much Matthew had deteriorated. In other words, she had not been totally open about the degree of upheaval that Matthew's cancer had created in her life.

Katharine was mourning the loss of the person that Matthew had been and the lifestyle that they had enjoyed. She found herself caught in a vicious circle: She would express impatience with Matthew, then she would feel resentful of the burden he was, and finally she would feel shame about having these reactions. She had taken family leave from her job as an advertising executive after Matthew was diagnosed, but she had not expected it to continue for so long. She was exhausted, frustrated, and depressed. To make matters worse, they had dipped deeply into their savings to pay the household bills while Katharine was not able to work.

Katharine, the sole daughter in a family of four children, had been socialized to take care of others and to put herself last. She had also been raised by parents who embraced the notion that strong people did not rely on others or delegate responsibility to others. This attitude had contributed to her successful career. At the same time, it left her isolated in the face of this crisis. As a result, her life had spiraled into a state of imbalance that was draining her very spirit.

Caregiver Burnout

Caretaking for a terminally ill loved one can easily become a full-time job. As Jane Brody reported in the *New York Times*, immediate family caregivers provide 80 percent of care for ill or disabled members in their last year of life. Fewer than 5 percent use caregiver support groups or respite care. Is it any surprise, then, that overworked and overly stressed caregivers can burn out and become mentally ill (depressed, anxious)? Is it surprising that the stress of caretaking can in turn compromise the caretakers' own immune systems and cause them to become physically ill? There are no sick days for family caregivers who administer medications and other treatments, provide nursing and personal care, shop, prepare meals, manage the household, pay bills, keep track of appointments, and provide or arrange transportation for medical visits.

The burden of caretaking is often further complicated by financial issues: loss of income, restrictions in insurance provisions, and limited resources with which to hire supplementary help. Primary family caregivers today are also affected by the fact that other family members likely live very far away; adding to the stress can be problems related to blended families. Research shows that the increasing number of people who find themselves sandwiched, raising children while simultaneously caring for elder parents, may experience such acute stress that it can jeopardize their marriages and their health. For this group, conflicting loyalties—most commonly, loyalty to one's spouse versus loyalty to one's elderly parents—have the potential to create destructively powerful feelings of resentment and anger.

Establishing Balance: First Steps

If you are one of the many who find yourself sandwiched, the first thing to do is to acknowledge the intergenerational needs that confront you. Our advice: *Don't be stoic, because being stoic increases your chances of burning out.* Your elderly parents may expect you to take care of them as they took care of you as a young child or as they may have taken care of their own parents. They may expect you to drop everything every time they have a crisis, no matter how minor. At the same time, your children and spouse may have competing needs that also place demands on you. Under these circumstances, it can be easy to lose sight of *your* needs: what *you* would like to do, and how *you* would like to spend at least some of your time.

✍ Jessica's Story

Jessica was preparing to attend her daughter's senior college piano recital when her father called from two thousand miles away to tell her that her mother had just had her third heart attack. The doctors had declared it minor, though as Jessica knew, no heart attack is truly minor for a sixty-five-year-old.

Jessica was torn. She had plane tickets to fly the next morning to her daughter's college to attend the recital. Yet she could hear the pleading in her father's voice. She had always responded to these crisis calls, feeling that she had no choice. This time, she was more conflicted. Her husband told her to go to her parents, and he would go to the recital. But Jessica knew how important this recital was to her daughter's musical career. It marked an important milestone not only in her daughter's life but in Jessica's life as well.

For the first time, Jessica called her brother to ask him what he thought she should do. Up until then she had always assumed the caretaker role as the only daughter. Her brother heard her out and then, somewhat to Jessica's surprise, said "By all means, go to the recital. I'll fly out and see Mom. I'll call you to let you know if I think you really should come down after the recital."

Jessica attended the recital and treasured it. The next day her brother called to say that while their mother had looked fine when he first arrived, overnight she'd deteriorated. Bottom line: Jessica should come.

Jessica's mother died before Jessica could get there. She felt some guilt, but on reflection, she decided that she had made the right decision—for her daughter and for herself. Her brother later told her that he had always thought that Jessica wanted the caretaker role and that she would resent any offers of help from him and his wife. He agreed that she had done the right thing and that not getting there before their mother died did not negate all the times that Jessica had indeed dropped everything and run to her parents' aid.

Here is another example of someone who took a first step toward balancing caretaking with self-care:

✑ Frank's Story

Frank and his wife, Isabella, both came from very traditional Italian-American families, which emphasized family solidarity and interdependence. When they were growing up, if there was something that needed to be done, chances were that someone in one of their families—or else someone that someone in their families knew—could do it. Frank and Isabella had started dating during their junior year in high school. They have two children, one a sophomore in college and the other a junior in high school, and recently celebrated their twenty-fifth anniversary.

As time wore on, both families found they were increasingly separated by distance. Frank's two brothers had both pursued careers after graduating college. These careers required them and their families to move a number of times in the interest of advancement.

The closest of them was currently a few hundred miles away. Isabella had a brother and a sister, both of whom also had moved some distance away to establish careers and raise their families. In the meantime, Frank and Isabella took over his parents' family business, grew it into an even more successful operation, and stayed close to home.

Frank's mother had a stroke when his and Isabella's children were in middle school. They then added an in-law apartment to their home so Frank's parents could move in. This situation worked out well for a number of years. Then Frank's mother had a series of small strokes, which progressively weakened her, followed by a larger stroke that killed her.

After that, Frank's father fell into a depression. Once very independent, he became just the opposite. Rather than staying in his own apartment, he took to spending almost all of his time in their house—and in the middle of their family. He stopped cooking for himself and instead either ate with Frank and his family or would raid their refrigerator at all hours of the day or night. He'd complain whenever Frank wanted to take his family someplace without him. And in a most ironic turn, he began to call Frank ungrateful. "I handed you that business," he'd say, "and this is the thanks I get," referring to his feeling abandoned if he had to stay at home alone.

Guilt motivated Frank to avoid confronting his father and to giving in to many of his father's demands for attention. But then Isabella and the children began complaining. The kids complained about Grandpa always being underfoot. "He's always right there in the middle of things!" Frank's daughter complained, saying that her grandfather's intrusiveness made her reluctant to invite friends over to the house. And Isabella started making remarks about how she and Frank had no private time together.

Frank felt squeezed. "I'm like that little layer of cream in the middle of an Oreo cookie," he told a friend. The friend, who had known Frank and his parents since childhood, laughed, but then said, "Frank, if it was me, I'd choose my family. I love your father, but he's not your future. If you asked me, I'd say he was acting like a spoiled kid, and I've never believed in giving in to that kind of behavior."

This piece of advice was reassuring to Frank. It also made him feel less guilty about the idea of putting limits on his father, which he did by sitting his father down and letting him know that as much as the family loved him, they did not want him sitting center stage in their lives, day in and day out.

Frank's father did not take this news well and responded by announcing that he intended to move into an assisted living facility. Frank and Isabella talked about this, and Frank spoke with his brothers by phone. Both were supportive of the idea of letting Frank's father do what he wanted. One brother said he did not know how Frank and Isabella had been able to tolerate the situation as long as they had.

Frank and Isabella told Frank's father together that they would be happy to have him stay with them, as long as they could come to some agreement about their family having its space. Frank's father scoffed at this, saying that families had no need for space. This attitude may well have reflected his own experience, growing up in an apartment in a building that housed not only his own family but the families of several relatives. In a sense he had indeed not known many boundaries growing up. But that did not render Frank and his family's desires invalid. So Frank and his brothers helped their father find a comfortable apartment in an assisted living facility that was only a few miles away from their home.

Frank visited his father twice a week, and Frank and Isabella visited for an hour or so every weekend. At first his father was cool and said little during these visits. In time, however, things gradually thawed between Frank and his father. Isabella was of the opinion that this was due to the fact that her father-in-law was having a lot more social contact in the assisted living facility than he'd had when he was living with them. "One reason he was always under foot, I think," she said, "was that he had no one else to interact with. Here he has men and women from his own generation to relate to. Sometimes he complains, but the staff all say that he's among the most active and social residents they have."

It is difficult to prescribe exactly how family members can begin to restore some balance into a lifestyle that has been severely skewed as a consequence of coping with chronic or terminal illness. Both Jessica's and Frank's stories, however, illustrate how people have taken some initial steps in that direction. The proliferation of senior communities (sometimes called lifelong communities), assisted living facilities that offer varying levels of service, and nursing homes can be a wonderful opportunity for families to ensure quality care, safety, and opportunities for social interaction for the ill. As Frank's case shows, families often overlook the fact that home care has its limitations as well as its benefits.

Some people express the feeling that it is somehow unloving to consider such placements. By the same token, some people who really need such care may feel that they are being abandoned by their family when they are placed in such a facility. They may resist it or attempt to make loved ones feel guilty for considering it. However, making such a placement decision, even when the ill or disabled family member disagrees with it, can in fact be a loving act. This is where family unity becomes really important. Frank, for example, got the approval and support of his brothers. Jessica also got family support for her decision to attend her daughter's recital rather than flying to her mother's bedside. Without that support, these decisions would no doubt have been more difficult to make.

It is important to consider a number of factors when making decisions about placing an ill loved one in a care facility:

- *Geography and accessibility.* How far away is the facility, and how accessible is it to family?

- *Level of care.* What does the ill loved one need now? What are his or her expected needs in the future? Can the facility provide the services that are needed now and in the future or will a different placement be needed later on?

- *Finances.* What can the family and the ill loved one afford? What other sources of financial assistance could be tapped?

- *Programming and activities.* What kinds of social programs and activities does the facility provide? Is there a schedule? Does the facility provide transportation, for example, for shopping trips or medical appointments?

- *Family responsibilities.* Which family members will be responsible for providing what after the ill family member moves into the facility? What will the visitation schedule look like? Will the ill family member be attending family events, and if so who will be responsible for transportation?

In the film *Away from Her*, a husband must make the decision to place his wife, who is suffering from Alzheimer's disease, in an assisted living facility. He does so with great reluctance and only after concluding that her safety has become a factor. Their home was located in a place where the winters tended to be severe, and she had already wandered out of the house and into the snow more than once.

Initially, the wife is placed on the first floor of the facility, which provides housing for the relatively high-functioning residents. The wife is ambivalent, but she complies with her husband's decision. In time, she adjusts and seems happy. He visits her often and for long periods of time. They talk and play games. Eventually the husband also adjusts to his new lifestyle, though he still misses his wife deeply.

Then, when the wife's cognitive functioning further deteriorates— to the point at which she does not recognize her husband—the husband is informed that his wife needs to be moved upstairs, meaning to that part of the facility that is secure and houses lower-functioning individuals. This scene is poignant and sad. The husband has been resisting making that decision, holding on as long as he can to the notion that his beloved wife is not that ill. In the end, however, he agrees to the move. His decision is clearly an act of love.

Other Ideas for Balancing Caretaking with Self-Care

It has been our habit to solicit advice from those we work with and who are working their way through the stages of family grief regarding how to balance caretaking with self-care. What follows are some of the responses we have gotten.

Make a bucket list. This phrase comes from the film *The Bucket List*, in which two terminally ill men make up a list of things they'd always wanted to do before they kicked the bucket. One woman, after being diagnosed with a relapse of cancer, told her children to come up with their bucket list of things they would want to do before they died. She used the idea of a raft trip down the Colorado River that she and a friend had taken in her twenties as an example from her own life. Recognizing that in the months ahead her own care would place demands on her grown son and daughter, this woman funded an item that was on each of their bucket lists. She sent the daughter and her family to Yellowstone National Park for a week of cross-country skiing. Her son and his family, meanwhile, were treated to a week exploring the rain forests and beaches of Costa Rica.

Take time to pamper yourself. One man talked about his decision to join a fitness club. This was something he'd always wanted to do but had hesitated to spend the money on. After his father had to be moved to a nursing home, however, he purchased a family membership to a club that was located on the route between his house and the nursing home. Twice a week, after visiting with his father following a busy workday, he would meet his wife and two sons at the fitness club where they would work out or swim, and then have take-out food for dinner. He found this to be a great stress reliever. In addition, he felt that it helped make up for lost family time and brought his family closer together.

A woman we spoke with talked about how she signed up for yoga classes and arranged for a monthly massage as a break from taking care of her terminally ill husband. Initially, she said, she felt a pang of guilt doing this. "I think part of me felt that it was my duty to be with him every minute I wasn't either at work or doing something mandatory, like food shopping." When she brought it up, however, her husband strongly encouraged her to do these things. "He told me he'd be fine," she said, "watching the ball game on television. He said he sometimes felt guilty spending so much time watching ball games!"

Delegate! Not everyone is in a position to pay for help, but those who are can find a lot of relief by delegating time-consuming activities to others while they spend more time taking care of an ill loved one. One woman, who had a longstanding habit of spending at least half of every Saturday cleaning her house, opted to hire a cleaning service. This freed her up for several hours. Instead of visiting her mother, who was living in a nursing home, the woman and her husband spent this time hiking or canoeing and then going out for a late breakfast. They found the respite very rewarding and a welcome break in their hectic schedules.

However they choose to do it, and even if it means taking small steps, we encourage families to act on this issue of lifestyle balance—and in particular creating some space for self-care in each of their lives—as a means of mitigating the upheaval that prolonged illness in a loved one creates. Doing so represents the first steps that families can take toward resolving the crisis.

✹ Monika's Story

Monika is eighty-eight. "When Walter died eight years ago, I was already an old woman and all alone. I have no one, and I spent so many years taking care of him. I was so lonely." Monika said that Walter's death was the end of her whole world: She had spent many years caring for him, and then suddenly she had no purpose.

Monika and Walter lost their son, their only child, in an automobile accident when he was twenty-three years old. After that, she said, "It really felt like we were all alone. All we really had was each other." Between them they had only one family member, a nephew of Monika's, who lived reasonably close by. But he had a family of his own to tend to. And so Monika and Walter had gone on to create a lifestyle in which they were rather isolated but nevertheless happy.

When Walter became ill, Monika remembers feeling terrified of losing him as well and having no one to take care of her when she became older and possibly became ill. She was diagnosed with colon cancer two years after Walter died. After intensive surgery and rehabilitation, she returned to her home.

"I was all alone again, but now I needed a nurse to get by. I was alone before, but at least I had my independence. There were times when I almost wish they hadn't bothered treating me. For some reason—even after Walter was diagnosed with an illness we knew would be terminal—I didn't think about just how alone I would be after he was gone. Who would take care of me? My nephew helps me now and then, but he can only do so much. He has a family too, and it's not the same as having your own child to turn to." Monika sighed. "It's really a curse to have no children."

Walter had taken care of their finances, so when he passed away, Monika didn't know how much money they had and how she would take care of herself, "especially if I lived to a ripe old age, like many in my family." As it turned out, Walter had earned a good salary during his working years and had saved a significant amount of money.

He also had a great pension with a provision that paid half of his benefit to Monika for life after he died. "So at least I haven't had to worry about money," Monika said. "I am so grateful for that."

Two years ago, Monika sold the house that she and Walter had lived in and purchased a condominium in a lifelong living community. Her monthly fee pays for services such as cleaning and plowing the walks in the winter. In addition, she pays a monthly fee that entitles her to two full meals a day. She makes her own light breakfast every day in her kitchenette. Medical services are available on-site by appointment, and a van is available to take residents pretty much wherever they need (or want) to go. Finally, there is an active social calendar with a range of activities and interest groups.

Monika shared the following thoughts.

- She wishes she could have anticipated how hard it would be to lose her husband so late in her life, especially after the loss of their son. She thinks it was a mistake not thinking about that and advises women in similar situations to make a plan for that eventuality. She realizes that it wasn't possible to replace her lost son, but believes she could have put more effort into building a network of friends before moving into the community where she finally settled.

- She also wishes she had made the decision to move into her present residence much sooner after Walter died. She thought it would be helpful for people who are older and don't have kids to know that such communities exist and that they can provide much-needed support and friendship for those who don't have other family members in the area. Although she still misses Walter every day, Monika says it felt as if she had been "thrown a life preserver" when she moved in to the lifelong living community. "It's not the same as having Walter around," she said, "but at least it's a life."

Chapter Fifteen

THE FAMILY INVENTORY

REASSESSING FAMILY ROLES

In many of the stories of individuals and families going through the process of the new grief that we've shared with you, it is apparent that people establish the roles they play in their family at an early age. Then, even if many years have passed and we have changed in many other ways, we tend to "regress" to these same roles quickly in a time of crisis. Some people are completely comfortable with this, but many others are ambivalent: liking only some aspects of their role.

The upheaval caused by the family crisis you are in presents you with an opportunity to reassess the role you play in your family—and to change it. In chapter 10, we discussed family roles as part of a family's dynamics, which also includes such things as family traditions. Perhaps you have given some thought to the role that you have carved out (and that has been carved out for you!) over time. Many people have told us that their role seemed to have been defined fairly early. Firstborns, for example, often relate how they assumed a semi-parental role by the time they were eight or ten years old. In large families, the youngest child may find himself or herself gradually drawn into the role of taking care of aging parents. Meanwhile, middle children carve out identities and roles that diverge from those already taken. These can vary widely. Common roles include the family rebel, family clown, family adventurer, and family nonconformist.

In this chapter, we invite you to step back and look at the role you play in your family. With that perspective in hand, you can then decide if you want to leave it as it is or whether you would like to change it, and if so, how.

✍ Gregory's Story

"My sister still lived in Wisconsin, in the same rural town we grew up in," Gregory said. "I had moved away as soon as I went to college and never returned except for a brief visit once a year around Thanksgiving. She and I never had a close relationship, partly because of the distance and partly, I think, because she is ten years older than I am. She was always nice to me, however. Sheila would send me photos of her daughters, and periodically she would send an e-mail telling me about their adventures, how they were doing in school, and the like. I'd send the kids birthday cards with a check. I'd call maybe once a month or so, and we'd chat for five minutes. The truth is, I felt like I had somehow failed her when she died."

Gregory's mother and father both died of heart disease when he was in his twenties. "I lost my parents too young," he said, "I knew they were ill, yet I didn't really prepare for their death. I didn't even think about it. I was only twenty-five when Mom died. Even though I lived a thousand miles away and visited her rarely, I still felt her loss. She was my confidant, and I was too young to lose her."

Gregory was living in California when Sheila passed away from a stroke. He'd known that she was at risk because of her diabetes, which was very severe. She already suffered from chronic pain in her legs, and her vision was deteriorating. Once again, though, Gregory hadn't thought about his sister or her illness much, and he was caught by surprise.

Gregory was more than surprised when he got the news that his brother-in-law had also died, suddenly and unexpectedly, from a heart attack, barely four months after his sister had passed away. "That really jolted me," he said. "Up until then, even with the loss of both parents and my sister, I had paid little attention to my own health. And despite those losses, my lifestyle went on pretty much as it had. On some level I knew that Sheila was dying, but I think I was in denial and didn't want to face that possibility and what it would mean.

"But when Ben died, I snapped out of that state of denial. All of a sudden I found myself thinking intensely about two things: my own mortality, and the two grown nieces that my sister and brother-in-law had raised, but whom I'd rarely seen. Two beautiful, talented young women, and then suddenly they were orphans."

Looking back, Gregory definitely wished that he had maintained closer ties with his sister and her family. He felt that he had abandoned his family by moving far away and staying there. He wished he could have played a role in his two nieces' lives when they were children and teens. He was now forty-three, and having no family of his own, he wanted to get to know them. "I have my regrets," he said. "I pursued my career and have done well. Being gay, I wanted to get out of the small town I grew up in, and I did. But I wish I could have been able to do something to support my sister more, so that she would know that I really loved her. And I do intend to try to establish some kind of relationship with my nieces."

Gregory agreed that his role in the family was part prodigal child because of his being gay and not fitting in in the small town where he'd been raised and part adventurer because he wanted to pursue his interest in biology and become a college professor and researcher. Although he felt that his parents' deaths taught him a lot about what he called the pragmatics of death—funeral arrangements and so on, Gregory wished he could have played more of a role, especially in his mother's caretaking, even if only through more frequent contact and some financial support. No one had ever asked him for the latter, and he had never volunteered it.

With respect to his nieces, Gregory said that his goal now is to become more of a real uncle. He hoped that he could come to play a benign and supportive role in their lives and in the lives of their young children. He said that there were stories he wished he could have shared with his sister, and discussions he would have liked to have had. "I know she knew I was gay, but we never really talked about it. She didn't act like it mattered to her, but I would still have liked to hear her say that to me, face-to-face. And there are a lot of memories—good memories—that I have of things we did as a family, and things my big sister taught me when we were growing up, that I'd like my nieces to know about."

What's Your Role?

If you had to put a label on your role in the family, what would that label be? Gregory was able to put a label on both his and his sister's roles. Whereas he was the prodigal wanderer, she had been the settled caretaker for as long as he could remember. He never recalled her ever complaining about it, but he was sure it must have been a burden for her to carry.

As you prepare to consider changing your role in the family (or not changing it), and as you look at the role you have played in your family in the past, ask yourself the following questions:

- Did I feel that the responsibilities my family placed on me were fair?

- Did I believe that my family was proud of me?

- Overall, was I a "central character" in my family, or more of a "peripheral" one?

- When it came to making family decisions, did I feel that my opinion was heard?

- Did I speak up when I wanted to, or did I tend to be quiet even when I might have had something to say?

- How much did my family rely on me, for example, to make decisions, solve crises, or resolve conflicts?

- Who if anyone in my family have I been jealous or envious of, and why?

• Who if anyone have I felt lingering resentment or anger toward, and why?

CHANGING FAMILY ROLES

You can use your answers to the questions about your role as a guide to *whether* you'd like to change your position in the family and, if so, *how* you would like it to change. As much as you may feel sad, anxious, or even angry in response to the upheaval that family grief creates, this crisis also provides you with the opportunity to assess things and decide that they are either just where you want them to be, or to begin changing things for the better.

Our advice is to try to imagine what a new or revised family role would look like *before* you begin taking steps to change your role. For example, are there any aspects of the roles that others in your family play that you would like to incorporate into your own role? For example, Gregory seemed to feel that he would like to do more *caretaking* and play a more *central* (as opposed to peripheral) role in the lives of his nieces. In a word, he was ready to assume more *responsibility* in his family.

FAMILY ROLE DIMENSIONS

Caretaker (taking care of physical/ emotional needs)	1 2 3 4 5 6 7 8 9 10
Financier (providing financial support to the family)	1 2 3 4 5 6 7 8 9 10
Leader (making important or difficult decisions)	1 2 3 4 5 6 7 8 9 10

Peacekeeper (resolving conflicts between family members)	1 2 3 4 5 6 7 8 9 10
Keeper of traditions (holidays)	1 2 3 4 5 6 7 8 9 10
Coordinator of events (birthdays, weddings)	1 2 3 4 5 6 7 8 9 10
Family clown (providing comic relief)	1 2 3 4 5 6 7 8 9 10
Family rebel (challenging authority)	1 2 3 4 5 6 7 8 9 10
Nonconformist (being different)	1 2 3 4 5 6 7 8 9 10
Problem child (getting into trouble)	1 2 3 4 5 6 7 8 9 10
Family star (successful)	1 2 3 4 5 6 7 8 9 10

When considering in what direction they would like to move their family role, some people have found it helpful to use the chart given above. It lists a number of dimensions, such as *caretaker*. Each dimension has a range, from 1 (very little caretaking responsibilities) to 10 (extreme caretaking responsibilities). First, go through the list and, for each dimension, place the letter *N* where you think your role is *now*. Then go back over the list of dimensions, and for each one place the letter *F* to indicate where you would like to see yourself in the *future*.

When he went through the chart, Gregory placed an *N* at 1 on every dimension until he got to rebel, where he put his *N* at 3. He did so because he said that even as a child he tended to question his parents' values at times. "They were strong churchgoers," he explained. "On some level I knew, or suspected, that I was gay, and that the church thought I was a sinner condemned to hell for that. So I had a negative attitude about church." He placed his *N* at 8 for being a nonconformist, at 2 for being a problem child (he wasn't) and at 9 for being successful. "I knew my family was proud of me for becoming a professor and publishing scholarly articles, even if I was only a very distant success!" Gregory quipped.

In deciding how he would like to change his role in the little family he had left, Gregory was clear that he did not see himself playing a role as a decision maker for his nieces or their families; on the other hand, he did want to be able to be more of a caretaker and a potential source of financial support. He decided, for example, to establish a trust fund that was intended to be a college tuition fund for his nieces' children. He also hoped to become a more integral part of their lives by being there for family events, especially the big holidays. Finally, he wanted to make his own home, in San Francisco, a place that his nieces and their families could feel comfortable visiting and using as a base to explore the Bay area.

Maggie's story is another example of how upheaval can lead to positive change.

✹ Maggie's Story

The youngest of two daughters, Maggie was ten when she lost her mother to cancer. Before that, Maggie, her sister, Megan, and their mother, Mollie, were an inseparable team. Mollie taught her daughters how to ride a horse, how to cook and sew, and how to make pottery. She supervised their homework, played games with them, and took them shopping. Their father, Ned, meanwhile, was a steady source of financial support. A tall, burly, and affectionate man, Maggie said her father had always reminded her of Papa Bear from the children's story.

"After Mom died, I think we all felt lost for a while," said Maggie. "She had such energy, such a strong personality. She was the center of our family. Then she got sick. She lived for another year, and she

tried in that time to stay involved despite her weakness. We all pitched in a little to keep things going."

A year after Mollie's death, Ned introduced Maggie and Megan to Noreen, whom they immediately disliked. The feeling apparently was mutual. Ned eventually married Noreen, and she immediately took on the role that Mollie had played—being the center of the family, only with a lot less love and affection. "Noreen hated fat," Maggie explained, "and for some reason she decided that Megan and I were fat. She rode us constantly about it. We were always on forced diets. If we complained to Dad, he would listen, but then he'd explain that Noreen had our best interests at heart. What we believed was that she was out to starve us to death!"

Many years living with Noreen left both Maggie and Megan self-conscious about their weight and insecure about their attractiveness. These weaknesses eventually took their toll, in the form of two failed marriages—one each for Megan and Maggie. In time, however, both decided to seek counseling, and both managed to heal their wounded self-esteem well enough to go on. Megan married again and had a daughter. Although Maggie remained single, she felt that she had been able to have a few meaningful relationships that were not poisoned by her old self-doubts. By then both women were in their late forties.

Ned eventually retired, and he and Noreen moved into a condominium that abutted a golf course. They purchased memberships and played golf two or three times a week from early spring to late fall. They wintered in a rented condo in Florida. Maggie visited with them twice a year. The animosity between her and Noreen, while fading some over the years, was still strong enough that Maggie found it difficult to visit for longer than two or three days. She really liked being with her father, but found it difficult to get time alone with him. "Noreen is always there!" she said with obvious annoy-

ance. "Sometimes I think she had the place bugged so she can listen to everything my father and I say to each other!"

Meanwhile, Megan visited her father only once a year. She always brought her family along, and opted to stay in a hotel. "She can't stand to be in the same house with Noreen," Maggie explained.

When Ned was hospitalized and then diagnosed with lung cancer, Maggie and Megan flew out to see him and meet with his doctors. To their dismay, they were told at the hospital information desk that they would not be allowed in Ned's room. Noreen, it seemed, had asserted her authority as Ned's wife and instructed the hospital not to allow anyone but her into his room. When Maggie and Megan confronted her, Noreen stood firm, saying that Ned was not up to having visitors. Apparently, that included his daughters!

Ned returned home after four days in the hospital and began radiation therapy. At that point, when they were finally able to talk with him, Maggie brought up the issue of being barred from his room. She and Megan expressed concern that this could happen again. Ned looked surprised, then frowned. Then Maggie spoke up. "Dad," she said, "I've tried to stay out of your business all these years. I've respected your marriage, even though you know that Noreen and I do not like one another. I have not asked you for anything. But I am your daughter, as is Megan. We love you. We do not want to be left out in the cold when it comes to your medical care or any decisions you might have to make in the future."

Ned, usually mild and unassertive (especially around Noreen), replied, "What do you want?"

Maggie explained that she wanted either herself or Megan to share medical power of attorney with Noreen and to be given explicit permission not only to visit him if he were to be hospitalized again but to have access to his medical records and permission to communicate with his doctors. Ned listened, but said nothing. Maggie and Megan spent the next hour just talking with their father. When Noreen returned from running a few errands, they said goodbye.

Three days later, Maggie got a call from Ned's attorney. He informed her that Ned had just signed documents granting both her and Megan the powers she'd asked for. He said he was sending them copies by overnight mail, and that the signed originals would be on file in his office. Before hanging up, he added, "I've known your father for forty years, Maggie. I'm very glad you did this."

Maggie altered her (and her sister's) role in the family significantly with that single act of assertiveness. No longer content to stand on the periphery, she was now in a position of influence. At the same time, she took a step toward healing the resentment she'd long felt about the fact that Ned had never spoken up for her or for Megan, and had allowed Noreen to harass them relentlessly about their weight. From that day forward, both daughters would have unfettered access to their father as well as to his treatment. Noreen could no longer prevent Ned from hearing whatever they had to say.

How Would You Like to Change?

Even after completing the assessment of the roles they play in the family, some people conclude that they do not want to change. They are perfectly content with their roles and responsibilities. Others, however, like Gregory and Maggie, are not. Each of them took steps to alter their roles in directions that would make them feel better about themselves.

We are not advocates of change for change's sake or of upsetting the family apple cart for no good reason. In the stories described here, however, the family as a whole stood to benefit from one family member's decision to try to alter his or her role. Despite the fact that Noreen might have objected, for example, it is our opinion that Ned's family would be better off if his daughters were privy to his future medical care and medical decisions. Similarly, Gregory's nieces and their children surely stood to gain from having him become a more vital part of their lives.

Perhaps you have some notion now about if and how you would like to change the role you've played in your family's dynamic structure. If this means you must address some unfinished business, as Maggie did, see the guidelines in the next chapter.

✒ Jason's Story

"My mother was diagnosed with multiple sclerosis (MS) when I was small. She was usually okay, as I recall, but of course her attacks got progressively worse toward the end of her life. The worst thing was that there was nothing anyone could do to help her."

Jason recalled feeling helpless against MS and often feeling as if there were no hope. He described his mother's illness as being "like a shadow. It followed me around. Like all shadows, you sort of get used to it and most of the time you more or less forget that it's there. But it's there nonetheless."

As a child, Jason felt that his parents tried to protect him from his mother's illness and that it was easy for them to do that because she was not highly symptomatic during his childhood. Her main symptom then was periodic weakness. He could tell something was wrong, but his parents did not discuss it, and Jason did not even know exactly what it was. As a result of their silence, he became embarrassed to talk about his mother's illness. When he was in high school, his mother began to suffer from episodes of severe muscle weakness and spasms. At that point, she began to rely on a cane or walker at times to get around. Witnessing that made Jason extremely anxious.

"I know my parents were trying to protect me, but I think it would have been better to explain to me, even as a child, that my mother might seem fine now, but that in the future she might need more help and might someday even need to be in a wheelchair," said Jason. "It was as if I had no role in my family other than to be a child. I know that what I could have done would have been limited, but even doing a little might have made me feel less helpless."

As he entered college, Jason struggled with the idea that his mother's health was deteriorating steadily and that she would eventually die and that there was nothing he could do to help her. "My mom also eventually suffered from depression," he explained, "and it was really hard to see her suffer both physically and emotionally. My father put my mom's care first, and I often felt like a third wheel because he was so worried about her. And she spent more and more time in bed. So I just lived my life on campus, and even though school was only a couple of hours away, I went home pretty much only for holidays."

Jason was eventually able to get help in the form of information and support through the Multiple Sclerosis Association of America and National Multiple Sclerosis Society. He also sought out individual therapy to help him cope with his mother's illness and eventual death in his late twenties at the advice of his girlfriend (now his wife). Since then, he has been able to reconnect with his father, whom he sees regularly. He finally has learned much about his mother's

pre-MS life through his father's stories of their courtship and early
years together. Jason now feels that he plays a significant role in his
father's life through their relationship.

"I probably would have sounded pretty bitter and very angry if
you'd spoken with me a few years ago," said Jason. "I know I have a
lot of pain in me still. Sometimes I wonder if my parents would have
had me at all if they knew about my mother's diagnosis before I was
born."

Jason offered the following advice to families:

- If you are a parent with a serious illness, you need to talk to your children about it. Jason believes that it would have helped him tremendously to know what was happening with his mother's health. "I would have liked to have been included in what was happening. I know I couldn't have handled all of it, but it would have helped me to know more."

- As a father, he now sees the benefit to having a clear will and trust for his daughters should anything happen to him and his wife. He also feels that his daughters should know about anything major that happens with him and his wife and that he would prefer to keep them informed about any health issues that they might face.

- "Most important," Jason said, "I want my daughters to know me in a way that I never got to know my mom. My wife and I are much more open with them than my parents were with me. I think we're sensitive to their ages and how much they can understand, but we don't keep them in the dark, or on the outside looking in."

Chapter Sixteen

PUTTING UNRESOLVED ISSUES TO REST

In a story that was shared in the previous chapter, Maggie took a major step toward putting an unresolved issue to rest when she spoke her mind to her father. For years, she and her sister had felt largely locked out of their father's life. For years, she had chosen to bite her tongue and be quiet. But when the family entered the crisis created by her father's cancer diagnosis, the issue resurfaced, and this time Maggie did something about it.

Here is another example of someone for whom the upheaval created by terminal illness led to the resolution of an important issue.

✹ Jane's Story

"As a family, we have always been really outdoorsy people," Jane said. "As a child, I spent my summers on Cape Cod, playing tennis, biking, swimming. My mother, my sister, my brother, and I would all stay in a cottage my parents would rent for the whole month of July. My father would stay for a week and then drive down from his job in Boston for the other weekends. I don't remember my parents making a big deal out of sun block, and we never thought that the sun could harm us more than a beginning-of-season sunburn."

Jane discussed the pain of discovering that her father, Sid, had been diagnosed with melanoma three months before her wedding, and then learning a week later that the cancer had spread to his lymph nodes. He was able to attend her wedding but survived only another six months.

Sid had had two prior diagnoses of basal cell carcinoma (BCC) on his face; both were successfully removed through surgery and required no further treatment. Although everyone in the family knew that Sid might be at risk for further skin cancers, no one had anticipated such a serious and ultimately fatal diagnosis.

"My dad was very young for a sixty-two-year-old. He was in very good shape and he was very active. He could bike farther than I could. So it really hit me like a ton of bricks when he went in what seemed so short a time."

Jane said that while her father's diagnosis hit her hard, it absolutely devastated her mother, Ellen. "Not just because she loved him—which she did—but because she was so dependent on him. The truth is that we always knew this, and it actually bothered my sister and me, because we saw ourselves as independent, capable *women. Mom, meanwhile, relied on Dad for everything. But my sister and I kept our feelings to ourselves."*

Jane discussed how looking after her mother after her father passed away had been a daunting and frustrating task for her and her younger sister, Abbie. As Jane described it, her father had taken care of all the family's financial issues during the marriage: paying bills, arranging for home and car repairs, saving for college, and so on. He did this willingly and happily, Jane said. "They seemed quite content with the arrangement, even if my sister and I would not want it that way."

Whereas Sid had been the sole source of income for the family, Ellen was what Jane called its "emotional center." "In a way, Mom has always been at the center of our family life," she explained. "She planned all the special occasions. She's a great cook, and she actually likes doing housework! She was always there, and she was the one person my sister and I could talk to about anything. But when it came to finances, she was lost. After Dad died, Abbie and I found out that Mom not only did not know how to balance a checkbook but she didn't even know where the checkbook was!"

At sixty, Ellen still does not know how to use the Internet; nor does she have an e-mail address. Though she has a driver's license, when Sid was alive, she preferred to wait for him to drive her to one of the nearby malls, where he would sit and read a book while she shopped. "The one time Mom drove herself," Jane recalled, "was to meet with a small circle of friends for lunch once a week." Finally, when Sid died, Ellen had no idea exactly what was in their will, despite the fact that they had a lawyer friend draw up a joint will that both of them had signed. Fortunately, Sid had made provisions for that as well, having appointed that same law partner and close friend as executor.

"All us kids love Mom," said Jane. "She's a loving and thoughtful person. But she's also like a child in some ways. After Dad died, she needed us to do so much for her, and it was really frustrating and hard. My brother dropped out quickly, which left me and my sister to pick up the ball."

Jane thought it was very important for this book to address the problems that adult children have when one of their parents dies and the other parent is not used to taking care of things for himself or herself. Jane said that her mother is too young, too healthy, and too able-bodied to move to an assisted living facility, even though that would have made life easier for her and her sister. Instead, they got their heads together and decided to confront the issue of their mother's dependency.

"We made an appointment to meet her at her house for lunch. Then we sat down and laid our cards on the table. We explained that we did not want her to have to leave the house. At the same time, we did not want to continue having to do everything, from making sure she doesn't run out of heating oil in the winter to making sure that the cable or phone doesn't get cut off because she neglected to pay the bill."

Jane's solution was to hire a helper to take over some of the responsibilities that her father once handled, but whose goal was also to gradually teach Ellen how to do some of these things for herself. Jane recognizes that they are very fortunate in that Sid left Ellen with sufficient financial resources that she does not need to worry very much about money, even though the overall value of their investments and their home in Boston have decreased.

"Of course I still worry about Mom sometimes. I call her almost every day, just to check in. She doesn't complain, though I'm sure she

feels lonely at times. We all want her to be okay and we want her to be able to stay in the house. But we were also scared of her and the house becoming a burden for us. I don't worry about that so much now that we addressed the issue."

Jane said she hopes that her story will be instructive for people who need to help a parent become more self-sufficient. She wished that there were some kind of life-skills class that she could have sent her mother to after her father's death. "It felt so condescending in a way to try to parent my mother," she explained, "but we really had to teach her a lot that she'd never learned. I wish that my dad had made her do more, but that's the way he and Mom seemed to like it. And if he didn't like it, he never let on."

Would Jane and her sister have found a way to cope if they had not confronted their mother and found a way to address the issue of her dependency? We asked Jane. She replied that most likely they would have continued to take the path of least resistance and simply picked up where their father had left off. Sooner or later, though, she suspected that one or both of them could have chosen to gradually opt out of the picture, as their brother had. But this alternative would also likely have left both sisters harboring lingering feelings of both guilt (over "abandoning" Ellen) and resentment (over having to "parent" her) that could well have had an effect in the long run not only on their relationships with Ellen, but on their own families.

Our opinion is this: *Upheaval creates opportunities for resolution.* Jane and her sister chose to seize the moment and press for changes in the family dynamics. They risked offending their mother, who could have become indignant or decided to move into an assisted living facility. Instead, she heard her daughters out and complied with their request. A year later, she was more independent than she'd ever been.

Choosing Your Issues

Needless to say, it is neither feasible nor desirable to attempt to resolve every grievance we may have stored up over the years. On the other hand, the ongoing crisis your family finds itself in now does offer you the chance to pick one or perhaps two issues that have nagged at you and to make the kind of changes in your family dynamics that can put them to rest once and for all. Both Maggie and Jane did just that. Their stories illustrate how important it can be to sort through the various unresolved issues that may be on your mind and to choose wisely the one(s) to pursue. It can also be extremely helpful to have an ally at your side, as both Jane and Maggie did in their sisters.

This stage of the new grief is not the time to dredge up a litany of old grudges or complaints. Who among us could not come up with such a list if we really set our minds to it? As a guideline, we recommend choosing issues that directly bear on the role you've played in the family and that you would like to change in some way. That leaves out all those petty grievances that may populate the darker niches in our memories. If bringing them into the light of day would result in no meaningful impact on your role in the family, they may be better off staying where they are. One man, for example, had long found his father's continued smoking a source of irritation. When his father was diagnosed with lung cancer, this man was sorely tempted to vent his anger at his father. He thought better of it, however, and vented to his wife and friends instead. He chose not to say anything to his father because he concluded that expressing his feelings (again) at this point would result in no real change in his relationship with his father and would only make his father feel bad.

In a similar vein, a woman had long harbored anger at her father for having an extramarital affair when her mother was pregnant with her—a discovery she'd made when she inadvertently overheard her parents arguing when she was sixteen. Her mother, accusing her father of flirting with another woman at a wedding, brought it up. Her father had vehemently denied that he'd been flirting, but had also sounded profoundly sad. In this case, when this woman's father was diagnosed with a malignant and inoperable brain tumor, she opted not to bring up the issue with him, despite the fact that it had bothered her for many years. She had concluded that it would not significantly alter the father-daughter relationship. Her parents had decided to stay married, after all. Moreover, she knew her father loved her and that he was apparently remorseful for whatever it was he'd done.

The Importance of Trying

It is important to note that families often resist change. Like old habits, family dynamics are hard to break. Therefore, do not expect resolution and change to necessarily come easily. No matter how dysfunctional your family's dynamics may seem to you, they most likely crystallized long ago. It is reasonable under these circumstances to expect a family to attempt to block an individual from changing his or her role, not necessarily out of spite so much as inertia. That doesn't mean you shouldn't try.

The examples given earlier highlight how forming an *alliance* with someone in the system can help foster change. We know of many people, however, who have attempted to have end-of-life discussions, to resolve a conflict with a dying parent, or to change the family dynamics but who have been blocked from doing so— for example by a dying loved one who refuses to address an issue or by other family members who insist on maintaining control. We all have to acknowledge that it takes two to change and that if one party refuses to do so, the other party knows at least that he or she has tried to address an issue or make a change. Joy's story offers an example.

✒ *Joy's Story*

Joy was the youngest of three children. For as long as she could remember, her older sister, Maria, had taken on a parental role toward both her and her brother, James, who was the middle child and who'd never had many responsibilities placed on him. Joy loved both of her siblings, but ever since childhood she had felt that Maria was too bossy, while James got a free ride. For example, Maria would not hesitate to instruct Joy to empty the family dishwasher or put up a load of laundry, but James never seemed to be told to do anything. Joy recalled squabbling with Maria over this inequity at times, to no avail. Fortunately, Maria could also be warm and generous, which made up somewhat for her bossiness.

Joy and her family grew up in a comfortable middle-class, suburban community. They had their ups and downs—for instance, when Joy's father, an engineer, was briefly laid off from his job—but generally speaking, life went along smoothly. Joy's mother, Cindy, worked full-time as a licensed practical nurse in a nursing home (which was one reason that Maria had moved into a parental role), and although far from wealthy, the family wanted for nothing. They took annual summer vacations and rotated holidays among themselves and Cindy's two sisters.

Shortly after he retired, at age sixty-five, Joy's father suffered a heart attack. He survived and underwent emergency bypass surgery. After that, according to Joy, "He was never the same man he'd been." Many people who undergo cardiac bypass surgery suffer from depression after the surgery. Most eventually recover; Joy's father was one of the ones who don't. He became lethargic and sedentary. He became dependent on Cindy for everything, from cooking his meals to cleaning up after him to putting out his clothes for the day every morning before she left for work. He didn't want to venture beyond his own backyard. He lost interest in old hobbies, and he became generally irritable and pessimistic. At that point, he was a burden for Cindy, who had planned on working five more years but was finding herself torn between that plan and her husband's neediness.

Joy, Maria, and James all had families of their own by then. Joy was sympathetic to her mother's conflicted feelings. She also felt sorry for her father. She believed that, rather than retiring early, the best thing for Cindy to do would be to hire a home companion to stay with her father three or four hours a day while she continued to work. The companion could also do some of the light housework.

Joy's sister, Maria, thought otherwise. She wanted her parents to sell their house and move into an in-law apartment that she proposed to add to her home. Maria had three children and did not work. She believed that she could provide supervision for her father while Cindy was at work.

Joy really didn't think that her parents needed to leave the home that they had lived in for so many years. In addition, their friends all lived in the immediate area, whereas Maria lived more than half an hour away. Her father was depressed, but he did not require nursing care. Moreover, Joy thought that being isolated in a small in-law apartment might worsen her father's depression.

Joy talked to her brother and shared her concerns. James listened but was noncommittal when she asked him if he agreed. When she asked if he would be willing to meet with Maria to discuss the issue, he begged off, saying it really didn't matter that much to him one way or the other. In other words, Joy would have no ally if she decided to challenge Maria's plan.

Despite having to go it alone, Joy did ask to meet with her mother and sister to discuss Maria's plan. In that meeting, she laid out all of her thoughts about why it would be better to leave their parents where they were for now and to hire a companion. Maria's response was that it would be cheaper to add on an in-law apartment and have their parents move. "It's only a matter of time," she said, "before we will have to do this. So why not do it now?" Cindy listened. She had long ago come to rely on her oldest daughter's opinions, and she did not protest now.

Clearly, Joy was attempting to alter her role in the family, from the relatively passive and powerless one it had been when she was young to one in which, as an adult, she had greater decision-making authority. Having her parents move in with Maria would have been consistent with old family dynamics, in which Maria had much control.

In the end, Maria prevailed, and six months later her parents were living with her in an in-law apartment. Joy felt disappointed. However, she was consoled by the fact that she had voiced her opinion and made her case. She believed that Maria was advocating for what she thought was best for their parents. At that point there was nothing to do but agree to disagree and move on.

Guidelines for Change

Here are some lessons to be learned from Joy's and Jane's stories.

- Do not attempt to resolve too many issues at the same time. Rather, choose carefully from among the potential issues you would like to address or grievances you would like to remedy.

- Choose changes that relate directly to the role you play in the family's dynamics and try to move that role in the direction you would like it to go in.

- If possible, seek allies who agree with you and who will support your efforts.

- Show respect for the roles that others have played in the family. Give a voice to your opinions without coming across as though you are questioning the motives or intentions of others.

- Consider the possibility that you will not get the changes you seek or that you might get less than you'd hoped for. In that case, you still have not wasted your time because chances are you have already changed your role simply by asserting yourself.

✒ Bruce's Story

Bruce, a forty-eight-year-old attorney, described himself as "conflict avoidant." "I've always been a people pleaser," he said, and described himself as a placater and peacemaker in his family growing up. Ironically, when representing clients, Bruce could be quite assertive, though he said he was also always respectful, which had earned him a good reputation among the judges before whom he argued his cases.

Bruce had what he called a "very controlling" mother and a father who was rather submissive and who seemingly coped by working overtime as much as he could. Bruce had two older sisters, who often got into conflicts with their mother. In contrast, as the only son and youngest child, Bruce had taken on the role of making his mother happy. "I was the proverbial good boy," he said. He stayed close to home and to his mother. He never seriously dated until he had finished law school and passed the bar. By then he was well into his thirties.

When he was forty and finally living on his own, Bruce met and married a woman ten years his junior. He described Maria as smart, strong willed, and independent. As one might guess, Bruce's mother and his wife soon despised one another. The tension between them was so great whenever they were together that, when the opportunity presented itself, Bruce opted to take a position with a law firm that was located in a city a hundred miles away, just to avoid having his wife and mother spend much time together. He would make the hundred-mile drive to visit his family about every other month, but he and Maria would visit together only a couple of times a year.

Bruce's mother was diagnosed with end-stage breast cancer just after he'd turned forty-eight. By the time she went to the doctors and was diagnosed, the cancer had already spread to other parts of her body. She was told that chemotherapy was possible but that surgery was not a viable option. She called and told Bruce the news and then added that she wanted him to take a family medical leave and come home to be with her for the few months the doctors said she had left. Maria's response to this request was that Bruce's father should do this, not Bruce. He had his own family to take care of, she argued.

Bruce knew his wife was right. By this time they had three-year-old twin sons, and between the boys and his responsibilities as a partner in a law firm, there was no way Bruce could possibly comply with his mother's request without causing the rest of his life to become "a train wreck" as he put it. At the same time, he felt terribly guilty about not doing what his mother asked, and he was ambivalent. "One part of me knew that I couldn't just pick up, leave my family and my job, and spend who knew how long with my mother. But another part of me felt that I ought to—that I somehow owed it to her."

Bruce's ambivalence caused him to make the decision to drive to his parents' house every Saturday, spend the night there, and drive back the following morning. His father had stopped working as much as he had, but Bruce noted that he was still as passive as ever. To make matters worse, Bruce's mother continued to press him on each visit to take that extended leave from his job.

The conflict between Bruce and his wife that resulted from his decision to spend weekends with his mother led them to seek marriage counseling. Bruce had been in individual therapy for years when he was in his late twenties, and he credited that for enabling him to begin to date seriously, to leave home, and eventually to marry. However, dealing directly with his mother—and actually opposing her—had not occurred at the time. Instead, Bruce had used the

excuse of not wanting to put up with a long commute as a justifica-
tion for moving out and getting his own apartment. Then, once he
was out of his mother's sight, he was able to get on with his life.

The marriage counselor helped Bruce realize that he did need to
have the conversation he had always avoided with his mother. Over
several weeks, Bruce wrote a letter to his mother explaining that
while he deeply appreciated her devoted parenting, he was now an
adult with a primary loyalty to his wife and children. Moreover,
because he had already taken an extended family leave to be at
home with his wife and twin sons after they were born, he wrote, he
could not request a second family leave from the firm now. The bot-
tom line was that he would not leave his wife and children for an
extended period or even every other weekend, but that he would visit
as often as his other responsibilities would allow. Bruce read his fin-
ished letter to his wife and the counselor. Then he called his mother.

Apart from the issue of Bruce separating from his mother and
affirming his primary alliance to his own family, there was also
the issue of the animosity between his wife and his mother. Maria
fully understood the nature of her mother-in-law's illness and its
dire prognosis. Still, she felt that her husband had two sisters and
a father and that they could divide responsibilities among them. It
didn't all have to fall on Bruce.

That first visit after the phone call was enormously difficult for
Bruce. Despite the structured coaching he'd gotten through counsel-
ing, he felt himself wilting under his mother's ranting about his dis-
loyalty to her and his callousness in the face of her illness. Finally,
Bruce took his father aside and told him that he did not want his
mother to die with such bad feelings and that he needed his father's

help in talking with her. This conversation was a first: Bruce had never asked his father for help, and it had never occurred to his father to intervene on his son's behalf. His father reacted to the request with obvious discomfort; nevertheless, as events unfolded, it appeared that he rose to the occasion.

A week after he'd returned home, Bruce's father called and invited Bruce and his family over for Thanksgiving dinner. He said that everyone was coming and that he was having it catered.

This visit was very different from any other that Bruce could recall. His mother was pleasantly cordial to his wife, who, after her initial surprise, responded in kind. Everyone was indeed there, and the twins, being adorable, quickly took center stage. Bruce was a bit surprised at how affectionate and attentive his mother was to them. The talk focused on the children—Bruce's as well as his sisters'—and their future. At the end, hugs were given all around. "I don't know what my father did," said Bruce, "but it turned everything around."

Obviously, Bruce's father had intervened, and with surprising effect. Yet this happened only after Bruce had first set a limit on what he could do and then after they had that talk about Bruce needing his father's help. Subsequent visits were also tension free.

In the end, when Bruce's mother was admitted to a hospice (at her request), they took the twins to visit her. Maria was able to tell her mother-in-law how much she loved Bruce, what a great father and husband he was, and how she would always be there for him. While her mother-in-law never acknowledged her role in their conflict, which would have been nice for Bruce's wife to hear, no resentment lingered. She died peacefully, surrounded by family and holding her husband's hand.

Afterward, Bruce felt at peace with himself, accepting of what he'd done, and grateful to his wife for bringing him to counseling.

Bruce and his father went on to develop a closer relationship that added a new dimension to both their lives and that of Bruce's sons.

Bruce's story illustrates most of the guidelines described in this chapter. Naturally, not every story will have such a happy ending. Despite the fact that time may be running out on them, some terminally ill people are not open to hearing things they don't want to hear, to resolving conflicts, or to addressing issues, even though doing so could lead to serenity and greater peace of mind. Some, however, are. Again, it's important to remember that simply making an attempt to do one of these things during this upheaval stage is in itself significant for you.

STAGE 5

RENEWAL

Our love affair had lasted half a century and still goes on now, eight years after he died at the honorable age of one hundred. The love continues on my part, and on his side too, I believe. From where else could come the glad certainty every morning, evening, and hour of the day that I live in love and am charged with it—outgoing and incoming.

—HELEN NEARING

Chapter Seventeen

PLANNING FOR DEPARTURE

✔ Elise's Story

Elise, age fifty-eight, was aware she had symptoms of Alzheimer's disease even before she sought a medical consultation, and she suspected right off what was wrong. After her diagnosis, she told her husband and adult children that she was researching nursing care options and wanted to finalize arrangements before she was no longer able to do so. Her family wanted her to remain home so they could care for her, but ever independent and determined, Elise was adamant that her wishes be respected. If she waited too long, she knew that she might not be able to make that decision, and that her husband would balk at it.

Elise had seen her aunt progress through this disorder and was aware of the difficulties and burdens placed on her uncle and cousins. She never wavered in her plans, and after her placement, and as her disease progressed, her family was able to see the benefits. In a family therapy session held at the facility she chose, family members acknowledged their initial guilt and ambivalence about Elise's decision, and also their relief that she'd been so clear and certain about her decision. They felt her strength enabled them to deal with their grief more openly, and they refused to let others' judgments discourage them.

As they move into the final stage of the new grief, renewal, the family has worked its way through the crisis created by a terminal diagnosis. They've pulled together and marshaled resources to do what needed to be done. They've experienced the upheaval that a prolonged crisis creates. And also, we sincerely hope they have taken advantage of the opportunity to confront and resolve some unfinished business from the past and even assessed and, if needed, made some changes in the roles they play within the family's dynamics.

Making Choices

Elise made some choices and her family supported her. Fortunately, she had the resources that enabled her to make those choices. Not everyone does. Regardless of what resources the family has, however, the issue that we face as life's end approaches is the need to make some decisions. We also need to feel that we have the support of those who love us in making those decisions.

The process of planning for our departure does not have to be difficult. Elise did it by taking the bull by the horns: She faced her diagnosis, accepted her prognosis, and told her loved ones what she intended to do. There are others, though—both those who are terminally ill and their loved ones—who shrink from this task. Even today, talking or thinking about death is largely avoided in our culture, which prefers to focus on life extension, achievement, and preserving physical attractiveness. Many people no longer regard death as a natural part of the life process. One tragic consequence of this reticence is that our hospitals are increasingly turning into warehouses for those near death, where they linger and languish for lack of effective communication or planning.

According to a recent Harvard Medical School study, no more than half of terminally ill patients and their families say they have been able to talk about hospice or other end-of-life options. The study also noted that even fewer Latinos and African Americans discuss such issues. Even though the technology to extend life may justify delaying the conversation, we encourage patients and their families to begin the dialogue early, when a diagnosis that is terminal or potentially terminal is first confirmed. As much as we might wish families to do this, we recognize that the conversation often does not begin until the last stage of grief and often not until the end is in sight.

✒ Isabel's Story

Thirty years ago, Isabel, at age forty, was in an ICU dying of leukemia. She told her closest friend, who visited her daily, that she wished she could go home. When this friend discussed this possibility with Isabel's family, they were very resistant. They did not know

how they could manage, they said, and they were frank in admitting
that they found the responsibility intimidating and overwhelming.
They knew nothing about home care and did not even know whom to
ask for information about what kind of support Isabel might need or
be entitled to.

Isabel died, alone, her friend told us, in the hospital two nights later. Today, Isabel might have had the following choices:

- She could choose to die at home with hospice care.

- She could live her final days in a hospice.

- She could go to a palliative care unit of a hospital.

Today Isabel could choose with whom she wanted to spend her last hours, and her family would be more likely to have access to caring professionals skilled in home care and pain management as well as in emotional and spiritual end-of-life concerns. Today she would be more likely to be able to retain personal dignity and some degree of control, which would certainly have enhanced the quality of the dying process for her.

Isabel today would have more options because advances in medical technology have succeeded in making sudden death the exception and replaced it with a more or less prolonged process of decline leading to death. Along with the medical advances have come the emergence of supportive programs such as hospice, home healthcare, and palliative care units. Similarly, assisted living communities have emerged in response to our ability to extend life. Isabel could have these things, though, only if those closest to her were willing to engage in this conversation.

Starting the Conversation

All it takes to initiate an end-of-life dialogue within the family is for one person to speak up and ask other family members what their fears and hopes are about the immediate and long-range outcomes of the illness. There is no reason why this cannot happen at the outset, at the crisis stage. For most families, however, it usually starts somewhat later. Again, it may simply be our discomfort about openly talking about death that stands in the way of our taking this first step.

Once it becomes clear that life extension is no longer feasible (or desirable from the patient's point of view), and that death is therefore inevitable, this dialogue becomes even more important. Key questions that family members should first ask themselves, and then share with others, include the following:

- What scenario do you fear the most?

- What would be your idea of a good ending, recognizing that it must include the death of your loved one?

- If there are children in the family, who has spoken with them about terminal illness and death and what will they be told from here on out?

- How will the terminally ill loved one's end-of-life wishes and decisions be made known to everyone in the family?

We have known of families who called a family meeting to address these issues. In the best of circumstances, certain ground rules apply in these family meetings. First, family members are encouraged to speak their mind freely while everyone else listens. They share how they are feeling, what concerns they have, and what alternatives they have thought about for dealing with those concerns. If differences emerge (which is likely), they are respected, without judgment or criticism.

Next, family members together work on solving the problems and issues they've identified. Some people may offer suggestions, for example, about talking to children or volunteer to help do so. In one family, a sister offered to be with her brother when he told his two preteens that their grandfather's cancer had returned and that he was expected to live for only a few months. Another family set up a visitation schedule at hospice so that they could take care of their own families while knowing that a dying sibling would not be alone.

In addition to the family having an opportunity to think about and share their thoughts about end-of-life issues, the family can use such a meeting to discuss the dying person's final wishes, whether and how they can be met, and who will take responsibility for what. Obviously, to do this the patient must participate by making his or her wishes known.

The patient should be informed about the family meeting. If the patient wants to be part of that meeting, so be it. In any case, it is important that the ill person know that his or her wishes have been heard and respected, and that he or she will not be kept in the dark about who will be doing what. Often the terminally ill are concerned that they are a burden, and knowing that the family is working together can be a great relief.

In regard to end-of-life issues, our rule of thumb is: *Let the person with the illness have control as much as possible.* This means listening to what he or she has to say and respecting his or her wishes and decisions as long as these are feasible. Many people with terminal illness say that what upsets them the most is when they can't talk about their feelings and be heard, or share decisions they've made about how they want their life to end because one or more family members don't want them to do it that way. "It just seems to scare the hell out of them," one man complained. "Every time I try to talk about how I want things to end, they change the damned subject!" Whenever he wanted to talk about how he wanted his funeral to be arranged, for example, his two adult children would quickly hush him by saying something like: "Now let's not think that way. You're going to be around for a long time." "How do they know how long I'll be around?" he retorted in irritation. "So I finally decided to just write my plans down and put it in an envelope and tell them where it is."

What You Need to Know

The dying man's frustrations just recounted are all too common. Although we can understand that end-of-life conversations can be uncomfortable, it's easy to see how avoiding them can complicate things and create problems later on, as family members step in to make decisions and try to guess what their deceased loved one would have wanted. As Isabel's story shows, they may also allow their own anxieties to determine the nature of their loved one's last days, as opposed to the wishes of that loved one.

Here is what the family needs to know about their loved one's end-of-life wishes. The answers must come from the terminally ill person, not from other family members.

- Where do you want to die? Would you want to be at home in your own bed? In a hospital? In a hospice setting?

- What, if any, means do you want medical staff to use to extend your life? Which is more important to you: quality of life or extending life by any means?

- Do you want to sign a do not resuscitate (DNR) order in the event your heart stops?

- Have you signed a living will and a healthcare power of attorney? Who is authorized to make medical decisions in the event that you cannot?

- Who do you want to be with you at the end? Is he or she aware of this? Is there anyone you do not want to be there?

- Have you made funeral arrangements? Are these written? How can they be accessed?

- Have you finalized your will? Does it include instructions for how you will dispose of your most valued possessions?

Some people have told us that one reason they hesitated to have a discussion of end-of-life issues is superstition: On some level they believe that talking about death might make it come true. Since superstitions can never be disproved, they are impossible to challenge. Clearly, however, we have not seen any evidence to suggest that this is true. On the contrary, many people who have taken the time to make arrangements sometimes do not find themselves confronted with that moment for a long time, as in John's story.

✿ *John's Story*

John, fifty-one and dying of leukemia, had not only made his end-of-life decisions and requests clear and in writing but he had stock-piled pills after having researched the proper (that is, lethal) amount to take in the event he did not want to prolong his life. He kept these in a locked box on a shelf in a closet. His rationale was that he wanted to be the one to decide when to stop draining his assets and causing his family stress, particularly if he faced the prospect of going to a nursing home. He had other ideas about where he wanted his money to go, which included his children and grandchildren. His wife, Fran, was the only one who was aware of John's plan. His doctors believed that John had been taking all of his medications as prescribed.

Whenever John told Fran that he was thinking that he might not want to continue with his cancer treatments, she replied, "You will have to be the one to decide, but speaking for myself, there is always hope. No one's talking about a nursing home yet." This same scene was repeated several times over a period of two and a half years. During that time, John remained at home. Medical insurance paid for his treatment, and his resources were not unduly drained. He and Fran continued to enjoy life within the constraints of his illness. They went out on occasion for Sunday brunch, took in a movie now and then (their former favorite dating activity), and even went away once for the weekend. They let their children take over the responsibility for hosting holiday gatherings, and took on the roles of guests and doting grandparents.

John eventually requested hospice care, but he was only there for a few weeks before he passed. He made that decision when he concluded that his care was just too much work for Fran, and after coming to the conclusion that he would not be in hospice for long. As per his request, his family took turns being with him, so that they could go on with their own busy lives. The whole group was summoned to his bedside only when the end was near. Meanwhile, he'd instructed Fran to dispose of his stash of pills.

Was John suicidal? That's doubtful. Rather, his behavior—from making careful end-of-life plans to stockpiling medications as a means of making a quick exit—reflect a man who wanted to be in control of his life even as it neared its end. When he made the decision to enter the hospice, he apparently felt that he was still in charge and had made his final decision about where and how he would die. His ability to stay in control may even have helped extend John's life. A similar decision was made by the writer Scott Nearing, who decided to stop eating and to drink only water after he turned one hundred.

Robert's story is another example of why the terminally ill need to be encouraged to maintain control of what happens to them as death nears.

🖋 Robert's Story

Robert, age forty-four, decided that he did not want to continue with the experimental treatment he'd been receiving, because the side effects of this treatment were too difficult and severely impacted the quality of his living. His physician and parents tried to dissuade Robert from this decision. However, Robert's partner, Martin, was his primary caretaker. He and Robert had granted one another durable power of attorney as well as authority to make medical decisions on each other's behalf. They had written wills as well as living wills.

Martin understood Robert's agony, having lived with it every day for more than a year. Martin assured Robert that he would respect his wishes. Having the legal status to make decisions, he supported Robert's wishes and took leave from his work to provide care at home with some assistance from home healthcare aids and visiting nurses until the end. Robert's parents, who had never accepted Robert's homosexuality, hired a lawyer to contest Martin's rights, but the legal documents Robert had signed were airtight, and Robert died in Martin's arms surrounded by his family of choice—his close friends and an older sister.

As families near the end, it is important to review previous decisions and plans. It may have been some time since plans were discussed such as end-of-life wishes and funeral and burial choices. Difficult though it may be, it is important that someone in the family inquire whether there have been any changes or further thoughts the dying loved one has about:

- Any issues relative to his or her estate or intentions regarding gifts.

- Wishes regarding the type of funeral and burial (cremation, entombment, military, earth burial, body/organ donation, embalming).

- Type of service, who will officiate, where it will be, who will speak, and what music and/or recitations will be included.

Another consequence of medical life extension is that more and more individuals are preparing for their funeral in advance. One woman told us the story of how her parents, who were both in their eighties, had summoned her and her younger brother to a Sunday family meeting over coffee and pastries. They sat down around the kitchen table and then the woman's parents proceeded to go over in detail their respective plans for burial. They had written these down and gave each child a copy. The plans were comprehensive. Her parents, this woman learned, had already purchased a burial plot and even had a stone carved with their names and birth dates. All that would have to be added were the dates of their deaths. Each parent had also made out a list of what clothes they wanted to be buried in, where the service should take place, how they wanted it to go, and so on. They had set aside funds to cover all the costs, including the cost of postburial celebrations in their honor. These parents wanted to be sure that whoever survived would have ample help from their children, who would be well informed about what to do. According to the woman telling the story, "When my father first handed us these binders with all this information in it and I realized that he and my mother were going to tell us about their funeral plans, I felt my heart sink and I squirmed in my seat. But after it was over, I felt grateful to them for doing that. It made things a lot easier for me and my brother. All we would have to do is follow the instructions."

The Good Death

We recognize that the concept of a good death may be controversial, and some readers may object to the idea that any death is truly good. That notwithstanding, we have heard many stories—a number of which we have shared here—and we have concluded that some people definitely do meet death on better terms than others. These are men and women who, like Robert and John, at least experienced a degree of control, right to the end. They had made preparations and were able to make key decisions. Perhaps most important, they had established a pattern of open communication with their loved ones.

In her study of a good death, Julia Neuberger lists several defining characteristics:

- Knowing when it is coming and understanding what can be expected.

- Retaining control.

- Being afforded dignity and privacy.

- Having control over pain relief and other symptoms.

- Having control where one dies.

- Having access to emotional and spiritual support.

- Having access to information and required professional expertise.

- Having access to hospice care.

- Having control over who is present and who shares the end of one's life.

- Having the opportunity to issue advanced directives to be sure that your wishes are respected.

- Having the time and opportunity to say goodbye to loved ones and control over other aspects of dying.

- To be able to leave when it is time to go and not have your life prolonged pointlessly.

Many of the items on this list have no cost associated with them. It does not cost anything, for example, to be able to determine who we would like to be with at the time of our passing. Similarly, it costs little if anything to sign a living will, which is a fairly simple legal document that is widely available in generic form.

At the time these words are being written, however, the American healthcare system, despite recent reforms, still remains fractured. There are wide disparities among people with respect to what level of medical care they have access to. Not every citizen has the right, for example, to choose to enter a hospice. Not all medical treatments are available to all citizens. Therefore, in reviewing these criteria for a good death, families may have to consider them to be a desirable but not necessarily completely obtainable goal.

✎ Susan's Story

Susan was taken home from the hospice at her request three days before she died. The hospice nurse showed her family how to administer oral morphine and instructed someone to be with her at all times. The whole family gathered together, and the adults took turns administering the medicine, rubbing Susan's feet, talking to her, and caressing her. She was particularly interested in hearing her grandchildren, who periodically ran into the room and told her about what they were doing that summer. The youngest of them would gently climb onto the bed to hug and kiss Grandma.

On the third night, Susan hugged and kissed everyone good night. It was clear she was saying goodbye. Her husband stayed with her, and awoke in the middle of the night because the oxygen machine had ceased operating. He was pleased to find that he was still holding her hand and was curled up beside her.

This is one of the best examples we have heard of what might be called a good death.

Internet Resources

The Internet has given rise to a growing online community where individuals can seek both information and support on virtually any issue, including terminal illnesses. Two websites that facilitate the kinds of discussions we have been addressing in this chapter are Facing Death with Love (www.facingdeathwithlove .com) and Engage with Grace (www.engagewithgrace.org). No doubt additional sites will appear in the future. We encourage family members to use the Internet to better understand the nature of their loved one's illness, to understand treatment alternatives along with their prognoses and consequences, and to find support from others who share their circumstances.

✿ Theresa's Story

"My dad went to one of the best cancer treatment facilities in the Boston area," Theresa explained, *"but my impression was that once they realized they couldn't use him as a subject in one of their studies, they just dropped him."*

As an EMT, Theresa likely had more awareness of her father's medical issues than the average person and she found the bedside manner of some of his physicians to be lacking. She said that this is something that she'd seen as a result of working with emergency department (ED) physicians and nurses on a daily basis. She understood how working in that setting could eventually lead to a degree of detachment. After all, emergencies did not always turn out well. She'd seen staff suffer emotionally as a result of getting involved with the people they treated in the emergency room. They even had a name for it: ED burnout.

But Theresa was less sympathetic to some of her father's physicians. "I know that some surgeons and physicians are just full of themselves, so it was something I was able to help my dad deal with. We were also lucky to get some terrific nurses who cared for him. But I definitely think it would be really hard for someone who is not exposed to these kinds of people to cope with. I mean, you're there for help, and this person who's supposed to be helping you is being really cold and clinical. It's really unsettling. If I weren't there with him, I just know my father would have felt terrible."

Theresa strongly recommended that family members learn as much as they can about their loved one's disease or illness so as to be informed about any medical recommendations that are made. She felt that when physicians use medical jargon, many people get intimidated and overwhelmed. Being able to talk to family members who can research information and share information is one way around this issue.

Theresa also cautioned family members to be aware of what the risks are of participating in drug trials and studies through the hospitals where their loved one is getting treatment. "Those studies are important," she acknowledged, "but in my opinion the doctors who are conducting them have a conflict of interest. On the one hand, they do want to help; but on the other hand, they need subjects for their research."

"My dad lived a long time for someone with his type of cancer," said Theresa, "and they wanted to use him in more studies. But when he took a turn for the worse, all of the ancillary resources, like the psychological care he'd been getting by meeting with a staff psychologist once every two weeks, suddenly disappeared. It felt like once his doctors decided he could no longer participate, they just dropped him. Then I found out that these services had been funded by a research grant. They weren't part of my dad's health insurance plan.

"In the end my dad was bounced around between two hospitals, and I know it was disruptive for him and stressful for me. Families need to know that this can happen. It's not like you have one doctor for all of the treatment all the time. I think it's important for people to be prepared for this."

Based on her dad's experience, Theresa said it would be a good idea for families to supplement medical care with consistent psychological care for both the patient and the family members to help them through difficult decisions and in coping with the eventual loss of their loved one. She believed that any counselor chosen should have experience working with families in this situation. Theresa herself did not have difficulty asking for help from her friends and from medical and psychological providers. She said that this was very important to her, and she is grateful to have a trusted counselor and such good friends.

"It's important to take care of yourself," she explained, "to try to eat well, get sleep, and exercise while you are going through it all. Yoga, therapy, and friends really saved me. There were times when I felt guilty for doing these things while my dad was in the hospital, but I knew from the work I do that I needed to take care of myself."

Chapter Eighteen

CELEBRATING
A LIFE

⚰ Debbie's Story

"There is no pain like losing a child," said Debbie. "You wish you could have died in their place. It is the most terrible experience in life."

Debbie, who is now sixty, lost her daughter, Rose, to leukemia when Rose was just six years old. She had been Debbie's first child. She has had three other children since Rose died, and she believes that she and her husband, Tom, had them in part because they believed that if they had more than one child then they would never again have to experience what they went through when they lost their first daughter. "I know that sounds like a silly superstition," she explained, "and we never discussed it. But looking back on it, I think that on some level we believed that."

"Losing Rose was the most painful experience of my life. For years afterward I worried that my other children would feel like they lived with a ghost, because she died before they were born. When people would ask me how many children I had, I would respond by saying 'I had four, but only three are living'. I would say this even when my other children were present. Yet I resisted talking to them about Rose or her illness. I think that only mothers who have lost children could possibly understand this kind of loss."

Debbie discussed how due to her being a physician and her husband having a doctorate in biomedical engineering, they felt that they would somehow be able to help their daughter more than parents who did not have such backgrounds. "What fools we were! How absurd to think that we could save Rose ourselves! For some reason our education and credentials actually made it worse, knowing that we could not save Rose, but that I could go to work and help other children and my husband could work on ways to help amputees learn to jog. It was the most helpless feeling on earth: to be able to help another mother's child yet not be able to help my own."

Debbie said that losing Rose initially made her and Tom scared to have another child, and they hesitated for several years. Then, after they did take that step, they found themselves being very worried anytime a child became ill, had a stomachache, or even said they felt tired. Debbie also explained that less was known about Rose's leukemia twenty-nine years ago. "Ironically, had we known about the chance that one of our other children could contract leukemia due to the genetic links we now know about, that might have been enough to deter us altogether from having more children. But what a loss that would have been!"

Debbie experienced a tremendous amount of guilt and self-hatred over her inability to cure her daughter or even to help her sometimes when she was in pain. "It was so hard to talk to her about her illness and what its repercussions might be. This was my child, she was my responsibility, but I could do nothing to save her. Tom and I ended up just telling her that she was very ill and that everyone was doing as much as they could to make her better. I believe that on some level Rose knew that she was dying, but she and I never actually had that conversation. I don't know if it would have made a difference."

While Debbie remains somewhat cynical about her ability to help her own children with greater ease due to her medical background, she does believe that having a familiarity with the disease and what its treatment would entail was a benefit as Rose's illness progressed. "As awful as it was, I suppose it would have been worse to not know what was coming." She now recommends that parents educate themselves about any serious illness—terminal or not—that their children might have, and she directs them to resources for doing this. She is also a firm believer that parents who are facing the terminal illness of a child seek support immediately.

"There really were no support groups available back then. We grieved alone. At the end of each day we were all alone. That was the loneliest time of my life. I knew Tom was experiencing the same pain that I was, but we could hardly take care of ourselves let alone each other. It's amazing that we even stayed together after Rose died."

Shortly after Debbie and Tom's second child—also a daughter, Rachel—turned seven, she came over to Debbie, sat down on her lap, and said that she wanted to know about Rose. "For a moment I was breathless," Debbie said. "Then Rachel simply explained, in that calm, clear voice she's always had, that she often gazed at one of the few photos of Rose that we kept in the house. 'She was so pretty,'

*Rachel said. 'I want to know about her. Like what she liked to do,
whether she liked to draw like I do, and when was her birthday.'"*

*"I told Rachel that Rose's birthday was only a month away, and
that she'd been six when she died from an illness called leukemia.
Rachel said she'd heard of leukemia, and she even knew a girl who'd
been treated for it. I had no idea she would know such a person."*

*The next day Rachel approached her parents as they were sitting
on the deck enjoying an after-dinner glass of wine. She told them
that she and her siblings had had a meeting. "We want to have a
party to celebrate Rose's birthday," Rachel said. "We want to have
one every year. Just us."*

Tom and Debbie had grieved their daughter's loss, of course.
They had even tried to replace her—three times over. But the one
thing they had never done was to celebrate her life. When talking
about Rachel's desire to celebrate her dead sister's life, Debbie
thought it was important for parents to understand that while the
pain they feel over their loss may never fully dissipate, the experience of celebrating a child's life, however short it may have been,
can go a long way to balance their grief.

*Together Debbie and Rachel came up with a simple tradition that
the family then celebrated every year on Rose's birthday. The tradition was simple but poignant. Each year Rachel would go with Debbie and order a birthday cake—decorated, of course, with roses. The
family would share the cake, and Tom and Debbie would tell a couple of stories about Rose. One year Tom told a story about taking
Rose sledding when she was five and how the two of them had gone
so fast that their sled toppled, sending them rolling across the snow-
covered slope. Everyone laughed.*

After the cake was eaten and the stories were told, each child would get a small gift—from Rose.

Balancing Grief with Celebration

We have come to believe that the path to family renewal involves being able to strike a balance between grieving and celebrating the life of the person we have lost. The loss of that person creates a vacuum—a hole in the family that needs to be filled. Debbie's family was able to fill this hole thanks to her daughter Rachel's desire to learn more about the sister she'd never known and, in a sense, to bring Rose back into the family, even if her presence was only in the form of memories and a family ritual. Jay is someone else who found a way to fill that hole and move on.

✹ *Jay's Story*

Jay was ten when his father, Jim, was diagnosed with colon cancer, and he was thirteen when Jim died. This family, which also included an older sister, Cristina, and their mother, Lucia, had always been a cohesive and active unit, but father and son had an especially close bond. They went skiing, fishing, and hiking together on a regular basis and loved nothing better than being outdoors together. One of the activities the family liked to do together was go skiing in Vermont several times every winter.

Jim had always been a hale and hardy type, and his deterioration after his diagnosis, though steady, was not quick. Treatments would leave him drained for a day, but then he would seemingly bounce back, at least during the first two years. Though everyone was aware of the cancer, it wasn't a focus of discussion; Jay in particular avoided the subject.

In an effort to provide a project for her husband and son, Lucia suggested that they collaborate on finding a second home in Vermont that the family could use as a base of operations on weekends and school vacations. This was something they'd all talked about at times. Cristina, who was eighteen at the time and about to head off to college, said she would have preferred at that point that the family look for a house on the beach, but she raised no strong objections and left her father and brother to their pursuit.

The search for a suitable second home soon proved to be more of an elaborate exercise for Jim and Jay than a true hunt for a vacation home, though no one openly acknowledged that fact. Every week they would search the Internet real estate listings, looking for houses that met their criteria: being close to water (for fishing), having ample property (for hiking), and being close to ski areas. Every weekend, father and son would go over that week's accumulation of prospective properties. Then, as Lucia described it, "They would successively eliminate each and every one based on its not meeting one or more criteria. It became a ritual between them. They continued it even after it became more and more apparent that Jim did not have the stamina to be active in any of these activities."

On the family's last winter ski weekend together, Jim remained in the lodge while the rest of the family hit the slopes. Lucia described Jim as a man who was not given to self-pity and who did not seek a lot of attention. Instead, he expressed keen interest in Jay's and Cristina's experiences on the slopes.

Jim died in September, at age fifty. The next February, over Jay's winter vacation, Lucia suggested that they pick up on the search for a second home in Vermont—this time for real. Jay demurred, saying he was no longer interested. He had taken his father's death hard. "The hardest of all of us, I think," said Lucia.

Jay was very depressed, Lucia remembered, and his grades in school had declined. She was very worried about him. For her part, Cristina, who was then away at college, seemed to want to avoid grieving. "She didn't have time for it," Lucia explained. "Instead, she got involved in the church."

As April approached and another vacation was close at hand, Lucia again brought up the idea of looking for a place in Vermont with Jay. "I told him we should fulfill his father's dream," Lucia explained, "and that seemed to strike a chord in him." This time Jay, who had started seeing a counselor in February, agreed to help.

Lucia and Jay picked up where Jay and Jim had left off. Each week they'd each scour the online real estate listings. As before, however, they found few properties that came close to meeting all their criteria—and they'd agreed that anything the family bought would have to meet all the criteria.

Then one Sunday, Jay came downstairs after doing a computer search on his laptop. He was holding a piece of paper. He found Lucia sitting at the kitchen table, looking at a real estate listing she'd just printed out. "Then Jay handed me his printout, and it was the same as mine!" Lucia said. "That felt really freaky, but we both knew we'd have to check it out."

Jay and Lucia spent two days visiting available Vermont properties along with a local realtor. They saved the listing they'd both printed out for last. "As soon as we saw it, I could tell we both knew that it met the criteria," Lucia told us. "It was located on over a hundred acres of land that bordered a large lake. In addition, there were several other large lakes close by. About half of the land had been cleared, which made it great for snowmobiling. And last but not least, two major ski areas were less than an hour away."

"The only thing wrong with it," Lucia explained, "was that the house was a wreck." The former owner—a widow, the realtor explained—had died two years earlier, and in that time the family had not maintained it. After making some money by selling the logging rights, they put it up for sale. Probably because the house had become "a hovel," as Lucia described it, no offers had been made.

Then Lucia described the defining moment. "Jay and I climbed to the top of a rise that overlooked the house and the lake. Jay stared out for a minute then he turned to me and said, 'Mom, we have to buy this place.' He was very firm. After seeing the inside of that house, I wasn't so sure. So I asked him why he thought that. And he said, 'Mom, that house is just like our family—it's torn apart. We need to buy it and put it back together.'"

So Lucia bought the house. They had a sign made that read "Healing Acres," and over the next several years they oversaw the repairs. One of the best things about this, according to Lucia, was that Jay participated in the process. "We spent time finding local craftsmen with good references, whom we could trust, and Jay would work with them all the time. I think it did a lot for him: digging holes to pour concrete for supports, nailing down decking, repairing and painting walls. The more he worked on the house, the better he got. At some point I stopped losing sleep over him."

Lucia thought it was very important for others to know two things from her and Jay's experience.

- First, when a child loses a same-sex parent, it can be enormously helpful if he or she can establish one or more good relationships with same-sex adults. The craftsmen with whom Jay worked could not replace his father by any means; still, they were men with whom he could work shoulder to shoulder. They liked Jay for his personality and his work ethic, and they took him under their wing.

- The second point that Lucia made was that she now realizes that her son was left with "a hole in him" when his father died. If he had not found a way to fill that hole somehow—in this case, by repairing a house that had been torn apart—she wonders if he'd be doing as well as he is now, eight years later.

Striking a Balance

We do not believe that grief necessarily ever heals completely. The closer we are to the loved one we lose, the more likely it is that we will carry with us an emotional scar. Like physical scars, the scar of grief may fade with time, but it will always be there. Grief, after all, is a crisis of identity as much as it is a crisis of attachment and separation. We are defined in part by our attachments. Who are we, therefore, as individuals and as a family, without this family member? How much is each of us like this person? What will the family dynamics look like in the aftermath of this loss?

Part of celebrating a life is to recognize the ways in which it lives on: how our loved one has influenced us, and what parts of their personality live on in us. One man, in speaking at his father's memorial service, began his comments with a remark about how his father had been an intensely stubborn and frugal man. "You could say that my father was cheap and uncompromising," he said. Looking out on those assembled for the funeral, he could see a few faces tighten, and a few people shifted uncomfortably in their chairs. Then he said, "And I'm just like him, thank God!" The audience cracked up.

✿ Judy's Story

Judy, who lost her sister, Lynne, in a car accident when she was twenty and Lynne was twenty-four, established a tradition to celebrate her sister's life. "Lynne was my best friend," said Judy. "When she died, at first I thought I would just never stop crying."

Shy by temperament, Judy credited Lynne with helping to bring Judy out of her shell. "We'd go dancing together," Judy explained. "At first I didn't want to go, but she pushed me just enough that I did it. And we had so much fun! My sister was a scream. She was smart and funny and pretty. Everyone was drawn to her. She could light up a room. I like to think that just a little of her personality rubbed off on me."

It took Judy a full two years to reach the point where she could get through a day without having tears in her eyes at least once. A school administrator, Judy came from a family where feeling sorry for yourself was not allowed. Just as her sister had pushed her to overcome her shyness, their father had impressed on both his daughters the importance of being able to take care of oneself, of avoiding self-pity, and of persevering in the face of adversity. Therefore, even though she might cry every day, Judy pressed on with her career. "No one suspected," she explained with a laugh, "that I would go into my office after a meeting, close the door, and cry for five minutes. They would have been absolutely shocked!"

Each year on Lynne's birthday, Judy repeated the same ritual. First, she would stop by a florist shop after work and purchase two white roses, white roses being Lynne's favorite. She would then drive to the cemetery where Lynne was buried and place the roses on her grave. She would stand there for ten or fifteen minutes or so and talk to Lynne. "Usually I just fill her in on what happened in my life the past year. When she was alive, we would talk to each other several times a day, even after Lynne moved out and got her own place. We would tell each other everything."

After she was finished filling Lynne in on the goings-on in her life, Judy would visit one of the restaurants that had been on their list of haunts. "Lynne loved to eat at the bar of a good restaurant. We'd sit there and joke with the bartender, talk to each other, and kid around with anyone else who happened to be at the bar. Some restaurants have bars that are really good for that, and we knew them all."

Judy still sits at the bar on these occasions. She orders a beer and a salad. She still jokes with the bartender, and chats with the other patrons. Then she goes home. "I don't cry anymore," Judy said. "I just really feel close to Lynne on her birthdays."

As much as grief may never totally heal, there is no need for it to cripple us, or to take all the joy out of life. This idea is succinctly captured in the following ancient Chinese saying:

We cannot help the birds of sadness flying over our heads,
But we need not let them build nests in our hair.

The stories you have just read illustrate how it is possible if not to eliminate grief then at least to ameliorate it by balancing the sense of loss with the celebration of the life of our loved one. One way of doing this, as reflected in Judy's story, is to think about what part of our deceased loved one's personality or temperament lives on within us and to recognize and honor that part we share.

Including the Deceased in the Conversation

Many people have commented to us that others seem to avoid talking about the deceased loved one, as if he or she never existed. Some widows and widowers have said that after an initial period in which couples they knew and socialized with were supportive, they begin to feel shut out. "Some couples just don't seem to know how to relate to someone who is no longer part of a couple," said one woman whose husband had died of a heart attack after a year of treatment for cancer. This particular woman was of the opinion that she might represent a threat to a couple of her married women friends now that she was single. Others, she said, would ask her over, but would get obviously uncomfortable whenever she mentioned her husband. "They'll never bring him up in conversation," she said. "And that makes for a very uncomfortable situation, considering that I think about him and talk to him in my mind all the time."

Sometimes it is necessary for us to face the fact that we need to reach out and make new friends after the death of our loved one. Sometimes this is because others we've known have come to think of us less as an individual and more as part of a couple. This tends to be true for younger people. In contrast, older couples are more likely to have come to terms with the death of a partner and are more accepting of it. The reality is that the number of widowed Americans is increasing and will continue to increase as the baby boomer generation ages.

One strategy that seems to have worked for some people who have lost their partner is to take on the role of host. In addition, we have been told that it is often better to invite several people over for dinner or to watch the Super Bowl or a World Series game, for example. In such circumstances, if the subject of the departed loved one comes up, it seems to be less awkward.

More uncomfortable, according to people we have spoken with, is a situation in which it is not friends who avoid bringing up a deceased loved one in conversation, but other immediate family members. The MacDonald family was an example of this.

✿ Angela's Story

After her husband Michael died, Angela found that her grown children, two daughters and a son, suddenly seemed to want to avoid talking about him. When she would bring up his name in their company, one of them would immediately change the subject. Angela found this irritating, but not wanting to cause too much of a stir, she avoided a confrontation over the matter. In her mind, she thought that they might get over their discomfort after a while and that it would then be safe to talk about Michael again.

When six months had gone by and nothing had changed, Angela finally had had enough. She decided to take action. She knew the whole family was aware that Michael had wanted his ashes to be dispersed at sea off the coast of Ireland. He'd spoken about this several times over the years, beginning long before he was diagnosed. His parents had immigrated to the United States when he was seven, and Michael held some fond memories of his early years in Ireland and the family he'd known there. After Michael's death, though, no one brought the issue up, just like they didn't bring the subject of Michael up. But Angela had other plans.

Michael had left Angela with a significant life insurance policy as well as a pension. They had also been a frugal couple, so there were some significant savings. Thus Angela invited the three children and their families out for Sunday brunch, ostensibly to celebrate her birthday. When they had all sat down, she told them the news: She was making plans for a family trip to Ireland. All she needed from the family was a commitment to one week some time in the next six months. "We're going to scatter Dad's ashes at sea," she said, "and then we're going to see some of Ireland and visit some family." Her children looked at one another. Then Angela's oldest granddaughter, Makenna, age eleven, piped up. "Wow!" she said, "that sounds super!"

Angela pulled off Michael's dream. She, her three children, their spouses, and five grandchildren all traveled to Ireland during the kids' spring vacation. She completed all the necessary paperwork to bring Michael's remains along (he had dual citizenship), chartered a boat, and sailed with the family out to sea. While the boat cruised, each member of the family told a story about Michael, and when they were finished, his ashes, wrapped in linen and tied with satin ribbons, were set into a basket and placed on the water. They watched as the basket slowly filled with water and sank into the sea.

Then they spent a week together, touring Ireland, celebrating Michael's past, and getting in touch with that part of their shared heritage.

Loose Ends

Earlier in this book we wrote about taking care of business, meaning the necessary legal and other paperwork that needs to be attended to in order to avoid having treatment and end-of-life issues become a confusing mess. The more these things—wills, trusts, living wills, powers of attorney, and so on—are taken care of in advance, the fewer loose ends there will be later. Preparation makes terminal illness that much less of a crisis for the entire family at the same time that it allows the patient to be the one who controls how life ends. That said, after a loved one dies, there are still a number of loose ends that need to be tended to.

We hope that the details for burial of your loved one were worked out well in advance. Someone must attest to the actual death; typically, if the death occurs at home, it is the hospice nurse or the attending physician who does this. If organ donation has been approved, you can ask your loved one's physician to arrange for this. Once that occurs, someone must take responsibility for notifying the funeral home and the person who will officiate at funeral services and for putting a death notice in the newspapers. That notice should include the date of death. Most people also include the cause of death. If there is to be a public service, you will need to specify the date, time, and place where it will be held. Finally, if the loved one has stated a preference for donations in lieu of flowers, you will need to specify this. Some families have said that delegating these tasks among two or three people is a good way to get them done without putting too much burden on just one person. At least one set of parents we know used their family website to communicate to others about the death of an adult son. Their notice included information about the cause of his death as well as a series of photos, showing him from childhood through adulthood. At the end, they included information on where and when his funeral would take place.

Again, good planning would have included selecting a method of burial, selecting a funeral home, and planning the ceremony. More people today are making these decisions and paying for them in advance, to minimize confusion and to spare their family the considerable expense that a funeral can entail. If for some reason, however, no one has been in contact with a funeral home previously, it is important to ask about cost before signing any papers. If the deceased has indicated a military service, you will need to have discharge papers on hand.

Some families organize a phone tree that they then use to notify near and distant relatives, friends, healthcare providers, and work associates of the death. This task too can be divided among several people to make it less onerous. Making such phone calls can be emotionally draining.

Someone needs to take responsibility for feeding everyone, arranging for child and/or pet care, and taking care of home management issues at least through the period of burial, and probably for a few weeks afterward. We recommend that family members take turns answering the phone or the door or returning phone and e-mail messages. They should keep a record of such communications so family members can reply and have the comfort of knowing that others are thinking of them and their loved one. Detailed tasks such as these keep people occupied and keep the family working as a team. Most family members agree that these tasks gave them something to focus on. One woman said that being responsible for making sure that meals for the family were ordered and delivered gave her a reason to get out of bed in the morning for the week after her mother died. She was grateful for that.

Though some people report being very much in touch with their feelings (sadness, pain), others have said that they initially felt more or less numb after their loved one died. Whereas some people report that they cried at the drop of a hat after losing their loved one, others say that they could not have cried if they'd wanted to. We consider these to be normal variations on the grief process; in other words, there is not just one way to properly grieve.

The first few weeks after the death are typically taken up with attending to details that, while tedious, also keep family members busy and communicating with one another. Here are a few of such details that should be delegated to someone in the family:

- *Attorney and executor.* Obviously, someone needs to notify the deceased's attorney, executor, and/or trustee as soon as possible.

- *Accountant.* If the deceased used an accountant, for example, for tax preparation, this person should be notified.

- *Death certificates.* Someone must be responsible for obtaining a supply of death certificates. These will be needed to collect on any life insurance policies, for example, as well as for purposes of executing any will or trusts.

- *Banks.* It will be necessary to change the name(s) on any accounts that list the deceased as an owner. Also, it is necessary to empty the contents of any safe deposit box. The family member who has power of attorney will need to be the one to do this.

- *Social Security.* This government agency needs to be notified so family members can qualify for survivors' benefits.

- *Cars, boats, and so on.* Ownership of these things may need to be transferred.

- *Bills.* The family member with power of attorney needs access to incoming bills so that they may be paid.

- *Insurance.* Health, homeowners', and auto insurance policies will need to be updated to remove the deceased from them, which may affect premiums.

PERSONAL EFFECTS AND PROPERTY

One thing we encourage families to talk about before any firm decisions are made is how to dispose of the deceased loved one's personal property. Once again, because of the changing nature of death, more families report having had such discussions well ahead of time. A terminally ill parent, for example, may ask his or her children to make a list of things they would want. The parents can then review the lists, decide what to give to whom, and include this in a will. While not everyone may get everything he or she asks for, this approach tends to minimize any acrimony that can erupt when two children want the same thing, such as a car or jewelry.

Regarding possessions that are not distributed via a will, we recommend that two or more people do this. We have seen instances in which a grieving spouse has impulsively given away (or thrown away) all or almost all of their deceased spouse's possessions. They do so, it appears, in an effort to avoid having to look at these things, which only serve to remind them of their loss. Later on, some say they regretted having acted so quickly. Talking about this issue in advance and having more than one person involved in the process can reduce the chance of making a hasty decision.

✒ *Sarah*

Sarah had acted as a paid caregiver to her aunt Betty during the last year of Betty's life. She'd taken a leave of absence from her job as a paralegal, gave up her apartment, put her furniture in storage, and moved in with her aunt. Being single, and her aunt having no children of her own, Sarah felt that she was the only person in the family who was in a position to do this. She would perform functions ranging from cleaning the house and making meals, to helping her aunt take a shower, giving her medications, and massaging her. Betty lived alone, her husband having passed away many years earlier.

"Everyone thought Betty was nuts to want to come home to die. My sister and brother wanted her to go to a nursing home so she'd have around-the-clock care by professionals. But I thought we should honor her wishes."

According to Sarah, Betty was told that after she had major surgery to remove her colon and was fitted with a colostomy bag, she would not be treated with chemotherapy or radiation should the cancer reappear. Approximately a year after her surgery, Betty was informed that the cancer had indeed returned. At that point, her doctors offered her palliative care, which she accepted, to help ensure that she was comfortable. Sarah said that her siblings believed that Betty should not bother meeting with the doctors as there was "nothing they could do for her."

Sarah disagreed with her siblings and continued to bring Betty to see her doctors and receive the care that they could provide her. She recognized that if Betty stopped seeing her doctors that it could be a sign that she was giving up hope.

"I think it's very important to let people die with dignity," Sarah told us. "I believe that taking away someone's power by not respecting their decisions takes away their dignity. Until we go through it ourselves, we don't know what we'd want in that situation. I think it's wrong to tell someone to give up or stop their medical care, when maybe they are not ready to.

"It made me really angry that my brother and sister seemed to want to treat our aunt like a child, just because she had less power than we did because of her health. I hate to see this happen to older people. Just because she was relying on us for a lot of things didn't mean that we had the right to take away her choices. We will all be old someday, and I know I would resent being treated that way."

Sarah felt that it was important to address relationships like hers with her aunt, because other people will also find themselves in the position of having to care for and deal with end-of-life issues for a childless relative. "What happens," she asked rhetorically, "to people who have no one to care for them at the end of their lives?" Sarah said that although she did what she did out of a sense of compassion and obligation, she felt it was perfectly appropriate for people in her position to be compensated. She would have gladly found a nursing home for Betty, if she had wanted that. That would also have drained virtually all of Betty's resources. What Sarah was paid for taking a leave of absence to be with Betty full time cost only a fraction of what nursing care would have cost.

Sarah noted that people can become paranoid about their money and finances as they begin to give up some tasks due to illness. Sarah was responsible for paying her aunt's bills out of a trust. Sometimes Sarah thought, based on a few comments, that Betty became suspicious that Sarah might be stealing money from her, especially close to the end of Betty's life. "I know she didn't mean it," Sarah said, "but it was hard to not take it personally when I was doing so much for her. I had to answer to myself, and I know I am an honest person.

I would encourage people to not take it personally if this happens to them."

Sarah thought it was important to address the situation of coping with the aftermath of when a relative dies and leaves the majority of their assets to one relative, which was what happened in her case. "My aunt did not die rich," Sarah said, "but she did leave what she had mostly to me. I really didn't know about this until I was invited to her lawyer's office for a reading of the will. In it, Aunt Betty wrote that she wanted me to have a nest egg so that after she died I could start my life again. I wasn't getting paid very much for what I did that year, so my savings hadn't grown. But I was lucky in that the law firm gave me my old job back, and at my old salary."

Two years later, between what Betty left her and what she was able to save, Sarah was able to buy a small condominium. Before then, she had put roughly half of what had been left to her in a trust for her two nieces and a nephew, something she believes her brother and sister appreciate. "My comfort," she says, "comes not from any feeling that I'm some kind of martyr, but from knowing that I did what I'd want someone to do for me."

Chapter Nineteen

MOVING FORWARD

THE NEW FAMILY

Having lost a loved one, the family is now changed, and with that change will come changes in relationships and roles. The grieving itself, however, is not necessarily over. In our opinion, it is a myth that grief has highly predictable and defined stages and a finite end point; on the contrary, grieving is chronic. Although we may experience long periods of remission from grief, it never fully disappears. The pain, the actual heartache, eventually moves to the back burner, but it can still periodically be felt acutely—for example, at special times like anniversaries or birthdays or in places that were special to the lost loved one.

It is important for people to realize that there are no set rules for coping with the death of a loved one, just as there is no set process that leads to an ending of grief. Some people, for instance, suggest that major life decisions be postponed for a year; others recommend redecorating the house soon to minimize the things that can trigger grief. We have known people for whom each of these approaches seemed to have worked.

In any case, living with loss is somewhat of a roller coaster at first. Our pain—both physical and emotional—reappears at every family milestone: when a child graduates, when someone marries, when someone has a child. In each of these situations, we are likely to remember that the loved one is not there to share it.

Some people report that they find themselves having regular conversations with their loved one. Some do this in their mind, though some people (as in Judy's story from chapter 18) do it out loud. No matter what, we have our memories and if we keep mementos around and continue to allow ourselves to think about and talk about our lost loved one, we keep him or her in our lives.

Having said that, it is also true that now is the time for the survivors to move ahead with their lives. For some, that may mean getting back to former routines and more or less picking up life where they left it off; for others, it may mean making new life plans. Because of the nature of what we've chosen to call *the new grief*, many family members have experienced significant changes in their lifestyles during the upheaval stage. Some, for example, may have taken on considerable responsibility, either for the ill loved one or for other members of the family. Some—such as Sarah (whose story was told at the end of the last chapter), make major changes. For these people, moving forward involves much more than simply picking up where they left off. As much as they may have anticipated it, they may still feel lost or adrift at first.

✍ *Helene's Story*

Helene, age fifty-eight, had been the primary caretaker of her husband, Philip, for the two years that he was dying. During that time, they talked often about how she would live after his death. He advocated that she remain in the home they had lived in for over thirty years and also keep the small vacation home the family had used in the summer. Helene agreed with this plan.

Four years later, Helene had a talk with her rabbi. She was in great conflict, she told him. She was finding the house too big and cumbersome to manage. To make matters worse, the house was large and expensive to operate, whereas the value of the assets that she and Philip had built, along with the monthly income that these assets yielded, had declined significantly as the result of a severe recession. Finally, though neither she nor the rest of the family used the vacation home much, it too required ongoing maintenance and the payment of taxes.

Helene believed that Philip would not have approved of her idea, which was to sell both homes and downsize. On some level, she told the rabbi, it felt as if she would be breaking a commitment she'd made to him. She had not yet shared these thoughts with her children, for fear they would also object.

With the help of her rabbi, whom she found to be a sympathetic yet objective sounding board, Helene came to realize that circumstances had changed dramatically and that her loving husband would have wanted her to make whatever decisions were best for her. In the end, her adult children, though admittedly saddened, wholeheartedly approved of and supported her decision to sell the vacation home and pursue downsizing to a smaller primary residence.

✄ *George's Story*

George, widowed at the young age of sixty, had been living in an urban condominium with his ill wife, Ellen, for the three years before her death. They had sold the large home in which they had raised their family a year before her diagnosis. George primarily busied himself with his accounting practice after Ellen's death. Occasionally, he would go to a ball game with his best friend. But he was definitely lonely. Despite that, he was not interested in dating so much as he wished he had a social life.

George's children lived out of town and wanted him to relocate closer after retirement. Three years later, when he was ready to do that, he researched the Internet and learned of a new retirement community being constructed nearby that offered lifelong care. Without informing his children, George purchased a unit in this community. His children were shocked and angry that he had made this decision without consulting them. George explained to them that he needed to maintain his independence, that he never wanted to be a burden to them, and that he was lonely and was seeking community. George's wife had been the one who mostly arranged their social life. Being somewhat reserved and shy, George found it difficult to do this on his own; therefore, after Ellen's death, he found himself living the life of a recluse, largely missing out on social relations. Moving into this new community would be a relatively easy way to put an end to his isolation.

Facing Change: New Family Dynamics

In many Native American cultures, a family—indeed, an entire tribe—is likened to the individual. Each is a system of inter-

connected parts that must work in a coordinated manner to survive. If they work together really well, they not only survive but
thrive. If an individual loses a limb, he or she may very well survive. However, the way that individual's body functions after the
loss will certainly be different. So it is for the family after the loss
of a loved one. Change is inevitable. Change may also be painful.
And families, just like individuals and communities, can survive
a significant loss and go on to thrive, if only they are willing to
adapt and change to meet new circumstances.

In the stories you just read, Helene had anticipated resistance to
change and adaptation from her children, but it didn't materialize.
George, on the other hand, had thought he was changing his life in a
way that would make things better for everyone, and he encountered resistance. From our point of view, the mistake that George
made had nothing to do with his desire to end his social isolation
and avoid becoming a burden to his children in the future. Rather,
what George had failed to do was to recognize how the family is
indeed a system of interconnected parts and to respect the fact
that changing one part inevitably has effects on other parts. In fact,
this reality of family life accounts for many rituals and traditions
that most families once observed but that are increasingly falling
by the wayside. Birth rituals, coming-of-age rituals, engagement
and wedding rituals, and death rituals are all ways in which we
recognize that the system that is our family has changed.

It is for this reason that we encourage family members to be
public about changes they are contemplating as far in advance as
possible. That is not to say that the family has veto power over our
decisions but only that they have a right to know in advance of a
change that will affect how the family functions. To use George's
case as an example, his children had had conversations of how

they would handle things like holidays as well as how they might renovate the house if George moved in with one of them. Then, out of the blue, those plans were out the window.

Following are a couple of other stories that illustrate our point.

⚘ *Tom's Story*

Two years after his wife's death, Tom, forty-nine, became interested in a woman he met in a bereavement group that was sponsored by his church. With his two children off to college, Tom felt it was time to begin to date and so he began seeing Trudy. She was a divorcee with two high-school-age children. When Tom's children returned home for a Christmas visit, he invited Trudy and her children over to the house for dessert and introduced them. His children had no advance knowledge of this plan and learned about it only an hour before Trudy and her children arrived.

Tom's son, Ben, who was the older of his two children, was supportive and friendly during the visit. He said he understood his father's need for a companion and wasn't particularly bothered by the late notice.

Tom's daughter, Nancy, on the other hand, was enraged. She was offended at not being asked if she wanted to meet Trudy. She later admitted to her father that she regarded his relationship with this woman as a betrayal of her deceased mother. Her initial response was to tell Tom that if Trudy was to be in the house again, he was to inform her so she could make arrangements to not be there.

Tom said that his daughter's remarks and attitude had hurt him. He said it made him feel guilty at first. He felt bad that his daughter had lost her mother, and part of him wanted to make it up to her. He decided to reach out to Nancy. He made a point of calling her at least once a week, even if she didn't call him. He dropped her an occasional card or mailed a small gift. Then he wrote a letter letting her know that she and Ben would be well provided for in his will. Tom knew, of course, that what Nancy really wanted was for him to break off his relationship with Trudy, something he was not willing to do.

Two years later, Tom and Trudy decided to marry. Tom gave Ben and Nancy plenty of advance notice. Nancy did attend the wedding, which was a simple and informal affair, but many people commented afterward that she seemed unhappy.

Tensions continue to exist in this family. Nancy, who finished college and is now living on her own, visits only rarely. When she does visit, she is cordial but not particularly warm, and the visits tend to be brief. Tom says that Trudy has been enormously patient and continues to be kind to Nancy even if Nancy is sullen. Nancy sends Tom birthday cards but has not yet acknowledged either Trudy's birthday or Tom and Trudy's anniversary.

Tom's story is not at all atypical. When widowed parents begin to develop new lives, there may be family members who resist that change. In this case, Tom's son, Ben, was happy that his father had found someone to love. He tried to convey this to his sister, who nevertheless turned a deaf ear and chose to distance herself from the family. Fortunately, it does not have to be that way.

✒ *Gina's Story*

Gina, a fifty-two-year-old widow, developed a stable relationship with Carl, a fifty-four-year-old widower. Gina was an attorney who had worked throughout her marriage while she and her husband collaboratively raised three children. She took a family leave for the last six months of her husband's life and returned to work one month

after his death. She met Carl through a client, and the two estab-
lished a comfortable relationship. While they often spent the night
together at either of their houses and traveled together (their chil-
dren were all away at college during the academic year), neither was
interested in living together or remarrying. They enjoyed their separ-
ateness as much as they valued their time together. Over the years,
both sets of children came to accept this relationship, and even
urged them to at least move in together, but Gina and Carl insisted
that this arrangement suited them both very well and that they were
secure and satisfied with this arrangement.

The point of these stories is to illustrate how there are many
different choices that people can make as they begin to carve out
a life after loss. As a rule, it is better not to spring decisions on the
family that will affect everyone, but that is no guarantee that a
life-altering decision will be fully embraced.

Final Thoughts on Change

In order for the family to grow, it needs to accept the inevitability
of change. When any system—a marriage, a family, a community—accepts the inevitability of change and takes the position of
adapting to it rather than resisting it, it grows stronger and more
resilient.

✹ Sonny's Story

Sonny, thirty-two, had her first child, a daughter, one month after her
mother died after a five-year struggle with lung cancer. Sonny had

always wanted her mother to be with her when she had her baby, and she was pleasantly surprised to discover that she and her husband (who substituted for Sonny's mother in the birthing room) were able to bond to one another and to their baby so strongly and develop a family unit as a threesome from the moment of birth. Sonny believed that having a baby and losing her mother almost simultaneously somehow enabled her to integrate her beloved mother into her own role as a mother. "She'd been involved with my pregnancy right up to the end," Sonny explained. "In a way, it was like she was also there when Hayley was delivered."

Three years later, when Sonny was pregnant with her second child, her mother-in-law offered to assist her in the birthing room—again, along with Sonny's husband. Although Sonny loved her mother-in-law, her initial response was to say no, but that she would like some help after she got home from the hospital.

Sonny's mother-in-law was very sensitive. She understood Sonny's rationale, and she did not feel or act offended. Then, one week before she went into labor, Sonny called her mother-in-law, saying, "I've thought about your offer. If it's still on the table, I'd like to take you up on it. I'd love to have you in the birthing room with me."

Letting go and moving forward can sometimes be a gradual process. Taking a page from Sonny's story, there is no need to be discouraged if someone in your family takes longer than others to change. Time is a critical ingredient in this recipe—no need to rush it. Who knows, even Tom's daughter might eventually soften her stance and rejoin the family.

CONCLUSION

In this book we have presented what is best thought of as a template that describes the experience that many families have after one member is diagnosed with a terminal illness. As we have said before, however, it would be a mistake to think that the five stages we discussed were sharply delineated or that grief has a final end point. Although the vast majority of people we talked with related to these stages and the experiences that define them, many also commented on how the five stages tend to blend into one another. This makes sense to us. By analogy, consider what we call developmental stages for humans: infancy, toddlerhood, childhood, adolescence, adulthood, midlife, and old age. These stages also tend to blend into one another, rather than being sharply divided.

Another caveat to our five-stage model is that not every

member of a family will go through all five stages. We have known people, for instance, who felt so wounded by abuse or abandoned by their families that they choose not to join in at what we have called the unity stage. Instead, they elect to detach themselves. Similarly, while almost everyone recognizes how their lifestyles have experienced upheaval as a consequence of a loved one being terminally ill, not everyone says that they were able to clearly identify and/or resolve the issues that came up. This makes sense as well because what we have termed the resolution stage represents an opportunity for change, not an inevitable fact of life.

Our hope is that this book—and especially the stories that others have so generously shared—will be both a source of useful information and a source of comfort to families as they navigate their way through the new grief. Contemporary medicine has dramatically altered the nature of death and dying. As a resilient species, we humans face the challenge of adapting to those changes. There will always be loved ones lost, and people will always grieve, although that grief process appears to have changed along with the medical advances that have allowed us to extend life. The best we can hope for is to be able to allow all of us as individuals to preserve our dignity through the process of dying and death.

ACKNOWLEDGMENTS

The authors would like to acknowledge the following people, all of whom played a part in shepherding this book from concept to reality. We are indebted to them for their support, advice, and counsel: Drs. Norma Zack and Michael Miller for suggesting and encouraging the development of this book. Honora Kaplan, Esq., and Dale Robeson, Esq., for their invaluable input regarding legal issues. Nina Lewis-Schroeder for her assistance in the development and implementation of many of the interviews. Elizabeth Markle for her assistance in compiling the resources. Linda Konner, Dr. Julie Silver, Denise Silvestro, and Candace Levy for their support, critiques, encouragement, and editorial feedback. Our patients, friends, colleagues, and families who contributed their stories and advice, and who provided invaluable encouragement and support.

RESOURCES

General

These websites can lead you to more specific resources for coping with terminal illnesses and end-of-life issues.

Growth House

www.growthhouse.org

Comprehensive website offering resources for individuals and families coping with terminal illness and end-of-life care. Includes a large database of Internet resources, recommendations for print materials, online bookstore, and online radio station. Topics covered include hospice and home care, palliative care, pain management, grief, death with dignity, and practical matters (including estate planning and financial issues). They provide disease-specific guides for those struggling with cardiac disease, renal disease, and cancer.

Recommended Pages

Find a Hospice (www.growthhouse.org/nhpco): Searchable database of hospices in the United States and links to international search sites.

Search Our Databases (www.growthhouse.org/search.htm): Search engine for exploring databases of reviewed resources for end-of-life care.

Bookstore (www.growthhouse.org/books/books.htm): Includes reviews and recommendations for a wide variety of materials related to illness and end of life.

Coda Alliance

www.codaalliance.org

Coda is a nonprofit organization that helps individuals and families plan for end-of-life care. It promotes exploring values and goals, facilitating advance discussion with family members and healthcare providers, providing access to quality information and education around care options, and encouraging collaboration between families and institutions to overcome barriers to high-quality end-of-life care.

USA.gov: End-of-Life Issues

www.usa.gov/Topics/Seniors/EndofLife.shtml

Extensive site with links for estate planning and wills, consumer guides for funeral homes and other services, hospice care and the selection of a hospice, resources for caregivers, coping with loss, and legal issues (living wills and advance directives).

USA.gov: Caregivers' Resources

www.usa.gov/Citizen/Topics/Health/caregivers.shtml#vgn-find-help
-providing-care-vgn

Page devoted to supporting caregivers with links to information on assisted living, hospice comparison, nursing home comparison, respite care, government benefits, Medicaid and Medicare basics, legal matters, long-distance caregiving, and support organizations for caregivers.

On Our Own Terms: Moyers on Dying in America

www.pbs.org/wnet/onourownterms

Site devoted to the PBS television series that focused on quality end-of-life care. Includes community support, forums, end-of-life planning tools, and discussions of both practical and emotional matters.

Grief and Support

In addition to your local community resources, the following websites can help you find online resources for information and support.

NewGrief

www.newgrief.com

The authors' website offers links to resources, blogs on various issues related to the new grief, as well as a portal for asking questions and sharing experiences.

GriefNet

www.griefnet.org

An online support community of individuals and families dealing with grief, death, and major loss. Griefnet.org facilitates nearly fifty e-mail support groups for adults and children, some of which are topic specific to different types of loss.

LotsaHelpingHands

www.LotsaHelpingHands.com

An online community that helps coordinate volunteers to provide support and help to local community members in need.

Kidsaid

kidsaid.com

A site for youth who are dealing with grief and loss, hosted by GriefNet (www.griefnet.org). Offers e-mail support groups, places to share and view stories and artwork of other children, and forums for parents and children to ask questions and find information.

Kids Konnected

www.kidskonnected.org

Provides written materials, groups, and programs for children who have a parent who has been diagnosed with cancer.

Gilda's Club Worldwide

www.gildasclub.org

A network that provides social and emotional support for families with cancer.

The Compassionate Friends

www.compassionatefriends.org

A national resource providing support to families (parents and siblings) who have lost a child.

Hospice

Hospice organizations differ in regard to services provided and attitudes about pain management, and it is important to research carefully which hospice program will be best suited to your family's needs. They also differ in eligibility for their services, physician's estimate of time remaining, and whether one can still be treated while in hospice care.

Hospice Foundation of America

www.hospicefoundation.org

Organization devoted to providing information about hospice care, such as different types of hospice programs, locating and choosing a hospice, grief and loss, end-of-life issues, and publications and videos.

Hospice

www.hospicenet.org

Extensive information for patients and caregivers on hospice care, choosing a hospice, bereavement, and talking with children about death.

Funerals

Funeral arrangements vary in regard to cost, options, and services. It is important to research alternatives and to determine eligibility for military and other benefits. Seek recommendations from clergy and healthcare staff.

Funeral Consumer's Alliance

www.funerals.org

A nonprofit organization dedicated to protecting consumers' right to choose a meaningful, dignified, and affordable funeral. Site includes information on legal rights, burial and cremation options, and state-specific materials for planning logistical matters before death.

FunPlan.com

www.funeralplan.com

Website devoted to helping individuals and families plan a funeral. Includes information on finding and choosing a funeral home, grief and bereavement education and resources, obituaries, and supporting children through loss. Also has a free "ask the expert" feature, which allows viewers to send questions to a panel of funeral directors and grief counselors and get personal replies via e-mail.

Medical Issues, Specific Diseases

It is critical for the family point person to aggressively pursue all options for healthcare. Many people find they are eligible for clinical trials or other treatments, and today alternative treatments are often combined with conventional treatments.

ClinicalTrials.gov

clinicaltrials.gov

This site is hosted by the National Institutes of Health and provides information on understanding clinical trials or experimental treatments, exploring the potential risks and benefits of a given treatment, and making decisions related to clinical trials. Includes a large database of all current clinical trials in 171 countries, searchable by medical condition or intervention.

Cancer*Care*

www.cancercare.org

A national nonprofit organization that provides free support services to anyone affected by cancer. Services include counseling, support groups, educational workshops, publications, financial counseling, youth programs, and information specific to different types of cancer.

National Cancer Institute: Clinical Trials

www.cancer.gov/clinical_trials

Information about ongoing clinical trials.

American Heart Association: HeartHub

www.hearthub.org

Offers information, tools, and resources to help patients understand their conditions and make informed decisions. Includes a video library.

> *Recommended Pages*
> Health Centers (links in the sidebar): Information specific to heart attack, heart failure, high blood pressure, stroke, diabetes, and other cardiac-related concerns.

American Heart Association (www.americanheart.org): Includes links to pages geared specifically for caregivers, offering
information, support, and e-newsletters.

Counseling and Therapy

When choosing a therapist, it is important to ask for recommendations from your medical team as well as from friends and relatives. If you do not feel comfortable after meeting with a therapist,
discuss whether he or she is a good fit for you and your family.

Psychology Today: Find a Therapist

therapists.psychologytoday.com/rms
Database of psychologists, psychiatrists, therapists, and counselors in the United States and Canada. Searchable by location and
specialty, including grief and loss.

TherapistLocator.net

www.therapistlocator.net
A service of the American Association for Marriage and Family
Therapy (AAMT); offers an international database of marriage
and family therapists.

American Association of Pastoral Counselors

www.aapc.org
Online directory of certified pastoral counselors.

Services for Veterans

Many people find that there are resources within the VA system if the person with the illness or a member of the family has served in the armed forces.

U.S. Department of Veterans Affairs

www.va.gov

If you do not have Internet access, you can find out about eligibility for VA benefits by calling 800-827-1000. Available information includes benefits relating to burial, medical programs, pensions, and life insurance.

Recommended Pages

Burial and Memorial Benefits (www.cem.va.gov).

Compensation & Pension Services (www.vba.va.gov/survivors/index.htm).

Legal Issues

In selecting an attorney, be sure to inquire about estate planning experience and interest.

U.S. Living Will Registry

www.uslivingwillregistry.com

Online registry of advance directives. Anyone can register their healthcare wishes and make them accessible to healthcare providers.

American Bar Association: Consumer's Tool Kit for Health Care Advance Planning

www.abanet.org/aging/toolkit

Provides materials for clarifying choices regarding healthcare advance directives (including living wills and durable power of attorney).

American Bar Association: Estate Planning FAQs

www.abanet.org/rppt/public/home.html

Extensive information, glossary, and frequently asked questions regarding wills, power of attorney, state-specific laws, living wills, and information for executors and trustees.

REFERENCES AND
RECOMMENDED READINGS

De Vries, Peter. (2005). *The Blood of the Lamb*. Chicago: University of Chicago Press. The most poignant of all of De Vries's novels, this is a thinly veiled fictional account of his young daughter's death from cancer.

Didion, Joan. (2007). *The Year of Magical Thinking*. New York: Vintage. This book is a memoir focusing on Didion's long marriage to John Gregory Dunne as well as the intense story of his sudden death from a heart attack after visiting their only child, who was in a coma in the hospital. Didion describes in unflinching detail the pain, fury, alienation, and disorientation that engrossed her during her first year of bereavement.

Genova, Lisa. (2009). *Still Alice*. New York: Pocket Books. This novel about a Harvard professor's descent into Alzheimer's disease is written from the inside out and depicts the progress of the disease in the patient and her family. The author realistically discusses the issues that anyone coping with this illness will relate to.

Groopman, Jerome. (2004). *The Anatomy of Hope*. New York: Random House. Using the examples of real patients, Groopman elucidates the critical role of hope—for both doctors and patients—in struggling with the complexities of disability and illness. Neurological research has validated the significance of hope and compassion in managing illness, and this inspirational and comforting book blends humanism and science.

Kessler, D., and D. Kessler. (2007). *The Needs of the Dying: A Guide for Bringing Hope, Comfort, and Love to Life's Final Chapter*. New York: Harper. Explores the needs of the dying and those who support them. Discusses the physical, emotional, and spiritual experiences of terminal illness, and offers compassionate insight into common concerns and challenges. Includes accounts of others' experiences of navigating medical care, family relationships, and important communications.

McFarlane, R., and P. Basche. (1999). *The Complete Bedside Companion: A No Nonsense Guide to Caring for the Seriously Ill*. New York: Simon & Schuster. Comprehensive handbook for caregivers. The first part provides information on relating to doctors, building support networks, legal and financial issues, and the emotional and practical aspects of preparing for death. The second part covers specific diseases, such as cancer, heart disease, and liver disease. For each disease, symptoms, treatment options, common caregiving challenges, and recommended readings are provided, supplemented by stories of caregivers who have dealt with these issues.

Nearing, Helen. (1992). *Loving and Leaving the Good Life*. White River Junction, VT: Chelsea Green. A beautiful memoir of a fifty-year relationship. It includes many authors' and poets' reflections on life and death.

Neuberger, Julia. (2008). *Not Dead Yet: A Manifesto for Old Age*. New York: HarperCollins. A rabbi, baroness, and member of the British House of Lords, Neuberger decries the current conditions of the old in Britain, particularly what happens to them when they become ill. She makes some very sensible suggestions about what should be done based on meticulous research and focuses on medical care and end-of-life issues.

Pausch, Randy, with Jeffrey Zaslow. (2008). *The Last Lectures*. New York: Hyperion. Pausch was forty-six when diagnosed with pancreatic cancer, and in his last year and a half of life, he not only fought the disease but prepared his last lectures to Carnegie Mellon University where he was a professor. He lived his dreams, helped his wife and young children plan for life without him, and provided inspiration to all by reminding us to laugh, seize each moment, and appreciate what we have. He shows us how to live and die with integrity and dignity.

Roiphe, Anne. (2008). *Epilogue: A Memoir*. New York: HarperCollins. This depiction of late-life widowhood and aging acknowledges how generational issues affect coming to grips with loss, change, and taking charge of all aspects of one's life. Roiphe's husband had handled most of the financial and management issues in her life, and she was left thinking that she needed a man to survive. Common pitfalls and amusing anecdotes can open our eyes to the necessary changes after the loss of a life partner.

Schreiber, Jennifer Kaplan. (2010). *Young Adults Coping with Death: You Are Not Alone*. Available at jenny@manitouexperience.org. This workbook is written by a social worker who has worked with a variety of youth who have experienced the death of a family member. There are exercises that can be used individually or in small groups. The purpose of the text and exercises is to give people the opportunity to talk about their loss and understand how normal their thoughts and feelings are.

Strongin, Laurie. (2010). *Saving Henry: A Mother's Journey*. New York: HarperCollins. The detailed description of a family's seven-year battle against their son's fatal genetic disease. A depiction of how one family member's illness is a family system challenge and how proactively they navigate the five stages of saying goodbye.